MANAGING CAREERS INTO THE 21st CENTURY

HUMAN RESOURCE MANAGEMENT SERIES: FOREWORD

The two integrating themes of this series are organizational change, and the strategic role of the human resource function.

The 1990s have witnessed a further shift in thinking with respect to the organizational role of the personnel function. That shift has been reflected in the change of title – to human resource management – and revolves around the notion that effective human resource management is a critical dimension of an organization's competitive advantage. Personnel or human resource management is thus now more widely accepted as a strategic business function, in contrast with the traditional image of a routine administrative operation concerned with hiring, training, paying and terminating.

The range of issues with which personnel managers must now deal has widened considerably, as has the complexity and significance of those issues. Conventional texts in this subject area typically have the advantage of comprehensiveness, by offering a broad overview of the function, its responsibilities, and key trends. Such coverage is always purchased at the expense of depth. The aim of this series, therefore, is not to replace traditional personnel or human resource texts, but to complement those works by offering in-depth, informed and accessible treatments of important and topical themes, written by specialists in those areas and supported by systematic research, often conducted by the authors themselves.

The series is thus based on a commitment to contemporary changes in the human resource function, and to the direction of those changes. This has involved a steady shift in management attention to improved employee welfare and rights, genuinely equal opportunity, the effective management of diversity, wider employee involvement in organization management and ownership, changing the nature of work and organization structures through process 'reengineering', and towards personal skills growth and development at all organizational levels. Further significant trends have included the decline in trade union membership, the increased interest in 'non-union' organizations, and the potentially shifting responsibilities of the human resource function in this context. This series documents and explains these trends and developments, indicating the progress that has been achieved, and aims to contribute to best management practice through fresh empirical evidence and practical example.

David Buchanan, Series Editor
De Montfort University School of Business, Leicester

MANAGING CAREERS INTO THE 21st CENTURY

John Arnold

The Business School, Loughborough University

P·C·P
Paul Chapman
Publishing Ltd

Paul Chapman Publishing Ltd
A SAGE Publications Company
6 Bonhill Street
London EC2A 4PU

Reprinted 2003

British Library Cataloguing in Publication Data

Arnold, J.
   Managing careers into the 21st century.
   – (Human resource management series)
   1. Career development
   I. Title
   650.1'4

ISBN 1 85396 317 8

Typeset by Dorwyn Ltd, Rowlands Castle, Hants
Printed and bound in Great Britain

   G H   3

BIOGRAPHY

The author joined The Business School, Loughborough University as Senior Lecturer in Organizational Behaviour in February 1996, having previously been Lecturer and then Senior Lecturer at Manchester School of Management, UMIST. He has directed several research projects on career development, especially in early career, and also conducts consultancy work in this area. Much of his work has involved graduate groups. His interests span all areas of career management, particularly those most closely connected with personal change and development. He has published numerous articles on career development in academic and practitioner journals, and together with Professors Ivan Robertson and Cary Cooper, has written the successful textbook *Work Psychology*. The third edition will be published in 1998. He is co-author of the 1996 monograph *Managing Careers in 2000 and Beyond*, published by the Institute for Employment Studies. He is a Chartered Psychologist registered with the British Psychological Society.

CONTENTS

List of tables and figures   xi
Preface   xiii

1. INTRODUCTION   1
    The context of careers   1
    The context of career management in organizations   2
    Career management interventions off the job   3
    Career management interventions as part of day-to-day work   5
    Career decision-making   6
    Development and careers   8
    Managing career transitions   9
    Diversity in careers   11
    Concluding comments   13

2. THE NATURE AND CONTEXT OF CAREERS   15
    Defining careers and career management   15
    More terminology   18
    The times they are a-changing (well, quite a lot)   20
      Workload   21
      Organizational changes   21
      Organization of work   22
      Outsourcing   22
      Short-term contracts   23
      Disappearance of organizational career structures   23
      Changing skill requirements   24
      Diversity in the labour force   25
      Ageing populations   25
      Small organizations   26
      Working at or from home   26

Insecurity   27
A recap: careers and their context   28

3. MANAGING CAREERS IN ORGANIZATIONS – AN OVERVIEW   31
Delayering and downsizing   31
Devolution and decentralization   32
Outsourcing   34
Competencies – a new language for careers?   35
The psychological contract   39
    Some cautions   42
    Negotiations   43
The management of careers by organizations   44
Self-development   48
Fertile ground for career management?   50
Integration of career management interventions   51
Summary   54

4. CAREER MANAGEMENT INTERVENTIONS IN
ORGANIZATIONS I   55
Succession and succession planning   56
Development centres   59
Workshops and workbooks   62
Outplacement   64
Career counselling   67
Summary   70

5. CAREER MANAGEMENT INTERVENTIONS IN
ORGANIZATIONS II   72
Developmental work assignments   72
Performance appraisal   76
Personal development plans   78
Career action and resource centres   80
Networking   83
Mentoring   85
Managing the career plateau   91
Summary   94

6. CAREER DECISION-MAKING   95
Readiness for career decision-making   96
Information about the self and the world of work   98
    Personality   99
    Interests   101
    Talents   102
Accuracy of self-assessment   103
Self-efficacy   105
John Holland's typology of people and occupations   106

The Self-Directed Search   108
Tests of Holland's theory   111
The process of decision-making   114
Computers and career decision-making   120
Summary   121

7. DEVELOPMENTAL APPROACHES TO CAREER MANAGEMENT 123
Erik Erikson   124
    Life stages and developmental tasks   124
    Critique and practical applications   125
Donald Super   127
    Life stages, roles and concerns   128
    Critique and practical applications   130
Daniel Levinson   131
    Phases of life   131
    Critique and practical applications   134
Women, men and phases   136
Anchors and themes   140
    Schein's career anchors   140
    Life themes   142
Ageing   143
Wisdom   146
Summary   147

8. WORK-ROLE TRANSITIONS   148
Definitions and types of work-role transitions   148
Stages   153
The transition cycle   155
Preparation   157
Encounter   159
Adjustment and stabilization   161
Organizational commitment   165
Entering employment   167
Retirement   168
Relocation   170
Summary   176

9. DIVERSE PEOPLE, DIVERSE CAREERS   177
Managing diversity   178
    Diversity initiatives   179
    Some cautions and speculations   181
Dual-career couples and families   182
    Leave entitlements   185
    Child-care facilities   185
    Career breaks   186
    Training   186

Flexible working patterns   186
Fostering a family-friendly culture   187
The future   189
Women's career success   189
Unemployment   191
Entrepreneurship and self-employment   194
Careers of technical specialists   197
Summary   200

POSTSCRIPT   201
Education and career guidance   201
Information technology   202
Individuals   204
Organizations   204

REFERENCES   209

INDEX   229

LIST OF TABLES AND FIGURES

Table 3.1 Doing the career deal I   44
Table 3.2 Doing the career deal II   45
Table 3.3 Career management interventions in organizations   46
Table 3.4 Use of career management interventions by
           organizations in three countries   47
Table 3.5 Inputs to organizational career management   52

Table 5.1 The Developmental Challenge Profile   74
Table 5.2 Organizational Analysis Survey   75
Table 5.3 Potential benefits of mentoring   87
Table 5.4 Career management interventions for plateaued people   93

Table 6.1 Aspects of career exploration   98
Table 6.2 Selected occupations and their Holland codes   109
Table 6.3 Some computer packages for career management   119

Table 7.1 Super's adult career concerns   129
Table 7.2 Levinson's phases of adult-life development   132
Table 7.3 Coping responses and behaviours in the establishment stage 139
Table 7.4 Schein's career anchors   140

Table 8.1 Socialization tactics in organizations   163
Table 8.2 International assignment policy documents   175

Figure 3.1 Four psychological contracts   41

Figure 6.1 A hierarchical model of vocational interests   100
Figure 6.2 John Holland's six types of vocational personality   107

Figure 6.3   Prediger and Vansickle's career dimensions
             in relation to Holland's types   113
Figure 6.4   A schematic diagram of the sequential elimination model   117

Figure 7.1   Model of development in adulthood   133
Figure 7.2   Warr's classification of work tasks   145

Figure 8.1   Self-esteem changes during transition   154
Figure 8.2   The transition cycle   156
Figure 8.3   Four modes of adjustment   162
Figure 8.4   Framework of international adjustment   174

PREFACE

This book concerns how we as individuals can manage our own careers, and how organizations, particularly employers, can be involved in the management of individuals' careers. The world of employment has changed significantly in the last two decades of the 20th century and continues to do so. It is important that the notion of career is not confined to predictable upward movement over a long period of time within one organization or occupation, simply because this pattern has become rarer. Instead, a career concerns *any* sequence of employment-related positions. It includes people's subjective experiences of that sequence, not simply an objective account of the jobs they hold. Interest in careers is very high at present, due partly to the increasing complexity of managing them and the increasing importance of doing so well. This book is a response to those trends.

Three areas of research, practice and theory are brought together in this book. The first concerns changing patterns and types of employment within economies as a whole and within employing organizations. The second concerns organization-based perspectives on career management: in particular how techniques such as mentoring, succession planning, relocation and flexible working patterns can facilitate the achievement of organizational goals whilst also honouring individual career aspirations. The third area is a more uniquely individual perspective on careers and their management. This particularly concerns the making of career decisions and the ways in which people's careers and whole lives develop during adulthood.

I attempt to provide an accessible and scholarly analysis of what is known about career management in the areas described above. Emphasis is placed upon the usefulness or otherwise of this knowledge given the changing employment context as we approach and enter the 21st century. The probable future of careers and career management in the 21st century is also analysed. I hope and intend that there is much useful guidance in this book for individuals and organizations on how careers can and should be managed. However, this is not primarily a 'do-it-yourself' guide about how to have a successful career. Rather, this book aims to offer a wide-ranging and dispassionate account of different forms of careers, different techniques for managing them, and the conditions in which those techniques are used and in which they can be successful. Although written by an author based in the United Kingdom, the book is international in content and application.

Given its aims, this book is intended for several different audiences. In no particular order, they are as follows. First are managers with responsibility for devising or implementing career management strategies in organizations. Second are students on postgraduate or undergraduate degrees in business, management and applied social sciences taking modules in career or human resource management. The third intended audience is those working for professional qualifications such as, in the UK, membership of the Institute of Personnel and Development (IPD). The fourth and final target group is individuals looking for an understanding of their own past, present and future careers – an understanding which goes deeper and wider than can be achieved by the completion of some self-assessment questionnaires or participation in a career development workshop.

The role of organizations in careers is prominent in many sections of this book. I am acutely aware of the dangers inherent in referring to an organization as if it was an individual, speaking and acting with one voice and single intention. Organizations are of course made up of many coalitions with competing goals and views of reality. Nevertheless, for the sake of clarity I do, on occasions, refer to the organization as a single entity. I do so as a convenient shorthand for the goals and intentions of the dominant power group within the organization, which typically is senior management.

Many people have contributed to this book, even though some of them may not be aware of it. I am particularly grateful to Charles Jackson at the Institute for Employment Studies, Kate Mackenzie Davey at Birkbeck College and Tony Watts at the (UK) National Institute for Careers Education and Counselling, who have all been stimulating discussion partners over the last several years. The publisher Paul Chapman and series editor David Buchanan have both provided helpful feedback and encouragement. My family have endured with fortitude the writing process, particularly in the latter stages when we could really have used some more time together. Colleagues at Loughborough University Business School have also contributed significant ideas, and been remarkably tolerant when I have whinged about how difficult it is to find the time to write a book and do everything else one is supposed to do in higher education these days. Irene Moody in particular has taken the brunt of this, and has provided reliable and expert help in word-processing, reference-checking and formatting. Without her assistance the book would have been a long time coming. It almost goes without saying, however, that any shortcomings of the book are solely my responsibility.

I would welcome feedback about the book from readers, so if you want to tell me what you think, please do so. I am at The Business School, Loughborough University, Ashby Road, Loughborough, Leicestershire LE11 3TU, UK. Phone (+44) (0)1509 223121; fax (+44) (0)1509 223960; email J.M.Arnold@Lboro.ac.uk.

Loughborough
November 1996

1

INTRODUCTION

The purpose of this initial chapter is to present an overview of the rest of the book. I have described in the Preface the aims and style of the book as a whole, so I will not repeat those now. If you are unfamiliar with careers and career management, you should find this chapter helpful in orientating you to the remainder of the book. If you are more familiar with the topic area, you may also find it useful as a refresher, and as a guide to which parts of the book are likely to be most useful to you. But this chapter is not intended as a kind of executive summary, or as a substitute for the rest of the book. The research and practice upon which this chapter is based are cited and described in subsequent ones.

THE CONTEXT OF CAREERS

In Chapter 2, I set the scene by starting with definitions of key terms. I want to be clear that careers encompass a wide range of sequences of occupational experiences, not just conventional ones. They do not necessarily involve promotion, and they may well cross occupational and organizational boundaries, frequently in many cases. Careers are subjective as well as objective – they include people's interpretation of what happens to them as well as what can be observed objectively. Career management consists of attempts to influence the way the careers of one or more people develop. This can include managing one's own career as well as the careers of other people.

The context in which careers are being played out has changed and is changing, though perhaps less radically than is sometimes claimed. The composition of the work-force is changing in most Western countries. The numbers of men and women in the labour market are now nearly equal. The average age of the work-force is increasing and the work-force is becoming more culturally and ethnically varied. Self-employment, limited-term contracts and part-time work are all symptoms of increasing global competition and a consequent surge in labour flexibility (flexibility from the employer's point of view, that is). People are on average less secure in their jobs and certainly feel more insecure than used to be the case. Many organizations have reduced the number of people who can be considered core employees – that is, those who are employed (usually full time) on medium- or long-term contracts. They make more use of outside contractors for functions such as cleaning and catering, and for highly specialized technical or managerial tasks, usually with a limited duration.

So careers are becoming less predictable. They involve more frequent changes of job, employer and skill requirements. They involve more varied hours of work, work colleagues and forms of employment relationship. There is also more need for (re-)education and (re-)training, commonly referred to collectively as lifelong learning. There is a real danger that the gap between the haves and have-nots will widen further. Those with marketable skills and the resources and know-how to maintain them will survive, but those without, or with limited skills and resources, may find themselves in highly insecure and low-paid work, if at all.

THE CONTEXT OF CAREER MANAGEMENT IN ORGANIZATIONS

Chapter 3 gives an account of the context in which careers occur within organizations. It is argued that downsizing (i.e. shedding staff) has often been done rather unthinkingly, with the result that some organizations have lost too many people and/or the wrong ones. Those who remain are often disillusioned and fearful. They are encouraged to be committed to their organization's mission and culture, but know only too well how readily expendable they are.

Human resource managers are increasingly inclined to think in terms of the competencies required by the organization, and some commentators predict that the very notion of a job may fall by the wayside and be replaced by sets of competencies that can be deployed to accomplish a range of work duties. The growth of competency-based training and qualifications is consistent with this. There is a risk in all this that innovation, risk-taking and excellence will be sacrificed for conformity to set procedures, adequacy and avoidance of mistakes. Staff in severely downsized organizations are especially wary of risk-taking in case it gets them noticed for the wrong reasons. Yet many organizations claim to value innovators and have, at least on the surface, attempted to empower individuals to solve problems in their own way.

Many employees of organizations believe that the understanding they thought they had with their employer concerning their respective rights and obligations has been undermined in recent years. This understanding is often termed the psychological contract. It once revolved around mutual trust, training and development, a potentially long-term relationship, and helping each other out in times of trouble. Now it seems to mean more work, more responsibility whether one wants it or not, less security and less training and development. People who feel that their employer has broken the psychological contract are understandably less inclined to 'go the extra mile', and more inclined to insist to the letter on whatever entitlements they have. According to some observers, the old unwritten 'you scratch my back and I'll scratch yours' employment relationship can never be reinstated. Instead, there needs to be explicit negotiation between individual and organization concerning what each side expects to give and to get. There should subsequently be monitoring to make sure the deal is kept, and renegotiation if necessary. Even if the labour market power of some organizations might suggest that they do not need to negotiate, it can be argued that doing so is the only way of establishing a harmonious and productive employment relationship.

In the downsized, delayered and outsourced organizations there is often a very 'hands-off' approach to career management. Individuals are seen as being responsible for looking after themselves through what is often termed self-development. Yet self-development can be presented in either an aggressive or a supportive manner. The former says, in effect, that the organization is too subject to change and too poor to develop its employees, so they must look after themselves. The latter approach, in contrast, acknowledges that the organization will not manage people's careers for them as it may once have done in the past, but it will play a role in supporting staff in defining and meeting their development needs for themselves. Further, in some organizations there is still a concerted attempt to have a co-ordinated approach to career management through, for example, succession planning. Other career management interventions include career workshops, mentoring, developmental job assignments, career action centres, career counselling, development centres, personal development plans, networking and, as a last resort, outplacement.

It is probably better to have a small number of career management interventions working well than a larger number working not so well. It is also crucial to be clear about what they are trying to achieve. For example, is a career workshop primarily about helping people to identify career options, or is it aimed at equipping them with the skills to achieve options already selected? A tricky balance must be struck between on the one hand confidentiality and ownership of the process for individuals, and on the other hand integration of information from career management interventions with other human resource practices so that the organization as a whole can profit from them. Messages about careers must be honest and open.

CAREER MANAGEMENT INTERVENTIONS OFF THE JOB

Having discussed the organizational context of career management interventions, it is necessary now to assess in more detail some of the available interventions. Some of them are events or processes which occur separately from the day-to-day work activities and venue of the people whose careers are being intervened in. These interventions are analysed in Chapter 4. One of them, succession planning, can happen without the person or persons concerned being aware of them.

Succession planning concerns the planned replacement of one or more people in an organization by new individuals. It is most commonly carried out by relatively senior managers. It may focus on one particular individual such as the chief executive officer, or it may be directed at a whole cohort of individuals whose development is being monitored. Succession planning may occur on quite an *ad hoc* basis as and when someone announces he or she is leaving. In this case it is not much different from selection. On the other hand, succession planning may be a strategic activity where individuals with appropriate competencies are earmarked for development. The succession of chief executive officers has attracted a lot of attention. Research has shown that it is often not sufficiently planned, and CEO succession does not necessarily lead to improved organizational performance.

Development centres use techniques such as work simulations, role-played group discussions and presentations to establish the competencies and development needs of existing employees. Information about their own performance at the development centre is often the property of the participants rather than those who assess their performance during the centre. It can be used to provide feedback on work behaviour and competencies, thus equipping staff to plan their development. The organization may also use information about employees' competencies to inform its training and development policies in the light of its strategic plans. Although development centres are not generally designed to select individuals for posts, there is sometimes an element of selection about them – for example, they may aim to identify people who could benefit from a fast-track training scheme. However, this runs the risk of making participants less willing to be candid about their development needs, and perhaps less receptive to feedback.

Career development workshops usually provide groups of people with the chance to undertake structured exercises and discussion in an attempt to clarify their career plans and preferences. Workbooks or their computerized equivalents do something similar, though obviously they have less potential for discussion than workshops. Some common fears about career management interventions in general tend to be particularly evident regarding workshops. The bosses of participants often fear that they will want to leave, or demand opportunities that cannot be provided. The available evidence suggests that this is not generally the case. On the other hand, claims by advocates of workshops that they improve the fit between individuals and organizations have little concrete evidence to support them (or, indeed, to refute them).

Outplacement is a career management intervention offered to people who are leaving the organization, usually not voluntarily. It is a catch-all term for the use of a number of career management interventions to help leavers prepare for their departure and successfully identify and obtain alternative employment. Outplacement is usually provided by agencies external to the organization, which can create some interesting dilemmas since the service is provided to employees but the client is the organization.

Career counselling is provided in some organizations, staffed by trained counsellors from inside or outside the organization. Counselling is not advice-giving, but an attempt to use empathy and other interpersonal skills to help clients solve their own problems to their own satisfaction. Confidentiality must be maintained – certainly nothing discussed in a counselling relationship should be revealed without the client's permission, and possibly the very fact that counselling occurred should be confidential. As with many other career management interventions, evidence for or against the effectiveness of counselling in organizations is sparse, but what there is tends to be positive.

CAREER MANAGEMENT INTERVENTIONS AS PART OF DAY-TO-DAY WORK

I continue to examine career management interventions in Chapter 5. This time the focus is on interventions which form part of a person's day-to-day work activities and/or take place as part of the usual course of the person's work. The clearest case of this is developmental work assignments. These are projects, or more often whole jobs, which are designed to develop a person's competencies and experience in service of personal and organizational future needs. In recent years, research has suggested that organizational job rotation schemes do have more gains than losses, and there are also tools available to analyse the developmental potential of a particular job.

Performance appraisal can be a source of information for career management. It is usually necessary to separate the assessment of past performance from the review of developmental needs, possibly in terms of both time and the person doing the appraising. Individuals are unlikely to be frank about their development needs if it might mean their performance ratings suffer. The more proactive developmental elements of appraisal nowadays sometimes take the form of personal development plans (PDPs), which constitute another career management intervention. A PDP is a developmental action plan for which the individual takes primary responsibility. A key issue for PDPs is where the information and ideas that feed into them come from. It might be from appraisal, or from a developmental centre, or perhaps discussion with a mentor. There is some evidence that PDPs are received with most enthusiasm when they invite a person to consider his or her development holistically, and not just in terms of his or her present job, or indeed a future one. A tightrope has to be walked between on the one hand having PDPs that are very detached from the organization's HR processes, and on the other hand having PDPs closely scrutinized by members of management. The former line invites a reaction of 'why bother?' from potential PDP users, whilst the latter takes ownership away from individuals and turns PDPs into just another management tool.

Career action centres (CACs) have been formed by some organizations, and also by professional networks. CACs are essentially drop-in centres where a variety of career-related services is available. The 'dropping in' may be electronic via computers rather than physical. Resources available in CACs often include many of the interventions discussed in this book, particularly perhaps counselling, self-assessment tools and career workshops. Training in job-seeking techniques and career information is also usually available. The relatively informal flavour of CACs is even more prominent in another career management tool, namely networking. This is the effective initiation and maintenance of social relationships for career-related purposes. As careers become less governed by organizational and societal structures, the importance of informal social contacts increases. Furthermore, it is important to have these contacts before one hits times of trouble. They can act as sources of support, advice and information, but one must be prepared to offer these things as well as receive them since like many social relationships networking is often based on the social norm of reciprocation. Networking may be particularly important for members of disadvantaged groups who might otherwise find it difficult to gain access to opportunities.

Mentoring is a very popular career management technique at present. It usually involves a relationship between one more and one less experienced person where the former helps the latter find his or her way in the world of work. Like networking, mentoring can particularly assist people who would otherwise be at some disadvantage in the work-place. The potential benefits for the person being mentored, the protégé, are considerable, and also for the mentor and organization. Some research suggests that these benefits do indeed often occur, but most of it is far from conclusive because of deficiencies in research design. The key is to replicate the benefits of mentoring relationships that spring up spontaneously in relationships which are formally organized and 'brokered' within the organization.

Career management interventions are certainly not confined to the upwardly mobile. Most organizations are populated by many people who are plateaued – that is to say, they have reached the highest level of responsibility they are likely ever to reach. The reasons for plateauing are many, and it is not necessarily a problem for either individual or organization, though it may be. Interventions such as developmental assignments and being a mentor may help to maintain plateaued employees' performance, motivation and adaptability.

Overall, then, career management interventions are many and varied. Most can be used for more than one purpose. They can be aimed principally at individual or at organizational needs. On occasions these needs may conflict. Interventions which prosper in the 21st century are likely to be those which involve the least interruption from work whilst also being effective and relatively cheap in helping a person and/or organization to assess and/or fulfil developmental needs.

CAREER DECISION-MAKING

In Chapter 6, I investigate how career decisions are made and how they should be made. I also examine the conceptual and practical tools available to assist the making of effective decisions. In spite of the broad definition of careers used in this book, it has to be said that the literature on career decision-making normally concerns decisions about what occupation to enter. The unstated assumptions are that a person has a choice in these matters, and that what occupation he or she enters is the key aspect of choice. There is a case for arguing that related but different questions are the most important, such as the competencies a person wishes to develop or the lifestyle he or she wishes to lead.

Career exploration is the collection of information about self and the world of work, together with the drawing of appropriate inferences about the kind of person one is and the characteristics of occupational environments. Exploration can occur by a variety of means, some systematic but others more haphazard. Activities can include reading careers information, asking friends, shadowing someone going about his or her work, taking some psychometric tests, and trying out a certain kind of work. Other things being equal, this should lead to more accurate and complete knowledge of self and the world of work.

But that does not in itself guarantee an effective decision. Some people lack self-confidence about making decisions which may make them reluctant to try. Sources of career indecision are many, and some (e.g. being strongly attracted to more than one occupation) are not necessarily dissipated by good knowledge of self and the world of work. Styles of decision-making may also make the task easier or harder, depending on the suitability of the style used. More optimistically, it seems not to be the case that only one style can work. Being passive and waiting for a decision to be forced by circumstances or another person is not usually a good idea, but other styles such as being rational and systematic or being intuitive may be equally effective for different people.

A sound conceptual structure for thinking about people and work environments is a great aid to effective decision-making. It allows a person to interpret information in a way which reflects real characteristics of people and work-place, and also facilitates the integration of information about self and work that is necessary if an effective choice is to be made. A dominant theory here is that of John Holland. He has proposed the existence of six different vocational personality types. Any person resembles each of the six types to varying degrees. Occupational environments have their force through the people who work in them. Effective career decisions are therefore ones which enable a person to work in environments with others who are similar to him or her in terms of vocational personality. Holland has developed easy-to-use self-assessment devices, and has collated massive amounts of information about a large number of occupations so that people can check which occupations they appear to be best suited to. Other ways of looking at the occupational world may be useful, but the validity of Holland's typology has some powerful evidence to support it. On the other hand it is possible that his definition of vocational personality gives insufficient emphasis to some aspects of self that people bring to their career decisions, particularly perhaps their values and lifestyle preferences.

DEVELOPMENT AND CAREERS

Human personality tends to be relatively stable during adulthood. Nevertheless, some people change. Even those who do not change in terms of their characteristic ways of thinking, feeling and behaving, encounter different personal concerns and issues at different stages of their life. For example, a man in his mid to late thirties may be preoccupied with an attempt to achieve major success at work in order to maintain his employability and demonstrate his worth to himself and to other people. These phenomena are examined in Chapter 7. If it was possible to identify which career concerns are typically dominant at which ages, then attempts at career management could be closely age-linked. However, in a world with increasingly unpredictable careers and increasingly diverse work-forces (see Chapter 9) the idea that certain concerns reliably come to the fore at certain ages seems less plausible than it might once have been. A more flexible approach is to identify the different career concerns people may have at whatever age. If there are identifiably different concerns, career management interventions should take them into account.

A number of attempts have been made during the latter half of the 20th century to map out the course of human lives. Erik Erikson suggested that there are four phases of psychosocial development during adulthood. Each is characterized by a key developmental task which must be accomplished before a successful transition to the next phase can be made. Erikson attached age-bands to each of the stages, but stressed that these were very inexact since different people tackle developmental tasks at different rates and with different levels of success.

Daniel Levinson and colleagues proposed a particularly controversial theory of lifespan development. Primarily on the basis of in-depth interviews with 40 men, they suggested a series of closely age-linked phases of adult life. The phases alternate between stable, structure-building ones where the person attempts to establish a particular lifestyle, and transitional ones where the life structure is actively questioned and perhaps revised. The best-known transitional phase is often referred to as the mid-life crisis. Levinson and colleagues reckoned that this occurs in a people's early forties as they realize they are no longer young and feel a sense of urgency that if things are going to change it needs to be now. The stable phases are not necessarily experienced as relaxed and happy, because a person may not be successful in building the life structure he or she desires. Levinson has avowed repeatedly that he did not expect to find such neat phases, or necessarily any phases at all, but others have criticized him for interpreting his data in a way which guaranteed the phases would show up. Not surprisingly, doubts have also been raised about whether the theory applies to women's lives.

Another big name in this field is Donald Super. He started out shortly after World War II by suggesting some career stages which were quite closely related to age and which rather assumed an adult lifetime of employment. Later, however, his ideas became much more flexible. He detached the stages from ages and renamed them concerns. So, for example, one concern is *consolidating*, which means making oneself secure in an occupation and demonstrating one's value in it. Another is *holding*, which refers to retaining one's position in the face of changing technology, competition from younger employees and other pressures. Knowing what concern or concerns is or are uppermost in a person's mind may influence the utility and design of career management interventions. Super also broadened his ideas to encompass the different potential arenas of a person's life – not just worker but also student, leisurite, parent and other roles. Super's work can best be described as a framework of concepts rather than a theory.

A now well-known typology of career concerns is Edgar Schein's notion of career anchors. A career anchor is defined as an aspect of self-concept that one would not give up, even if forced to make a difficult choice. Schein argued that an anchor does exactly what the word suggests – it keeps a person near a fixed point (in this case a set of values) and pulls him or her back when he or she drifts away. So, for example, one anchor is technical/functional competence. A person for whom this is the dominant anchor will be most concerned to exercise, develop and be rewarded for his or her expertise in a particular functional or technical area. He or she will not welcome a general management role. Schein has argued that a person's dominant anchor emerges during early career, and that it has significant consequences for the way his or her career unfolds and how it should be managed.

Yet another approach to lifespan development is the study of age-related change in thinking style and capability. Whether performance of cognitive tasks increases, decreases or remains static during adulthood depends on the relative requirements for quickness or flexibility of thought and use of accumulated experience. Older people tend to be less good than younger ones at the former (though the age-related deterioration is less than once was thought) and better at the latter. The related notion of wisdom is broader than simply using experience. It also refers, among other things, to recognition of multiple points of view and tolerance of ambiguity. As the 21st century arrives, it looks as if the use of wisdom to manage one's own career will be increasingly important.

MANAGING CAREER TRANSITIONS

Some, though not all, research indicates that people are moving more often between jobs, as well as into and out of employment, than used to be the case. These so-called work-role transitions are examined in Chapter 8. They vary a lot in terms of how expected, welcome, controllable, novel and commonly experienced they are. So not all transitions are the same. For managers at least, sideways and even downward moves are more common than they were in the 1980s and before. In spite of this, it is dangerous to assume that transitions are necessarily experienced as stressful. On the other hand it is also the case that they are often managed rather poorly by individuals and particularly by organizations. This matters, not least because the speed with which a person adjusts to a new job, and the kind of adjustment reached, have important implications for his or her value to the employing organization. Whilst transitions out of an organization are often supported by outplacement provision (see Chapter 4), those within the organization are frequently left to chance.

It is helpful to think of transitions into or between jobs in terms of interrelated stages. Each stage throws up somewhat different issues for individual and organization. Perhaps the most neglected stage is the one before the transition actually happens – often referred to as anticipation. Often, though not always, individual and organization have considerable prior warning that a transition is going to happen. Often, though not always, they fail to make good use of the opportunity to prepare. Later adjustment problems can often be averted if an organization resists the temptation to make a job sound wonderful in every way, and instead tries to portray it as experienced by those who do it. This is often called a realistic job preview.

The way newcomers to a job or an organization are dealt with can influence greatly not only their satisfaction but also the way they do their job. Highly structured induction and socialization help a newcomer to feel at home, but also tend to lead him or her to adopt a rather traditional, un-innovative approach to the job. The extent to which newcomers seek out information from other people, particularly about how things are done in the organization, also affects how well they perform and how satisfied they are. This re-emphasizes the need, made explicit in some organizations, for newcomers to be allowed to ask 'idiot questions', without fear of scorn.

One longer-term outcome of transitions often desired by organizations is commitment to the organization by the person who made the transition – though, as we have already seen, this does not sit easily with the reality of insecure and short-term employment. Furthermore, the kind of commitment desired is a positive one based on a sense of attachment and belief in the organization's values rather than a resigned sense of not having alternatives. Most of the copious research in this area suggests that the commitment of staff depends more on their experience of work challenge, skill development and perception of future long-term career paths in the organization than on salary. There is a certain irony here, since long-term career paths are exactly what many organizations are saying they cannot provide these days.

Transitions into work at the start of working life and out of it at retirement perhaps have more potential than others to be difficult and to require careful management. But on the whole it seems that, at least from individuals' points of view, they are not usually experienced as significantly more taxing than other transitions. This may be because their occurrence is usually anticipatable, and there are plenty of other people around who have done it already and can offer advice and support. Also, like some other transitions, these are becoming fuzzier. The transition from education to work is less clear cut because of work experience during education. Subsequent returns to education as part of lifelong learning may also mean the transition is experienced more than once. Gradual retirement is becoming more common, and changes in pension scheme rules may accelerate this trend.

Relocation of employees, either as individuals or en-masse, is a requirement of some organizations. Its prevalence is influenced by the economic cycle, and by the competing forces of globalization, which increases the relocation and teleworking, which reduces it. It is clear that not everyone is willing to relocate when asked, though of course sometimes there may be little choice. For those who do, any problems that arise are more likely to surround family and education than the work itself. Here again, organizations often seem unaware of the need to manage relocations with sensitivity and thoroughness.

DIVERSITY IN CAREERS

The work-force in most Western countries is becoming much more evenly balanced in terms of gender and ethnicity, and thus less dominated by white males. There is also a slowly increasing acceptance that other individual differences such as sexual orientation and disability should be better reflected in the work-place. It is a fair bet that career patterns are becoming more diverse, with more moves between organizations and occupations, more periods of unemployment and more participation in education during adulthood. All these trends (particularly regarding gender and ethnicity) have contributed to an increased concern in organizations with managing diversity, and this is discussed in Chapter 9.

A good business case can be made for managing diversity, but implementing meaningful processes to support it is not simple. A few seminars on cultural or gender differences probably will not change an organization's culture very much on their own, and run the risk of creating as many stereotypes as they dispel. Managing diversity is different from equal opportunities or affirmative action because it emphasizes the recognition, utilization and development of individual differences, not just equality of treatment when opportunities arise. Nevertheless, an organization which is effective in managing diversity will certainly take steps to ensure equal access to opportunities for different groups of people. Thus managing diversity is a substantial extension of equal opportunities, not a competitor with it.

The increasing participation of women in the labour market has contributed to an increase in the number of dual career couples. Life in dual career households can have both high rewards and high pressure. To varying degrees in different countries, the norm is for the man's career to take precedence over the woman's, and for the woman to perform the lion's share of housework and child-care. Dual career couples are subject to a number of difficulties and constraints, some practical such as ensuring satisfactory jobs for both partners, and some less tangible but still important, such as guilt at 'leaving' children with a child-minder.

Various forms of flexible working and support can assist members of dual career couples to juggle their various commitments and to be effective performers at work. These include a broader range of leave entitlements (e.g. paternity, special leave to care for a sick relative), career breaks, variable working hours and job sharing. Some organizations have tried initiatives of this kind and found that the benefits seem to exceed the costs. The extent to which such initiatives become established may ironically in the long term depend on the extent to which men as well as women make use of them.

In the meantime, there remains clear evidence that women enjoy less success than men in terms of material rewards and hierarchical advancement, and that this cannot fully be explained by rational factors such as less training or work experience. It is also the case that the causes of women's career success are less well understood than those of men's career success. On the other hand, the increasing diversity and fragmentation of career paths means that, on average, men's careers are becoming more like women's have been for some time, and hierarchical position and salary are becoming less appropriate as measures of career success.

Writers have disagreed about whether the net effect of technological change is to eliminate or to create jobs. Either way technological and organizational changes in the 1980s and 1990s have led to spells of unemployment for many people, including many who did not expect it. The evidence is conclusive that unemployment is a debilitating experience for most people who experience it, probably because it hampers achievement of personal goals whether or not these are related to employment. In the 21st century it will be important for both individuals and societies to view unemployment as a time for properly resourced support and development for roles in or out of employment.

Another consequence of downsized, outsourced organizations and more customer-focused cultures has been increasing numbers of entrepreneurs and self-employed. They would not all have chosen these roles given a free hand, and relatively few people in Western countries seem to have a clearly entrepreneurial orientation to their career. There appear to be at least two types of entrepreneur – those who primarily want freedom to do things their own way, and those who primarily want to create new and/or better products and services. On the whole, most entrepreneurs are not greatly different in terms of psychological make-up from other people, which suggests that successful ones can be made (via training and education) as well as born.

In an information-rich, knowledge-based work-place the role of technical specialists is likely to become increasingly important, though as already noted they need to work effectively in teams with non-specialists. It is possible to identify distinct stages in technical careers, and interestingly these appear to be only very loosely connected with age. A key point in many technical careers is a transition from primarily technical to primarily managerial work. Many specialists do not want to make that transition, and are in any case ill-equipped to do so. But the use by organizations of technical career tracks rising to quite senior levels separate from generalist tracks seems less than appropriate now that organizational integration and information-sharing are so highly prized.

CONCLUDING COMMENTS

So the concept of careers will be just as relevant in the 21st century as it ever was, but now more complex and in need of more skilful management. There needs to be clarity at societal level about how they are to be managed, and this involves integrated policies regarding education, training, employment, careers guidance and welfare. People who are unemployed need resourcing to maintain or enhance their employability, or the prospect of a viable alternative lifestyle if this is not realistic. Information technology will progress much further and increasingly be a medium for career management as well as the day-to-day performance of work in the 21st century. But social as well as technical networking will remain important as a career management tool for individuals.

Individuals working within organizations should take any opportunities offered to manage their career, and be aware of additional opportunities to do so within local communities. All individuals need to be aware of labour market trends which might affect their employability, and respond accordingly. We need also to be clear about our own preferences and values in a 21st-century world in which many alternative lifestyles are visible to everyone and attainable to some. Everyone needs to be open to lifelong learning of new skills and from experience. The need for personal development places particular strain on people already under pressure to achieve immediate performance targets at work, and on those who are unemployed and lack psychological and material resources.

Twenty-first-century organizations should remain involved in career management, principally through supporting self-development but also on occasions through a more controlling organization-centred approach to ensure that human resources are developed appropriately to organizational needs. Organizations must avoid being too greedy in what they ask of their members. Members have valued roles and identities other than their work ones. Whilst they can legitimately be asked to commit themselves to organizational objectives at work, the other areas of their lives should be respected, particularly nowadays when employment relationships tend to be more transitory.

The increasingly blurred boundaries within and between organizations can cause some ambiguity about exactly who is a member of which organization or part of one, and about exactly who should be eligible for career management interventions and what interventions would be most appropriate. But the blurred boundaries also represent a chance for multi-organization partnerships to pool resources and career opportunities. Career management interventions may serve a particularly wide range of purposes in organizations where most or all employees are telecommuters or for other reasons rarely in the same place.

The success of career management interventions in organizations probably depends upon a number of factors. Prominent among these are doing a small number of things well, acknowledging and valuing diversity, achieving a balance between individual ownership and integration with organizational processes, and evaluation of the impact of interventions on employee behaviour.

2

THE NATURE AND CONTEXT OF CAREERS

DEFINING CAREERS AND CAREER MANAGEMENT

Let's start at the beginning. What is a career? The word is used a lot, but in different ways by different people. If this book is to be useful, we need to have a clear idea of what we are talking about. Please pause for a couple of minutes right now and jot down what the word career means to you. This isn't a test, but a clarification. The rest of this page is blank for your jottings.

Right. Thank you for taking the time to do that. Here is my definition of career for the purposes of this book:

A career is the sequence of employment-related positions, roles, activities and experiences encountered by a person.

You might think this is just the kind of definition you would expect from an academic: rather woolly and using four words where one would suffice. There might be some truth in that, but there is method in my madness. Let's think for a while about the implications of using this definition of career, and then let's compare it with yours.

Notice first that my definition of career treats it as personal. It is in a sense a possession of a person. It is not simply an occupation, like law or hairdressing. You or I might have a career which involves work in law or hairdressing, but the career is ours. Law or hairdressing is simply the context in which our career takes place.

Second, and related to the first point, if a career is personal then it has a subjective element. That is, it is partly the product of our own ways of viewing the world. Hence two people who had exactly the same sequence of jobs in the same places at the same times would almost certainly not have had identical careers. In my definition, the word 'experiences' gives this game away. Two people experience the same sequence of events differently. For example, one might regard it as a success, the other as a disappointment. One might find it easy to explain why things worked out as they did, but the other might not. And so on. So, whilst some aspects of career are objective in the sense that they can be verified by an observer, e.g. employment-related positions, others are not.

Third, and perhaps most important, careers concern a *sequence* of employment-related positions, etc. We are concerned with how an individual's positions, roles, activities and experiences unfold over time, connect with each other (or not), change in predictable or unpredictable ways, match (or not) a person's changing skills and interests, and enable (or not) a person to expand his or her skills or realize his or her potential.

Fourth (yes, there's more!), notice that my definition of career refers to employment-*related* positions. In other words, positions, roles, activities and experiences that feed into or result from the person's employment are part of a career. (Employment is taken to include self-employment, entrepreneurship, consultancy and freelance work.) Although there is undeniably an element of ambiguity here, career can include some aspects of, for example, leisure activities, education, domestic tasks and family roles if these link with employment. To take a personal example, I have been learning Spanish in evening classes. This may affect my future roles at Loughborough University Business School as, for example, our links with Spanish universities and teaching of Spanish as a stream in our European Business degree develop. Notice also that individuals' careers can influence the functioning of the organizations in which they work.

Finally, a career is not necessarily confined to one occupation, nor does it necessarily involve promotions or other indicators of increasing status such as income. So, whereas some people distinguish between jobs (low status, few promotion prospects) and careers (high status, many promotion prospects), I am firmly rejecting that line. That's really all there is to say on this point, but I want to emphasize its importance. Everyone who spends time in and/or seeking employment has a career.

To illustrate the point here are two very different careers considered sufficiently noteworthy to be featured in newspapers. To repeat, both are careers, neither yet complete. From the *Loughborough Echo*, 29 March 1996, a local career:

> Plumber Clive Jones joined William Davis Ltd in February 1946 as an apprentice at the tender age of 14, and now half a century later he plans to finally down tools next year when he retires. Clive completed his five years training on site while working on the Loughborough council house building programme and other schemes in the area. Chairman Eddie Davis congratulated Clive on his 50 years' service saying . . . 'Over the years he has shared his knowledge of plumbing with many young apprentices. We can all learn from his example of dedication and commitment to the trade.'

From *The Times*, 20 March 1996, a story from the USA:

> Louise Rafkin has quit academic life to become a charwoman. As a career move it may sound like an old warplane, smoke trailing from its engines, plummeting to earth. But listen to Miss Rafkin and you start to see it differently. Life as a cleaning woman is, she says, more satisfying than as a college lecturer – and more lucrative. 'I really don't think I was very good as a teacher, so I stopped. I'm really good at cleaning. I am thorough and fast and I enjoy leaving a clean house behind.' Acquaintances from university days are told on a need-to-know basis about her new life. . . . The family are slowly getting used to her new occupation, though it has been 'a little awkward' for her mother.

As well as showing how varied careers can be, these examples also hint at a few phenomena that will be explored further in subsequent chapters. Clive Jones has worked in the same trade and the same company for half a century, but you can be sure that the tools, skills, techniques, materials, practices and standards have all changed. So has his role in the company – from learner to mentor, among other things – and so have the people around him. Louise Rafkin is a particularly good example of the importance of subjectivity in careers, though notice that her unusual perspective causes some tensions in her relationships. She made an assessment of her skills and personal style and acted upon it.

To recap, it is important to remember that careers, as they are construed in this book:

(1) are defined in personal terms;
(2) have a subjective element;
(3) concern *sequences* of employment-related experiences;

(4) are *not* confined to employment itself;

(5) can include employment in different occupations;

(6) do *not* necessarily involve high status occupations;

(7) do *not* necessarily involve promotion.

How does this compare with your definition? I would guess there are some differences. In my experience of running classroom exercises, there is a fair chance that your definition concerned solely activities at work, high status occupations and upward movement in terms of promotion. But I could be wrong! I'm not trying to score points off you; only to make the important point that career is a broader concept than it is often given credit for. The particular relevance of my relatively inclusive definition as we approach and enter the 21st century will shortly become apparent, but first a few more introductory comments are in order.

MORE TERMINOLOGY

You may have noticed the word 'roles' in the definition of career given earlier. How do roles differ from positions or activities? Well, let's take an example. Imagine a factory manager who moves from one company to another similar one, let's say in order to increase her salary. The position changes since it's a new job in a different place. But probably the change is small in terms of the job description. In both the old and new job it is likely to include responsibility for meeting production requirements, minimizing waste, maximizing product quality, recruitment training and discipline of staff, health and safety, plant purchase and maintenance, and so on. If we watched the factory manager working in her new job, we would probably observe similar activities. But the *role* may or may not change. The notion of role includes intangible but important elements such as the informal status accorded to the person, the style of personal relationships he or she adopts (and/or is expected to adopt), and the relative priorities he or she assigns (and/or is expected to assign) to the various tasks. In other words, role includes elements of how things are done as well as what is done. It also makes reference to how the post-holder fits into the pattern of social relationships in the work-place.

Now, I don't want to tax your patience for semantics too much but it is necessary to pin down the meaning of a couple of terms that include the word career. First there is *career development*. This is all too readily reduced to promotion, but I'm sure that by now you won't fall for that one. Career development is more helpfully seen as the particular way that an individual's career unfolds – i.e. how that career develops. This has both descriptive and explanatory elements. We need to be able to describe how the careers of individuals unfold using language that does justice to their individuality whilst also allowing some comparison between the careers of different individuals and groups. The explanatory aspect of career development refers to identifying *why* the careers of individuals or groups of people unfold in the way they do. This relies on adequate description so we know what we're explaining. In turn, explaining why careers turn out as they do helps direct attempts at change if this is felt necessary. The word 'development' has positive overtones, but note that for our purposes this is not necessarily the case. Some people's careers can develop in unwelcome ways, or in ways about which the individual feels neutral.

However, given the title of this book, we need to be clear above all about what we mean by *career management*. This can be thought of as attempts made to influence the career development of one or more people. These attempts might be made by that person or those people themselves, or they may be made by other people – for example their bosses, human resource managers, professional associations or partners. Straight away we can make some further observations:

First, there are many phenomena which can contribute to career management. For now let's simply make distinctions between (1) personal thoughts and actions such as reviewing one's past experience or seeking careers guidance; (2) organized events such as career development workshops; (3) policies laid down by organizations, e.g. employers, government, professional bodies.

Second, career management always has (or, at least, should have) defined goals. The notion of managing careers implies that they can turn out for better or for worse. The first step in career management is of course to define what counts as better or worse in any given context, and for whom. The second is to specify what 'better' means in terms of achievable and verifiable goals. The third is to plan actions geared to achieving those goals. The fourth is to put those actions into practice. You might think that's the lot, but it isn't. The fifth step (rarely done, I would say, and I'm not alone) is to evaluate the success of the career management, and the sixth is to use the results of the evaluation to alter the goals or actions if necessary (Hirsh, Jackson and Jackson, 1995).

Third, different stakeholders in careers may have different aims. A marketing trainee may aim to gain wide experience quickly and attempt to manage his or her career by networking with people in different parts of the company and applying for various internal vacancies. On the other hand senior management in the company may wish employees to specialize, and introduce policies which, for example, restrict certain kinds of job move. So your career or mine may be subject to various attempts at career management, and these attempts may be directed at different goals, or even contradictory ones.

Fourth, given that careers have a subjective element, the management of careers can theoretically include not only attempts to influence the sequence of activities, positions and roles, but also attempts to influence how individuals *experience* them. We are dealing here with attitudes, opinions and emotions. Let's take a topical example which will recur throughout this book. In delayered and downsized organizations, individuals' initial expectations about what frequency and level of promotion counts as success may be unrealistic. Career management by individuals and their employing organization may therefore include attempts to scale down expectations.

THE TIMES THEY ARE A-CHANGING (WELL, QUITE A LOT)

There is no shortage of gurus telling us all that the world of work is changing fast – see, for example, Handy (1994). There is a respectable case to be made that we are experiencing change on something like the scale of the industrial revolution involving transformation from mass production in bureaucratic organizations with semi-skilled labour to small-batch production with computer-controlled machines and small teams of highly skilled workers, and more emphasis on information (Piore and Sabel, 1984). Global competition and technological change are the major triggers of this. They have created, or maybe simply accentuated, needs for cost competitive production and organization, high speed to market of new products/services, high responsiveness to customer wishes, high product/service quality and high innovation. At least, that is the conventional wisdom, though journalist Will Hutton (*Guardian* newspaper, 28 December 1995) has argued that in fact technology is currently making little significant impact on the way people live their lives, and that the big changes happened earlier in the 20th century. In the UK, there has been a substantial transfer of many activities and organizations from public to private sector, with consequent changes in organizational goals, culture and work requirements. Perhaps the most important trend is the overall pace of change – little remains the same for long in this brave new world. This has led some to assert that the only constant is change. Others go further, and say that the only constant is ever-increasing pace and scale of change. Most commentators see an inevitability about this – a kind of technological determinism. Adler (1992) argued that the biggest threat to jobs was not too fast a pace of technological change, but a pace that was too slow in comparison with competitors. Not that technology alone is the whole story. Carnevale (1995) has suggested, on the basis of much research on the impact of new technology, that the technology itself accounts for 20% of any competitive improvements, education another 20%, and that the other 60% is down to the way in which technological and human resources are used.

So is this the end of life as we knew it, or at least employment as we knew it? One author at least has heralded the death of the job (Bridges, 1995), let alone career. Yet for millions of people in employment the world is still a first cousin of the one they inhabited a few years ago – more uncertain and more difficult, yes, but not unrecognizable. What has changed is that few people can look forward to a predefined sequence of job roles within one general line of work in one or a small number of similar organizations, with periodic promotion. In truth, this kind of career was always the preserve of a minority of people (not everyone even wanted one like this), but now it is even rarer.

Peter Herriot (1992) has pointed out that this may seem like a strange time to be promoting the notion of career, but it is strange only if we restrict the notion of career to the one described in the previous paragraph. Of course, we are not going to do that, and neither does Herriot. It is exactly because maps of the employment terrain are harder to come by that we need to pay more attention to careers and their management. Careers are still important to the people who own them. As Jackson *et al.* (1996, p. 7) have stated:

> Whatever soothsayers about the future of careers may assert, individual men and women remain passionately interested in . . . their personal development through work experience over the course of their lifetime. People are more concerned about their skills, competencies, future roles and opportunities for self-determination than they are about most other areas of their work experience.

So if careers are more difficult to describe, predict, explain or manage than they once were, all the more reason to devote time and effort to doing so. It is no coincidence that this book and others like it are being commissioned by publishers. The market is there.

So exactly how are things changing in the world of work? Economic and technological change combine with demographic trends to produce a pretty long list. I have chosen to describe a round dozen. Here they are, in no particular order:

Workload

In the UK at least, there is no doubt that people in employment perceive themselves to be working harder and longer than was previously the case (Coe, 1993). Schor (1991) has reported a similar picture in the United States, with workers working more hours but earning less than a decade earlier. This obviously brings significant stress and strain, as well as probably some benefits. From a career point of view, it *may* mean a perception that things aren't working out as hoped, that the rewards once expected aren't worth the effort, that there is little or no time for reflection on one's career, or that the 'psychological contract' about what employer and employee can expect of each other has been broken. We will return to some of these themes in subsequent chapters.

Organizational changes

A whole range of changes in organizational structures has occurred. Common ones are reductions in labour force numbers (often referred to as downsizing or even rightsizing), and reductions in the number of layers in the organizational hierarchy – so-called delayering (Wheatley, 1992). Of course, for plenty of people this means redundancy, which might be an unexpected feature of their career. For others, as well as meaning increasing workloads, organizational changes also lead to more difficulty in gaining promotion and bigger jumps in responsibility when it does occur. It may also mean less close scrutiny of their work, and more chance to do their own thing. Although perhaps less publicized than downsizing and delayering, there has also been a tendency to break up large organizations and devolve more responsibility, or at least accountability, to staff who are in direct contact with customers. This tendency to empower staff can mean more decision-making than some had expected or wanted (see also Chapter 3).

Organizational changes have occurred partly to reduce costs, but also partly to increase the speed and appropriateness of response to customer demands. They have been characterized as breaking boundaries and barriers within the organization, for example between departments, and between the organization and its environment, for example via joint ventures, secondments, and people working *in* the organization who are not employed *by* it. The need to change perpetually and reflect on experience and learning is more apparent than was once the case.

Organization of work

Several other organizational changes have also been geared towards more effective use of labour. These include project teams, where, instead of or as well as functional-based structures, organizations are structured around teams assigned responsibility for certain tasks. For those involved, this may mean working with a wider range of people than they had expected, and carrying out new tasks with new skills, not least interpersonal ones. It may also provide an opportunity to discover new avenues for future work. Related to project teams is labour flexibility. This takes two general forms (Legge, 1995): first, flexibility in terms of numbers in the work-force. This is sometimes achieved using part-time and/or limited-term employment contracts. Second, there is flexibility in the way labour is deployed. In other words, instead of being able to do just one job, staff at a variety of levels may be trained to do several so that they can switch between them. Here again, a wider range of skills and experiences is involved, almost by definition. High demands of people's time and adaptability may be made, but there may also be a wider range of subsequent job possibilities, and easier transitions between them, than was once the case. A striking example of how labour flexibility might transform the operation of a factory can be found in an article by Merrick (1995), which describes the turnaround at a Rank-Hovis mill in England. Increasing labour flexibility went hand in hand with other changes such as a more participative management style, however, so it is not certain that flexibility was the key factor.

Outsourcing

Another form of labour flexibility is referred to as outsourcing. This is where people are brought in to perform various functions for an organization, even though they are not employed by it on a long-term basis, or even at all. Two general kinds of work are most likely to be treated in this way. One is relatively low status and portable work such as cleaning and catering. The other is highly skilled specialist work such as information technology consultancy. Although the two groups of people involved in outsourced work are obviously very different, both are sometimes referred to as peripheral because they are not employees of the organization in which they are working. This is in contrast to the core workers, who are. Outsourcing means that more people's careers involve roles as outsiders than used to be the case. For some it also means an erosion of employment conditions and security, whilst for others (chiefly the more skilled) it may present the opportunity to negotiate contracts involving more favourable work, development and rewards than they would have been able to as core employees.

Short-term contracts

There is some uncertainty about the extent to which limited-term contracts are being routinely used. The number of professional and managerial staff on short-term contracts rose by one-third between 1992 and early 1996 (David Smith, writing in the *Sunday Times*, 31 March 1996). This last fact may help to explain why short-term contracts have become prominent as an issue: the middle classes are more affected by them. Peter Robinson, an academic at London School of Economics, was quoted thus in the *Financial Times* of 14 December 1994:

> The tendency is to look around you and see what's happening in your own area. I and my colleagues are all on temporary contracts now, but when you look at the proportion of employees on temporary contracts you see it hasn't changed between 1984 and 1994.

More recently, Guest and Mackenzie Davey (1996) have reported only very limited use of short-term contracts in companies participating in the Careers Research Forum – mostly quite large and well-established ones. Gregg and Wadsworth (1995) reported that the proportion of full-time UK employees without tenure rose from 3.6% in 1975 to 14.7% in 1993, though this had a lot to do with an increase from a 6-month qualifying period for employment rights to 2 years. Martinez (1994) reported that in Spain close to half of employed people were on fixed-term contracts. This figure rose to 85% for 16 to 19 year-olds.

Even so, there is a clear trend towards senior managers being brought into organizations for only a few weeks or months to sort out specific problems. This presents a potentially interesting new element of careers for, among others, near-retirement executives, or those wanting intermittent not constant employment.

Disappearance of organizational career structures

Top managers in some employing organizations have responded to change by asserting that it is no longer possible to manage careers on behalf of employees, or even in partnership with them. Effectively, they are telling their staff 'you're on your own', and this remains a common stance even though some organizations have cautiously reintroduced attempts at career management (Hirsh, Jackson and Jackson, 1995). These matters are covered in more depth in later chapters. Here we need simply to note that more people are being expected to do more career management for themselves, though in truth the smarter ones probably never relied upon organizational career development systems, even comparatively effective ones.

Changing skill requirements

Another consequence of the pace of change is that in many occupations frequent retraining or updating is needed. This is most obvious in response to changes in production technology or information technology, but is also evident in other settings. For example, in recent years staff working in banks have been expected to be increasingly customer- and sales-focused as the financial services industry becomes more competitive. The logical consequence of such trends has been nicely described by Hall and Mirvis (1995a, p. 277):

> Careers too are becoming more complex. We would argue that what we are seeing now, instead of one set of career stages spanning a lifespan . . . is a series of many shorter learning cycles over the span of a person's work life. . . . As a result, people's careers will become increasingly a succession of 'mini-stages' (or short-cycle learning stages) of exploration-trial-mastery-exit, as they move in and out of various product areas, technologies, functions, organizations and other work environments. . . . Thus, the half-life of a career stage would be driven by the half-life of the competency field of that career work.

There are many implications for individuals of changes such as this. These too are explored in more detail later in this book. For now, we can note that attempts by governments (e.g. NACETT, 1995) and others to encourage lifelong learning are well founded, and individuals would be well advised to jump with alacrity on that bandwagon by seeking out opportunities for training and education throughout their working life. To some extent the UK education and qualification system is coming more into line with these needs, for example through NVQs and SVQs and credit-transfer schemes. But there is still some way to go. Action of some kind may well be necessary because the educational achievement of UK youngsters is not good relative to many competitor countries (Smithers and Robinson, 1991). The United States has some similar concerns (Fosler *et al.*, 1990), with about 13% of adults functionally illiterate. As Howard (1995a, p. 34) has put it: 'The bureaucracy era had dumb jobs and smart people; the post-industrial era threatens to have smart jobs and dumb people.'

Diversity in the labour force

The proportion of women in the labour force of most Western countries is increasing. In 1971, 37% of the UK labour force were women. By 1994 this had risen to 44% (Court, 1995). Of all the European Union countries Denmark has the highest percentage of married women who work, at 80%, with the UK next at 65%. By the year 2000, 48% of the American work-force will be female and so will half US entry-level managers compared with 15% in 1977 (Greenhaus and Callanan, 1994). New jobs tend to be occupied by women. For example, in the UK in the last quarter of 1995, the level of employment among women increased by 83,000 but only by 35,000 among men (*Financial Times*, 18 April 1996). The proportion of UK women in employment who have children is also rising: 66% in 1994 compared with 55% ten years earlier. Lone mothers have a lower participation rate, however, and this has not increased.

Many of the jobs occupied by women are part time and, consistent with their increasing participation in the labour force, there has been a rapid rise in the number of part-time jobs. The number of part-time workers within the active UK labour force increased from 15% in 1971 to 28% in 1994 (Naylor, 1994). Many of these jobs have low skill requirements and low pay. Similar patterns are also discernible in most Western countries. Also, about one and a quarter million people in the UK are known to hold more than one job – usually 2 or 3 part-time ones, but sometimes full-time. Most holders of multiple jobs do so not because they want to have what have been termed portfolio careers (Handy, 1989), but through sheer economic necessity. What all this adds up to is that more people's careers are involving part-time work, more women have careers as defined earlier in this chapter, and probably more people are experiencing careers where the number of jobs they hold, as well as what kind of job, is a significant factor. Although there are of course plenty of households where a woman is the only earner, the increasing participation of women in the labour force does mean that dual-earner households are becoming more common, with implications for the careers of both parties (see Chapter 9).

The working populations of many Western countries are also becoming more culturally diverse. In the US only about 15% of young people entering the work-force are white males. At the start of the 21st century white US-born males will constitute 29% of the work-force, down from 46% in 1990. In the UK, ethnic minorities form 5.5% of the total population, but more than this in younger age groups.

Ageing populations

Most Western countries also have ageing work-forces. In a UK labour force predicted to contain 30.1 million people in 2006, there will be a rise of 2.4 million in the number of people aged 35 to 54, and a fall of 1.6 million in the number under 35, compared with 1993 (Ellison, Butcher and Melville, 1995).

Some implications of this are hard to predict with certainty. However, a likely one is that older people will need to be increasingly adaptable – as is already the case to some extent. It is not possible to leave learning new ways of doing things to the youngsters. A possible implication of an ageing work-force is that pension funds will be under considerable pressure, and organizations may value older workers more than they do at present – if only through sheer necessity. So, as I write this at the tender age of 37, perhaps I can look forward to the dubious pleasure of another 30 years in employment, with considerable changes in role requirements along the way. Early retirement with enhanced pension deals at 55 or 57 may quite quickly be a thing of the past. Recalling that during my childhood my parents regularly reminded me how lucky I was to be growing up in the affluent 1960s and 1970s, I am now able to retaliate by telling them how lucky they are to be retired with pensions in the 1990s. Incidentally, another trend is that the transition out of employment, commonly known as retirement, is becoming even fuzzier. Disengagement is becoming rather gradual for some people, with part-time assignments or occasional projects over months or years forming a buffer between full-time employment and no employment (Feldman, 1994 – see also Chapter 8).

Small organizations

I noted earlier the tendency for some large organizations to devolve power and responsibility to local units, or even break up altogether. There is in fact an increase in the proportion of the labour force working either as employees of small organizations (less than 20 employees) or as self-employed, so that in the mid-1990s they represent respectively about 34% and 13% of the UK work-force (Employment Department, 1995). There is no doubt that more people than in the recent past are having careers that involve some time running their own business, for which development of entrepreneurial skills and interests will normally be needed (more on this in Chapter 9). The significant number of self-employed people and the high failure rate of new businesses attest to this. One recent survey of new firms in the UK (Cressey and Storey, 1995) found that less than a fifth of small businesses formed in mid-1988 survived to the end of 1994. Businesses started by people aged 50–55 had twice the success rate of those of 20–25 year olds. This was partly because some businesses, particularly those of younger people, were wound up when the person found a job, not because the business was failing. But even after allowing for this, the older people had more success.

Working at or from home

It has been estimated that about 3% of people in UK employment work predominantly or entirely from or at home using communications technology (Labour Force Survey, 1994). A fair proportion of these can be described as teleworkers (Chapman et al., 1995): that is, they use communications technology as an alternative to travelling to a work-place. Telecommuters are thought to constitute about 5% of the American work-force in 1992, which represented a doubling since 1988 (Caudron, 1992). It may be important to distinguish between those who work *from* home (that is, they travel much of the time) and those who work *at* home. The adjustment demands may be somewhat different. The number of people working from or at home does seem to be on the increase, with a doubling even within the 1990s (Davidson, 1996). Certainly at my children's school gate during the 1990s I have noticed increasing numbers of men who are working at home, at least part of the time, and less suspicion that we are either skiving or unemployed! The press has latched on to developments such as the construction in picturesque spots of telecottages and even whole televillages of dwellings equipped with an impressive array of communications technology already installed. It is not yet clear whether individuals or employers will welcome teleworking on a massive scale. For plenty of people the social contact that work brings is important, and much work, at least at present, requires a person's physical presence. Where two partners both telework in a home without innumerable spare bedrooms, there is of course an acid test of the extent of departure from old norms, as newspaper journalists presumably familiar with the problem have noted. Assuming there is one man and one woman, whose computer goes on the kitchen table?

Insecurity

Employment insecurity is perhaps here to stay, both as a reality and as a perception. The *Observer* newspaper of 5 May 1996 reported the results of an ICM poll of 1,440 UK adults conducted in April 1996. Eighteen per cent had suffered some unemployment since 1992, and 14% had taken a pay cut or increased hours to keep their job. In all, 57% had stayed in the same job throughout the four years. Only 54% were absolutely or fairly certain that they would keep their job over the next year, compared with 70% in 1991. One-third of the sample thought they would find it fairly or very easy to obtain another job if they had to; 53% said it would be fairly or very difficult. Peter Kellner, in his commentary on these figures, wrote:

a huge gulf persists between the economic state of the nation, as measured by the (mainly cheerful) data from the Government, and the economic mood of the people. The experiences of difficult times during the early Nineties have caused something akin to a huge national hangover. Millions of people are acutely nervous about their job prospects and the value of their homes.

O'Reilly (1994) reported that, in the US, whereas around 1980, 79% of management and 75% of non-management employees said their job security was good or very good, by 1992 these figures had dropped to 55% and 51% respectively. It seems that most European countries have been poor at job creation relative to the USA, though the UK has done better than the

European norm. However, many of the US jobs created are insecure and poorly paid. Even in countries with good job creation records, people tend to believe, probably accurately, that job security is more elusive than it was. From a career point of view, it looks as if long-term planning is virtually out of the question whilst equipping oneself as well as possible for the next move becomes ever more important. Charles Handy (1994) uses the analogy of the sigmoid curve, which is one that rises then falls. If you think about your future when you are already on the down, you are thinking too late. The time to prepare your medium-term future is when things are still good in your present role – and of course, that is not the situation in which most of us are prompted to think ahead.

A RECAP: CAREERS AND THEIR CONTEXT

A quick way of summarizing the impact on careers of the current context is to say that people will be (indeed, are now) working with more diverse colleagues and customers, in jobs with frequently changing skill requirements and limited security, more often part time, and spanning different organizations or even outside organizations altogether. From an individual point of view, it is often argued that your career goal and mine nowadays should be not so much to keep our job (that is outside our control) but to remain employable by collecting portfolios of skills and experiences which are attractive in the market.

Of course, to a large extent it was always thus. What Kanter (1989) termed the bureaucratic career was always open only to a minority and probably reached and passed its peak in the second half of the 20th century. In case you hadn't guessed, the bureaucratic career involves progression upwards through various jobs with increasing responsibilities and financial rewards in a formally defined hierarchy. In other words, it reflects the definition of careers I have already rejected as too restrictive. Many readers of this book will have, or have had, parents and maybe grandparents who experienced bureaucratic careers. But before that? I was struck by the story a Scandinavian student told me about his great-grandfather who tried his hand at various kinds of work. One of these was seafaring. On one voyage he travelled to a port in Spain, where it turned out that his country needed a diplomatic representative. He was the right nationality, he was there, so that's what he became – but only for a time before moving on again.

Kanter (1989) identified two other career forms, both of which are on the increase as the bureaucratic career declines. First is the professional career, in which people develop specialized, socially valued knowledge and skills. There is often a professional association, through which attempts are made to restrict access to learning and practice. Professional careers are based upon development of expertise which does not necessarily require upward status moves, or indeed any moves at all. The final career form identified by Kanter is the entrepreneurial career. This involves creating or developing products, services or knowledge in order to add value or profitability to an organization. The organization may well be one's own small business or even oneself, but the idea of the entrepreneurial career is also applicable in large organizations seeking to be more market responsive.

Michael Arthur (1994) has coined the term 'boundaryless career' to reflect current trends. This echoes the drive by Jack Welsh, of General Electric, towards a boundaryless company. Careers are boundaryless in the sense that, either by choice or from necessity, people move across boundaries between organizations, departments, hierarchical levels, functions and sets of skills. Organizations themselves become harder to define, and at the extreme become little more than 'legal fictions which serve as a nexus for a set of contracting relationships among individuals' (Badaracco, 1988, p. 87, quoted in Collin and Watts, 1996). This movement is possible partly because such boundaries are dissolving anyway, and partly because, to the extent that they are still there, maintaining employability requires one to make greater efforts to cross them than was once the case. According to Arthur, there is little point in thinking of entrepreneurial people or careers as separate types: all people and all careers must be characterized by entrepreneurship. Academics, if not others, have acknowledged for at least the last 20 years that most careers do not conform to Kanter's (1989) bureaucratic model, but Arthur criticizes much careers research for still reflecting too many of the assumptions of that way of thinking. You may or may not agree as you read about some of that research in later chapters of this book. My own view is that some of the recent research is more enlightened, but much empirical work, i.e. research in which data are collected, is based upon more bureaucratic views of career if only for the sake of simplicity and convenience.

Finally, though, it is important not to get too carried away with all this big talking about careers. Although things are improving, the United Kingdom is not noted for high levels of education and training attainment (Smithers and Robinson, 1991). There are many people who have very limited skills to offer in the labour market and probably negative experiences of education and training. All three of Kanter's career models are a long way removed from their experience – which indeed may be yours. Hutton (1995) has suggested that the UK can be described as a 30/30/40 society. The first 30% are *disadvantaged* in the sense that they are either unemployed or economically inactive. The next 30% are in and out of work – mostly work with little employment protection and few benefits. These people can be described as *insecure*. The remaining 40% are relatively *privileged*, in relatively secure employment or self-employment. Security here means not that their current jobs are safe, but that they have skills and experiences that are in demand in the labour markets. One might add that well-chosen or fortuitous education, training or job assignments might help members of the insecure group move to the privileged category. The absence of these might lead to mobility from the privileged to the insecure group. But mobility out of the disadvantaged group is difficult indeed, and perhaps ever more so as keeping up to date often relies upon information technology which is becoming cheaper but remains unaffordable for people living on social security. The societal task of enabling people to break out of the disadvantaged group is daunting indeed, but the moral and practical cases for devising ways of making it happen are strong. Who can justify a society where more than half the population have very limited opportunity to contribute to its economic well-being, and who wants to deal with the consequences for public order?

3

MANAGING CAREERS IN ORGANIZATIONS – AN OVERVIEW

Myth has it that medium and large organizations used to offer careers of the narrow 'onward and upward' type, and what's more they played a large part in helping individual employees manage their progress. The myth has some truth of course, though as I have already pointed out, it applied only to a minority of staff. Still, the game has changed. The previous chapter set the general scene for careers and career management, and contained clues as to why the game may have changed. This chapter picks up where the last one left off, and examines in more detail the current organizational setting of careers. We start by having a closer look at some of the changes briefly described in Chapter 2, particularly those most concerned with organizational structure and functioning. Analysis then moves to how jobs and careers can be described in changing environments. I will also discuss the in-vogue concept of the psychological contract as a means for understanding how people make sense of the changing employment relationship. Although the whole 'career thing' has become much more difficult for organizations to handle, it can be argued that they should try harder rather than give up. So the last part of this chapter looks in general terms at the career management interventions organizations can use, and how they may be integrated.

DELAYERING AND DOWNSIZING

First, many organizations have delayered and downsized. In English, that means that they have fewer employees and fewer levels in the status hierarchy. Lawler, Mohrman and Ledford (1992) reported that two-thirds of the leading one thousand US firms both downsized and delayered during the 1980s. In Japan too about two-thirds of companies downsized and/or restructured in the late 1980s and early 1990s. The UK picture seems to have been little more complex (Wheatley, 1992). About one-third of the companies surveyed seemed to be employing *more* managers in 1992 than they did in 1987, though about half employed fewer, and the majority of those also had fewer levels in the management hierarchy. Delayering and downsizing were most common in large organizations.

Wayne Cascio (1994) has argued that often when organizations downsize they make few adjustments to their ways of operating. They are still governed by what Cascio referred to as the three Cs: Command, Control and

Compartmentalization. So fewer employees are expected to do the same work, but that rarely happens. Downsizing is often done hastily and with little regard to the organization's aims and key competencies. It is claimed to be a last resort, but Cascio argued that few companies seriously consider alternatives such as pay cuts or a shorter working week.

Ironically, it seems that the cutting has been overdone in many organizations. They are often too lean to respond effectively to new opportunities. Some have suffered the organizational equivalent of memory loss, since many experienced members with much valuable knowledge have walked, or, rather, been pushed, out of the door. According to Martin Walker in the *Observer*, 19 May 1996, the word 'downsizing' has been replaced by 'dumbsizing' by some in the USA, who have seen companies like AT&T and People's Gas run into operational and public relations difficulties after overdoing the cutting. Management recruitment in the UK in the mid-1990s is on the increase again, and somewhat in excess of what the overall UK economic performance would seem to require – a likely sign that organizations dispensed with the services of too many of their managers (see, for example, Margaret Coles in the *Sunday Times*, 19 November 1995). Something similar seems to have happened in the USA, where Cascio (1994) indicated that 80% of companies had had to go back and re-recruit some of the people they had made redundant. An even deeper irony has also attracted attention: redundant ex-employees being hired back as consultants at a daily rate of pay far in excess of what they had earned as employees.

A number of consequences follow for careers. Most obviously, perhaps, a number of people are now pursuing, or attempting to pursue, careers in locations, organizations and types of work that they perhaps did not expect. Their earlier experiences in work may not have helped them very much in terms of their employability, or prepared them for coping with redundancy. For those who remain, and indeed those who find work in new organizations, different career rules now apply. In delayered organizations the jumps between levels are greater, so promotions are likely to be rarer and entail greater increases in responsibility than was once the case. Some senior managers are tempted to recruit from outside the organization because they cannot envisage current staff making the big step required (Hirsh and Jackson, 1996). It does not take great imagination to appreciate how the current staff (what remains of them) might feel about this. On the other hand, my own experience of what managers say about promotions in delayered organizations is in fact quite positive. The predominant opinions are that (1) the gaps between levels of responsibility used to be too small anyway, and (2) the greater significance of promotion forces more careful selection decisions, thus paradoxically reducing the chances of someone being promoted to the level of his or her incompetence.

DEVOLUTION AND DECENTRALIZATION

Many organizations have greatly reduced the size and significance of their head offices. This is partly to do with cost-cutting and delayering, but also partly a consequence of attempts to devolve decision-making power closer to the customer. In turn, this is designed to increase the quality of customer service and speed to market of new products and services. Charles Handy (1994, pp. 117–18) has given some good examples of this trend.

It isn't always genuine, of course. Herriot (1992) has pointed out that most organizations are a million miles away from achieving balances between various competing and potentially contradictory forces, or paradoxes as Handy (1994) likes to call them. Thus, people at the sharp end are expected to be innovative and explore new ideas, but are all too rarely supported with training, room for manoeuvre or tolerance of the mistakes that inevitably occur. Organizations still demand loyalty and commitment. But their attempts to bring everyone into line with new corporate values can very easily stamp out the free-thinking and diversity that are required for innovation and effective product/service delivery. Also, people want to retain their individuality because they believe that they need to keep their distance, psychologically speaking, from an organization that might easily spurn them at almost any time. They are probably right. Hirsh, Jackson and Jackson (1995, p. 15) quote one senior manager as follows: 'Companies are looking for highly committed, totally flexible and completely disposable employees.' This may have been a little tongue-in-cheek, but even so, many a true word is spoken in jest.

A certain amount of cynicism may also surround another aspect of devolution, which has come to be called empowerment. At its best, this means empowering individuals to act as mature, responsible, decision-making beings with the skills to do whatever is required to deliver quality customer service without needing to seek permission from superiors. On the other hand, it can mean heaping unwanted extra accountability on poorly trained and poorly paid people who possess neither the skill nor the inclination to take it, whilst simultaneously withholding any real decision-making power. The latter would not be considered real empowerment of course, and sometimes happens because first- or second-level supervisors feel unable or unwilling to let go of power they feel should be theirs. This has precedents in earlier literature on job redesign for shop-floor workers, where similar trends were often observed (e.g. Cordery and Wall, 1985). Real empowerment means the sharing of information, freedom of action and rewards throughout the whole work-force (Lawler, 1992).

Some aspects of the wider economic environment militate against empowerment. Hirsh and Jackson (1996, p. 17) have expressed this very nicely by asserting that external threats and the short-termism of the Stock Exchange have 'made the 1990s a paradise for the old-fashioned slave driver. For all the talk of empowerment, never have so many been disempowered by so few.' In a devolved organization there is also the problem of who manages careers. This is particularly pertinent where short-term productivity is the only goal, which is often the case. The line manager will probably want the person who can perform best now, not someone who will, with a bit of luck, grow into the job. Yet in reality, as Andrew Mayo (1991, p. 155) points out:

It is usually said that 'the best person for the job is the one to be appointed'. One cannot argue with that except to say that sometimes the choice between candidates is marginal and the development opportunities for personal growth of a candidate should then be part of the consideration.

We may nod our heads sagely in agreement with this, but a busy local manager might see things differently, and in a devolved organization there may be nobody with the power or credibility to enforce Mayo's wisdom.

OUTSOURCING

In the last chapter I noted increasing ambiguity about what an organization is, and where its boundaries lie. One reason for this is the increasing presence in a work-place of people not actually employed by the organization whose work-place it is. Instead, they may be employed by a person or organization holding a contract to deliver certain services to the host organization. Or they may work through a 'deploying' organization such as a recruitment agency. Adler (1994) has noted that in the USA there are nearly a million leased employees. The leasing company acquires staff, pays them and leases them back to their old employer, or to other employers. Another possible arrangement is illustrated by Cable and Wireless (Walker, 1996), which set up a business unit called Flexible Resource Ltd which acts as an in-house placement agency supplying external candidates for temporary posts to companies in the Cable and Wireless group. One implication for careers is how outsourced staff can ensure that their skills remain up to date. To a considerable extent the bigger deployers such as Manpower are taking responsibility for training, particularly in IT skills. In fact it might be argued that deployers are in the best position to do this, since they prosper or perish according to whether they can supply people who have marketable skills. It will be interesting to see whether this extends to facilitating the career development of staff on their books.

The presence of these so-called contingent workers in organizations can have some interesting effects. In a small-scale study, Pearce (1993) found that the commitment to the organization of contingent workers was only slightly lower than that of regular employees working alongside them. This may, however, say more about the erosion of employee commitment than the generation of contingent workers' commitment. Employees who worked alongside contingent workers trusted the organization less than those who didn't – presumably because the presence of contingent workers reminded them that they could be next for the chop. Also, Pearce found a tendency to assign tasks requiring co-operation to groups of employees, whilst more solo independent tasks were assigned to contingent workers. So the two types of staff may tend to develop rather different skills, preferences and styles of work.

COMPETENCIES – A NEW LANGUAGE FOR CAREERS?

There has been some frustration in the UK and elsewhere that whatever information the education system might or might not teach people, it didn't seem to equip them to *do* very much. Many surveys of employer opinion about education at various levels have established that this is a fairly widely held view. On the other hand there are other data which seem to show that the standards of literacy and numeracy of UK schoolchildren and the levels of qualification achieved by school-leavers and graduates are rising fairly consistently. Leaving aside questions of whether, for example, an upper second class degree means today what it did 20 years ago, the various data seem reconcilable if one draws the conclusions that (1) whilst standards are rising, requirements of the labour market are rising faster; (2) the knowledge and skills required to obtain some educational qualifications are not closely related to those required in most employment; (3) the qualifications most commonly obtained are not in subject areas most required in the labour market.

Partly as a result of the apparent gap between education and employment, the UK has seen considerable growth in qualifications based on what people can be observed to *do*, as opposed to what they can show that they *know*. Some argue that this is more a result of government concern about an educational establishment perceived to be hostile to vocationalism than a result of pressure from employees (Stewart and Hamlin, 1992). At the same time, psychological research has consistently shown that many factors dilute the connection between individual characteristics such as intelligence and personality on the one hand and work performance on the other (Mischel, 1984). So instead of selecting and appraising people on the basis of general statements about the kind of person they are, how much better it would be to do so on the basis of what they do. This is the main thrust of the notion of competencies. As Arnold and Mackenzie Davey (1992) have pointed out, there are many different definitions of competencies (also sometimes called competences). Some approaches seem to fly in the face of the rationale for their existence I have just described. In the field of management, Klemp and McClelland (1986) identified a number of competencies, some of which were very explicitly about general personality, e.g. self-esteem, not observable behaviour.

Again within management, Jacobs (1989, p. 33) provides a more specific definition of competency: 'an observable skill or ability to complete a managerial task successfully'. This definition can be generalized quite easily to other kinds of work, but sticking for a moment with management, the following performance criteria from the Management Charter Initiative can serve as examples (National Council for Vocational Qualifications, 1992).

In key role 'Management of finance', Unit 4 is 'Secure effective resource allocation for activities and projects'. Within this unit, element 4.1 is entitled 'justify proposals for expenditure on projects'. This element includes the following performance criteria, among others:

- Estimates of costs and benefits are supported by valid, relevant information
- Appropriate members of staff are encouraged to contribute to the recommendations
- Where challenges to the proposal are made, further explanation is given to promote acceptance
- Where proposals contain information and suggestions from other people, the final details are checked with them for accuracy prior to submission.

These performance criteria are clearly intended to be observable and measurable. Note, however, that nothing is entirely objective. The first two criteria listed above include the words valid and appropriate, which are partly matters of judgement.

The late 1980s and 1990s have accordingly seen the introduction of National Vocational Qualifications and Scottish Vocational Qualifications in the UK (see, for example, Jessup, 1991). NVQs and SVQs are designed for people in employment. They are available at different levels of complexity, and many are quite specific to a certain sector of employment or even a certain kind of job. Assessment is by observation of people in their real work environment or occasionally a simulated one. Observation is based on competencies as defined by Jacobs (1989): does the person display the skill or ability to complete his or her work tasks effectively? The skills and abilities concerned are defined at quite a specific, concrete level. For schoolchildren, General National Vocational Qualifications are being introduced which to some extent match the style of NVQs. They are based on types of work rather than academic subjects, and are assessed on the basis of portfolios of work demonstrating what the students can do, more than exams testing what they can write down about what they know.

Competencies may even take over from jobs as the basis of a new framework for organizing. This would in some ways be a logical consequence of the move towards observable performance and the rise of human resource management (see, for example, Storey, 1995). An organization's human resources as expressed in its core competencies (Prahalad and Hamel, 1990) may represent its key competitive advantage – an insight which really tests the reality of many a chief executive's rhetoric about how 'people are our greatest asset', 'our business is our people' and similar. As Lawler (1994, pp. 4, 6, 9) has put it:

> Instead of thinking of people as having a job with a particular set of activities that can be captured in a relatively permanent and fixed job description, it may be more appropriate to think of them as human resources that work for an organization . . . the capabilities of individuals are the primary focus . . . selection is best thought of as finding individuals for organizational membership not a particular job.

Along with such a change goes an emphasis on teamwork, on short-term projects, and on paying people for the possession, use and development of their skills, not for the status of job they hold. As we have already seen, there are significant changes in all these directions in many organizations. To illustrate how they tend to go together, consider this snippet from the *Observer* newspaper of 12 May 1996 concerning a leading UK financial services company:

> Abbey National is scrapping its present staff structure and introducing a more flexible, skills-based system for remunerating employees . . . the current 15-grade structure will be cut to four levels. Most pay rises will come as a result of learning new skills rather than being promoted to a grade.

Notice too that this is *not* quite the same as most performance-related pay schemes, which are usually based on a person's behaviour matched against a job description.

Another company to emphasize competencies is Chase Manhattan Bank. As their Vice-President for Human Resource Development Stephen Martin (1995, p. 20) explained: 'we are exploring the option of aligning what people can offer – their competencies – against the demands of customers, rather than against the ill-fitting and ill-designed demands of jobs'. Accordingly, the bank's human resource development and reward systems are being geared to the identification, measurement and development of competencies. Succession planning in this context is not an attempt to supply individuals for jobs, but an attempt to fill gaps in the bank's competencies when and where necessary. Whilst Martin is obviously enthusiastic about this, some questions do arise. Perhaps the most obvious is how the efforts of individuals can be effectively co-ordinated where their work is described in terms of competencies rather than sets of tasks.

You might not be surprised to hear that competencies, NVQs, etc. have been subject to some criticism from various quarters. I will briefly mention these shortly: they are yet another illustration that there is rarely if ever consensus about any 'one best way' in the field of human resources. First, though, let's think about what the competencies movement might mean for our careers.

We may see acceleration of a trend that is already visible for people to frame their curriculum vitae at least partly in terms of their competencies. Sooner rather than later we may construe careers as the sequence of competencies acquired. Indeed, at least one definition (Bird, 1994) is expressed in exactly that way. The positions a person has held may be more or less irrelevant, and indeed undefinable because positions in terms of statically defined jobs may scarcely exist. For individuals, career management will start from the question 'what competencies do I need to acquire and how can I do this?' rather than 'what job would I like to get if I could?' Many readers will probably recognize that already the first question often lies behind the second, which is itself a reflection of current changes in careers.

For an organization, the management of careers should also be framed around considerations of the competencies it requires for future competitiveness. If people are viewed as human resources, those resources need to be invested in and developed. Taken to the extreme, the shift in thinking would not only be away from jobs and towards competencies, it would also be away from individual people too. Instead of (or perhaps as well as) asking how S. Shah can be developed, the question might become something like how company competencies in the management of new start-ups can be developed.

Even within more orthodox job-based organization structures, there is no doubt that competency frameworks can provide a very helpful way of describing the requirements of jobs and identifying similarities and differences between them. For reasons I will mention in a moment, competencies are not always seen as ideal or complete for this purpose (Hirsh, Jackson and Jackson, 1995), but are nevertheless a useful tool for both individuals and organizations in considering future paths.

So what are the possible drawbacks of competencies and qualifications based upon them? A detailed examination of what they are and their strengths and weaknesses is beyond the scope of this book, but some have argued that the following problems exist:

(1) The notion of competency implies 'good enough' rather than excellence, which is increasingly required in every work-force.
(2) There are doubts about whether NVQs adequately assess the extent to which a person can perform his or her work tasks appropriately across different situations and at sufficient speed.
(3) Related to the previous point, to what extent are competencies and NVQs portable? Does being able to, for example, gain colleagues' commitment to a course of action in a factory with good industrial relations also mean that one could do the same at, for example, a health clinic with a history of labour disputes? There is a real tension here between two desired characteristics of NVQs/SVQs: portability and relevance to specific employers (Loan-Clarke, 1996).
(4) Some argue that there has been an overemphasis on competencies at the expense of knowledge and understanding (see, for example, the report by Authers and Wood in the *Financial Times* of 15 December 1993). To pursue the previous example, a broad and deep understanding of group processes might be required if a person is to be able to adjust his or her behaviour appropriately between settings.
(5) Finally, it could be said that competencies are a little like ingredients in a recipe. They are essential for good cooking, but the cook has to make appropriate choices about how and when to combine them, and how much of each to use. Thus it is perhaps not surprising that some people, when they see a competency-based profile of a job they know well, observe that somehow it doesn't quite capture what that job is really about.

THE PSYCHOLOGICAL CONTRACT

This might sound like a strange notion – after all, contracts are usually distinctly unpsychological documents which contain clear statements about what the parties involved can expect from each other, and about the penalties for violating the agreement. The psychological contract is not quite like that. The concept has quite a long history in organizational behaviour, with possibly the first recorded sighting being in Argyris (1960). Although it is possible to quibble at length about definitions, I did enough of that earlier in this book, so here is a definition of the psychological contract that I will not pick over – not much anyway.

> An individual's belief regarding the terms and conditions of a reciprocal exchange agreement between that focal person and another party . . . a belief that some form of a promise has been made and that the terms and conditions of the contract have been accepted by both parties.
>
> (Robinson and Rousseau, 1994, p. 246)

So, in the context of careers, the psychological contract represents informal, unwritten understandings between employer and employee(s). From the employees' point of view, the psychological contract is the agreement that they think they have with their employer about what they will contribute to the employer via their work, and what they can expect in return. This matters for one very simple reason. During the last part of the 20th century, and especially since around the mid-1980s, the trends described earlier in this chapter and in Chapter 2 have changed the careers landscape, and for the worse in many people's opinion. The deal many employees thought they had with their employer has turned out to be worth less than the paper it wasn't written on. As Herriot and Pemberton (1995, p. 58) put it in their book entitled *New Deals*, captains of industry 'have set in motion a revolution in the nature of the employment relationship the like of which they never imagined. For they have shattered the old psychological contract and failed to negotiate a new one.' So what was the old psychological contract that has been broken? Herriot and Pemberton draw on a well-established distinction between a relational and a transactional contract. The former refers to a long-term relationship based on trust and mutual respect. The employees offered loyalty, conformity to requirements, commitment to their employer's goals, and trust in their employer not to abuse their goodwill. In return, the organization supposedly offered security of employment, promotion prospects, training and development, and some flexibility about the demands made on employees if they were in difficulty. But global competition, new technology, downsizing, delayering and the rest of it have put an end to all that. Many employers no longer keep their side of the bargain. The new deal is imposed rather than agreed; it is transactional rather than relational. Instead of being based on a long-term relationship, it is much more like a short-term economic exchange. The employee offers longer hours, broader skills, tolerance of change and ambiguity, and willingness to take more responsibility. In return the employer offers (to some) high pay, rewards for high performance and, simply, a job.

According to Herriot and Pemberton (1995), many people have understandably responded very negatively to these changes. This might be particularly the case for managers, many of whom identify with the organization rather than a profession. Their sense of identity and self-worth is therefore particularly threatened when their organization 'rats' on the deal. Reactions vary, but include outrage, disappointment, anger, sullen conformity, fear, anxiety and probably lots of other negative things besides. The new psychological contract results from changes principally directed towards cost-cutting for increased competitiveness. However, this has gone about as far as it can go, and indeed even further if some of the research described earlier in this chapter is to be believed. Now and in the future, the UK economy will rely upon the knowledge, skills, creativity and perhaps most of all the goodwill of its work-force rather than further cost competitiveness. Unfortunately, relationships between employers and employees are not currently conducive to that. Herriot and Pemberton describe typical reactions to violation of the psychological contract as get out, get safe or get even – or, to put it another way: to leave, to stay and keep your head below the parapet, or to stay and take your revenge.

Nevertheless, it is not clear exactly how employees' behaviour is affected by their perception that the psychological contract has been broken. Parks and Kidder (1994) have suggested that employees' perceptions of the nature of the injustice, and its cause, are likely to influence the extent to which they engage in what have been called organizational citizenship behaviours (OCBs). The 'good citizen' behaviours include:

(1) compliance – conforming to job requirements;
(2) conscientiousness – conforming in a superior way, e.g. extra good attendance;
(3) sportsmanship – restraint and forbearance;
(4) courtesy – keeping people informed and trying to avoid problems;
(5) civic virtue – e.g. participation in meetings, training;
(6) altruism – helping others with their tasks and concerns.

The 'bad citizen' behaviours have been described as *mere* compliance (i.e. doing just enough and no more), shirking/negligence, negativism, theft, harassment/threats and overt damage. These good and bad citizen behaviours may well form a helpful framework for evaluating the impact of a broken psychological contract on work behaviour. Herriot and Pemberton's (1995) work rather suggests that many employees aren't impressed by employers' protestations that it's down to factors outside their control and that everyone in the organization is suffering, especially when they see their top managers receive big payoffs. Blaming the employer as opposed to more distant causes such as global competition or government policies may well be linked with reductions in OCBs.

This all has relevance to careers because it affects the sequence of people's work experiences. For many, the breaking of the psychological contract by employers has led to major disappointment and frustrated ambitions. Perhaps it also colours people's experiences of their work. Imagine that a new task has been added to your job. If you already believe your employer is exploiting you, your reaction is likely to be quite different from what it would have been if you felt you were in a more benevolent environment. The change in the psychological contract is also one expression of the trend towards people managing their own careers. It is less viable than it was to look toward your employer for future development. Some employers have withdrawn entirely from career management, and some are concerned with short-term profitability to the exclusion of virtually all else.

The American academic Denise Rousseau and her colleagues have been prominent in research concerning the psychological contract in the work-place (see for examples Rousseau, 1990, 1995; Robinson and Rousseau, 1994). Their research has supported the general distinction between transactional and relational contracts, though there is a little uncertainty about exactly what each consists of. An example of this uncertainty concerns training. This could be seen as an element of a relational contract because it suggests a commitment to employee development. On the other hand it might best be construed as part of a transactional contract because it enables the person to achieve more immediate results in his or her work, or because it enables the person to move quickly to his or her next assignment. Probably the safest conclusion is that the conceptual distinctions between relational and transactional contracts are clear enough, but the elements of each vary somewhat between organizations.

Rousseau and Wade-Benzoni (1995) have gone beyond the relational–transactional distinction in proposing a simple 2 x 2 matrix (see Figure 3.1).

		Expectations of performance (by both organization and individual)	
		Specified	Not Specified or Vaguely Specified
Expected duration of	Short-term	Transactional	Transitional
employment relationship	Long-term	Balanced	Relational

Figure 3.1 Four psychological contracts
Source: Adapted from Rousseau and Wade-Benzoni (1995)

Transactional contracts are short-term with clearly specified expectations of performance, whilst relational ones are exactly the opposite – long-term with unspecified or vaguely specified performance terms. Transitional contracts are in evidence in organizations formerly characterized by relational contracts but thrown into uncertainty by economic or organizational upheaval. Balanced contracts are probably what core employees can expect in the future. Like relational contracts, they are long-term but now performance standards are more clearly specified, though periodically reset as projects come and go.

In an interesting piece of research, Robinson and Rousseau (1994) found that 70 of their sample of 128 MBA graduates reported that their employer had violated their psychological contract at least once in their first two years of employment. What was more, violations by the employer increased the chances of the employee leaving the organization, and decreased the satisfaction of those who remained. This result was doubly noteworthy because it remained true even after taking into account employees' attitudes toward their employing organization when they first joined up. The three areas where the contract was most likely to be violated were training/development, pay/benefits and promotion opportunities. Promises concerning the nature of the job, job security, feedback, management of change, responsibility and people were all less often broken, but were nevertheless reported broken by a third or a quarter of the sample. Other research with the same sample (Robinson, Kraatz and Rousseau, 1994) found that employees tended to reduce their felt obligations to their employer whilst increasing what they felt their employer owed them. Furthermore, true to the reciprocal nature of the psychological contract, violation by the employer was associated with a reduction in employees' felt obligations.

Some cautions

The psychological contract looks like a powerful and helpful concept in understanding people's behaviour at work, and some aspects of their subjective career. The term is enjoying increasing use, and even the most cursory literature search turns up a lot of articles where it gets a mention. Before we get too carried away, however, it is necessary to point out a few problems. One has already been covered: the ambiguity concerning the content of relational and transactional contracts.

The psychological contract concerns each party's perceptions of what they have promised and been promised. Given that the psychological contract is implicit and unwritten, there is plenty of scope for interpretation. It doesn't take too much imagination to suppose that some employer violations perceived by an employee might be vigorously denied by the employer. In any case, who speaks for the employer? An employing organization has multiple constituencies (e.g. senior line managers, HR department, managing director), and they may not have the same understandings, or indeed any understanding, of the reciprocal obligations and rights of each party. If a psychological contract is *purely* one party's understanding of what is agreed, it might be more informative to investigate how and why they arrived at that understanding than simply to label it the psychological contract.

At its heart, the fulfilment or violation of the psychological contract has two components: what was promised and what was or was not delivered. Most analyses of the psychological contract assume that the broken promise effect is key. However, whilst the evidence suggests that is the case, there have been no direct tests of the proposition. Maybe simply getting less of what you like and want is what matters, whatever you think was or was not promised. Although I have made this point only briefly, I believe it is important. If it's a broken promise that matters, it should be possible to design research which shows that employee attitudes and behaviours are more affected by failing to receive something they believe was promised than by simply failing to receive something they would like.

Negotiations

A very valuable part of Herriot and Pemberton's (1995) book concerns their suggestions for how to deal with the new organizational context for careers. In particular, they go into some detail about how organizations and individual employees should negotiate and renegotiate explicit understandings of what they expect to give and receive. This is in fact a natural and constructive follow-on from some of Peter Herriot's earlier work in which he argued that the only way to make selection interviews effective was for both sides to drop what Schein (1978) referred to as the 'climate of mutual selling' and be honest with each other about how they see themselves, what they want and what they are willing to offer. The argument now is that there is such an atmosphere of distrust that the old implicit relational contract can never be re-established. But that doesn't mean there can never be mutually satisfactory relationships between employers and employees. Clearly understood agreements are required, based on the short- and medium-term perspectives of both sides (the long term is considered over-ambitious these days). These agreements might in fact be quite like the old-fashioned relational contract in content, depending on what each side believes they need and can offer.

Successful negotiations require not only negotiating skills, but also good knowledge of one's own situation together with an accurate appreciation of the other party's situation. From the individual's point of view, this implies a need to appreciate what one can already offer in terms of useful skills or experiences that the prospective employer will value. Crucially, it also requires some understanding of what further skills and experiences one needs to develop in future in order to remain employable and navigate oneself in directions one wants. The organization (or, rather, the person or persons representing it) needs a similarly strategic view of current and future skill needs, and a perspective on for how long, and how, this person might contribute. In turn, this requires continuing systematic reviews of staffing requirements possibly using some of the techniques described by Mayo (1991). In other words, both sides need to take a career perspective. Not a lifetime-of-employment type career, but career in the sense of a *sequence* of work-related experiences, roles, positions. The agreement also needs to be monitored to check whether it is being adhered to by both sides. Some subsequent renegotiation may well be required in response to changing circumstances or ambitions.

This all adds up to a fairly wide-ranging process. Just some of the formidable list of considerations for both sides are shown in Tables 3.1 and 3.2. Simply being able to answer the questions satisfactorily, let alone negotiate on the basis of them, would be quite an advance for most of us. In labour markets where employers have the upper hand, they might not feel a need to negotiate because they can always get someone else. That might be true, but on grounds of enlightened self-interest as well as ethics Herriot and Pemberton (1995) argue that negotiating deals is the right thing to do in terms of employee commitment and effectiveness. Note also that a highly individual employment relationship is implied here, as opposed to one characterized by collective bargaining. This too captures the spirit of the times, and raises some interesting possibilities such as you or I having an agent to conduct these negotiations. Perhaps this will be a future role for trade unions, professional associations or employment agencies.

Table 3.1   Doing the career deal I

Questions for the employing organization
How do employees discover what's expected of them now and in the future?
How do employees learn about how the business is going?
How can they understand the implications for their career?
How does top management learn how employees are thinking?
Are individual differences in wants discovered and considered?
Does the organization ever engage in career negotiations – i.e. does it change its offers to accord with employees' wants and offers?
What types of employee wants is the organization prepared to consider (e.g. family situation, functional preference, external employability)?
What sort of employee offer is the organization prepared to consider (i.e. existing expertise, development willingness)?
Who negotiates on behalf of the organization, and by what process?
Does the organization check whether it already has the skills and knowledge to meet its present needs? If so, how?
Does the organization check whether it is developing the skills and knowledge to meet its future needs? If so, how?
Does the organization review the nature of what it offers employees?
Does the organization monitor labour market trends in order to discover the likely availability of skills and knowledge?
Does the organization check up on the fulfilment of the contract? If so, how?
Does the organization monitor the satisfaction of both parties with the contract? If so, who does this, and what resources do they need?

Source: Adapted from Herriot and Pemberton (1995)

THE MANAGEMENT OF CAREERS BY ORGANIZATIONS

The previous sections might suggest that there is little fertile ground for organizational career management. The prevailing mood is expressed neatly in a number of vivid ways. One I particularly like is 'the ladder has unexpectedly turned into a hamster wheel' (Vaughn and Wilson, 1994, p. 44). Rather more analytically, Hugh Gunz (1989) has likened career

Table 3.2 Doing the career deal II

Questions for the individual employee
Do you know the organization's current business strategy, and what this means for its staffing policies?
Do you actively seek out information about what is happening in the organization, through official and unofficial routes?
Do you know what is happening in other organizations in the same sector?
Do you know who has the power base in the organization to help you get what you want?
Do you know what mindset you are bringing to your own career, and how this could affect your approach to negotiation?
How well developed are your negotiating skills?
Do you know what your own boundaries are for negotiating purposes, what is negotiable and what is not?
When moving job, do you consider the psychological contract you are seeking as well as the benefits package?
What time-span are you operating with in your negotiation? Are you sure it is realistic?
From the organization's point of view, what are your strengths and weaknesses? Can you use your strengths to offset your weaknesses?
Have you rehearsed selling your case in terms of business benefits rather than personal ones?
Do you know with whom you should be negotiating?
Are you monitoring the operation of the contract, including any ways in which you and/or your family and/or the organization are changing?
Do you monitor how much support the organization gives you, and whether this is enough to enable you to deliver your side of the contract?
Do you monitor changes in the prominence and satisfaction you get from your various life roles?
How does your organization signal that you are valued? Are you the recipient of these signals?
Do you monitor the external environment, so that you can put your experiences and skills into a wider context?

Source: Adapted from Herriot and Pemberton (1995)

structures in organizations to climbing frames rather than ladders. There may or may not be a single pinnacle and, for the sure-footed, movement is possible in a number of directions, including laterally and downward. It is even possible to jump off. Some people can see a particular point on the frame they would like to reach, whilst others prefer to move around and try out different locations on it. Others again would prefer not to be on the frame at all. This theme of disillusionment was taken up by Goffee and Scase (1992), who found that many managers felt their future progress was less assured, the timetable was less clear than was once the case, and it was even less clear what counted as progress. Out of a large number of job characteristics, promotion showed the biggest gap between what was desired and what was available.

Nevertheless, as we shall now see, attempts are made to manage careers in many organizations. Table 3.3 shows a menu of what I have called career management interventions available to organizations. Some of these are examined in detail in later chapters. It is very difficult to obtain definitive information concerning the uptake of these interventions. Iles and Mabey (1993) have summarized some of the relevant research on this matter, and also provided data of their own about the UK situation. It looks as if internal vacancy advertising is nearly universal. Mentoring seems to be becoming increasingly common, with perhaps close to half of organizations running

Table 3.3   Career management interventions in organizations

Internal vacancy notification. Information about jobs available in the organization, normally in advance of any external advertising, and with some details of preferred experience, qualifications, and a job description.

Career paths. Information about the sequences of jobs that a person can do, or competencies he or she can acquire, in the organization. This should include details of how high in the organization any path goes, the kinds of inter-departmental transfers that are possible, and perhaps the skills/experience required to follow various paths.

Career workbooks. These consist of questions and exercises designed to guide individuals in determining their strengths and weaknesses, identifying job and career opportunities, and determining necessary steps for reaching their goals.

Career planning workshops. Cover some of the same ground as workbooks, but offer more chance for discussion, feedback from others, information about organization-specific opportunities and policies. May include psychometric testing.

Computer-assisted career management. Various packages exist for helping employees to assess their skills, interests and values, and translate these into job options. Sometimes those options are customized to a particular organization. A few packages designed for personnel or manpower planning also include some career-relevant facilities.

Individual counselling. Can be done by specialists from inside or outside the organization, or by line managers who have received training. May include psychometric testing.

Training and educational opportunities. Information and financial support about, and possibly delivery of, courses in the organization or outside it. These can enable employees to update, retrain or deepen their knowledge in particular fields. In keeping with the notion of careers involving sequences, training in this context is not solely to improve performance in a person's present job.

Personal development plans (PDPs). These often arise from the appraisal process and other sources such as development centres. PDPs are statements of how a person's skills and knowledge might appropriately develop, and how this development could occur, in a given timescale.

Career action centres. Resources such as literature, videos and CD ROMS and perhaps more personal inputs such as counselling available to employees on a drop-in basis.

Development centres. Like assessment centres in that participants are assessed on the basis of their performance in a number of exercises and tests. However, development centres focus more on identifying a person's strengths, weaknesses and styles for the purpose of development, not selection.

Mentoring programmes. Attaching employees to more senior ones who act as advisers, and perhaps also as advocates, protectors and counsellors.

Succession planning. The identification of individuals who are expected to occupy key posts in the future, and who are exposed to experiences which prepare them appropriately.

Job assignments/rotation. Careful use of work tasks can help a person stay employable for the future, and an organization to benefit from the adaptability of staff.

Outplacement. This may involve several interventions listed above. Its purpose is to support people who are leaving the organization to clarify and implement plans for their future.

an organized scheme or actively encouraging the formation of informal mentor–protégé pairings. Formal career path information is also quite common – around one-third of organizations. This is perhaps surprising given the structural changes in organizations, and the difficulty experienced by at least some groups in discerning what these paths are (Arnold and Mackenzie Davey, 1994). Self-assessment materials, development centres, career planning workshops and career counselling probably feature in about one in four or one in six organizations, though in the case of career counselling this conclusion depends a great deal on how the term is defined. Of course, the proportion of organizations using an intervention is not the same as the number of people experiencing it. Any intervention may involve just a few members of the organization or all of them.

Table 3.4 Use of career management interventions by organizations in three countries

	Australia (%)	USA (%)	Singapore (%)
Career workshops	28	34	24
Career workbooks	18	18	10
Career action centres	14	20	2
Counselling	31	41	20
Succession planning	62	65	69
Job rotation	58	54	60
Mentoring	29	21	44

Source: Drawn from data reported by Gutteridge, Leibowitz and Shore (1993)

An international study of career management interventions has been reported by Gutteridge, Leibowitz and Shore (1993). A number of organizations in several countries and continents were surveyed via their human resource managers. The data were not reported fully and were only partly comparable between countries, but Table 3.4 shows some of the comparisons it is possible to make. It looks as if, internationally, the use of mentoring is a little lower than found by Iles and Mabey (1993), whilst counselling and career workshops are somewhat more commonly employed.

But why might interventions like this be used? What can they achieve? One quick answer is that little is known about what they *do* achieve. Evaluation studies are difficult to carry out. There are usually many things happening simultaneously in an organization, so it is hard to be sure whether any changes that occur are due to the intervention. Also, evaluation studies are often in-house, and not for public consumption (Russell, 1991). One might add that interventions tend to be evaluated either against very 'soft' immediate criteria such as whether people enjoyed them, or against quite 'hard' and distal criteria such as organizational performance. There are other intermediate criteria that could be used, as long as they reflect the aims of the intervention. These might include people's commitment to, and intention to stay in, the organization; the extent to which people engage in career planning and exploration of options; the extent to which people fulfil roles which develop competencies vital to the organization, and so on.

The claims made about what career interventions will achieve (London and Stumpf, 1982; Gutteridge, Leibowitz and Shore, 1993) often include:

(1) increasing employee commitment, satisfaction, motivation;
(2) increasing productivity, performance, person–job fit;
(3) identifying which employees have the most potential;
(4) identifying how well employees match organizational requirements;
(5) developing employees in line with business needs;
(6) socializing employees into the organizational culture.

However, as noted above, it is often not clear whether such claims are justified. This uncertainty can often make senior managers quite sceptical and unwilling to spend money on career development interventions.

Hirsh, Jackson and Jackson (1995, p. 30) point out that the many interventions in reality probably serve only a small number of important purposes. Different interventions may achieve the same purpose, and the same intervention may achieve different purposes in different settings. These purposes might be:

- Filling vacancies
- Assessment of potential, competencies, skills or interests
- Development of skills, competencies
- Identification of career options
- Action to implement career plans

Notice that with the exception of the first of the five possible purposes, each could be primarily serving the needs of the organization or those of the individual. So, assessment could be undertaken to help the organization review or implement a person's future assignments in the organization, or it could primarily be to help the person do that. Indeed, the person could do the assessing him- or herself (more on that in later chapters). The same applies to development, identification of career options, and action to implement career plans. The options and plans could be those of the individual or of the organization. People responsible for career management in organizations need to be clear about which purpose(s) are served by which interventions, and primarily for whose benefit, and communicate this clearly.

That said, it is undoubtedly the case that some interventions more obviously contribute to career management on behalf of the organization than that on behalf of the individual. Guest and Mackenzie Davey (1996) equate succession planning, appraisal and counselling with the former. Mentoring and self-development are lined up with the latter.

SELF-DEVELOPMENT

In one sense self-development can be taken to mean something like:

> this organization is so chaotic and strapped for cash that there is no point waiting for something to be organized for you. Anyway, it wouldn't have any payoff for the organization. You'd better find your own way around, organize your own training, use your networks outside the organization, buy a 'plan your own career' book and work things out for yourself, by yourself. Oh yes, . . . good luck!

Yet it can be much more constructive than that. Mackenzie Davey and Guest (1994) have observed that although some organizations take the line described above, others have recognized that they can provide a helpful context in which people can engage in self-development. This can take the form of financial support to engage in learning – just about any kind of learning as far as some employers, such as Ford and Rover, are concerned. Some organizations produce or sponsor career workbooks that employees can complete in their own time, or set up career action centres that people can use or not as they see fit. The availability of mentors as part of a fairly unmanaged scheme, or provision of career development workshops, might also be construed as self-development. So the message in this version of self-development is something like:

> Things are changing too quickly to guarantee a certain sequence of posts in this organization, even if you perform well. However, it is in your interests and those of this organization that you should maintain or enhance your competencies and employability, and that you should become accustomed to learning new things and taking the initiative. Therefore this organization will provide some supports which enable you to do those things, but it will not do them for you.

So really, the first message is saying that none of the interventions described in Table 3.3 will be available, whereas the second is saying that some interventions will be available but employees must do most or all of the work required to benefit from them. The first message is difficult for just about everyone. The second message too is little consolation for two main types of people. First, there are those who for whatever reason do not have, or believe they do not have, the skills to manage their own careers. On the other hand, this second message is not nearly as daunting to these people as the first, and effective support for self-development will include some training or orientation in how to play the new game. The second group are those, usually senior in the organization, who worry that any attempt at career management by organizations runs the risk of raising people's hopes too much, and/or helping them to realize that they want to leave. What's more, they say, career management in the hands of staff themselves is doubly likely to do that. This is rather reminiscent of an episode of the now legendary British television series *Yes Minister*, in which the senior civil servant, Sir Humphrey Appleby, is horrified to discover that the Minister, Jim Hacker, is out of sight and unattended by a minder. His use of expressions like 'escaped' and 'on the loose in the building', as if Hacker was a dangerous beast, amply demonstrated his desire to prevent the Minister acting autonomously. Yet all Hacker was doing was talking to people he hadn't yet had much contact with, so that he could be more effective. In organizations where people are supposed to be thinking more for themselves, it is not appropriate, or even possible, to bottle them up.

An example of self-development in action is provided by Macaulay and Harding (1996). They describe how software company SCO introduced measures such as substantial outsourcing and partnerships with other organizations which reduced promotional opportunities and made career paths less clear. There was concern about employee commitment and motivation. Human resource staff decided that centralized career management systems would not meet business and employee needs. Employees needed encouragement toward managing their own careers:

The HR department issued a self-development guide, with input from senior management, which was issued to all employees. It . . . included inventories and questionnaires . . . pages on which to record training, achievements and a personal development plan. It spelt out for the first time the joint nature of future development.

(Macaulay and Harding, 1996, p. 34)

Self-development wouldn't have got very far if that was all that happened. So, coaching in how to use the guide was made available. Career planning workshops were too. Problem-solving workshops and lunchtime training sessions are now held. These developments are all consistent with increased use of project teams and continuous improvement by SCO.

Macaulay and Harding were employees of SCO involved in the introduction of self-development so their account may be a little optimistic. Even so, they do report that some new initiatives have had a mixed reception. They also say that it is still too early to judge how far the culture has moved towards self-development, even after four years. This emphasizes the long-term view required by career management interventions. The whole case suggests that self-development needs to be managed if it is to be effective.

FERTILE GROUND FOR CAREER MANAGEMENT?

Hirsh and Jackson (1996) have argued that the rapid swing of the pendulum toward individual responsibility for career management is now being reversed to a limited extent. There is a tendency for more organizational control to creep back in. This is because:

(1) Setting up facilities for self-development is not an easy or cheap option.
(2) In some organizations there has been a proliferation of career development initiatives. Nobody knows which ones are currently operating, how they fit with anything else, or what they are supposed to achieve.
(3) Self-development is not sufficiently linked to business needs. Ann Segall (1995) has provided a good example of how balances between individual and organizational interests have to be struck in her account of career development interventions at the British Broadcasting Corporation. A scheme for radio staff to learn about television and vice versa through job secondments foundered because key BBC managers realized that they didn't actually need radio and television staff to be interchangeable.

More generally, some very organizationally driven interventions such as succession planning are being reinstated but operating in a much less secretive fashion than before. On the other hand, attempts are being made to link potentially very individualistic tools such as personal development plans (PDPs) to organizational skill requirements. There are very sensitive issues here concerning who owns the information that arises from attempts at career management, as well as what is done with it. There is something of a 'devil and the deep blue sea' situation: if information from an intervention does not influence organizational processes, people not surprisingly tend to assume there is no point in participating in that intervention. On the other hand, if the information feeds into organizational systems, or is even owned by the organization, there are dangers of breaches of confidence, and possible use of the information in ways which do not suit the person who has generated it.

Drawing on a number of sources, it seems intuitively reasonable to suppose that career development interventions will be successful when:

(1) There are high levels of openness and trust between organizations and individual employees. As we saw earlier in this chapter, these days (and perhaps in the old days too) such trust and openness are rare commodities.
(2) The interventions have stated goals which encompass both business needs and employee needs.
(3) There are not too many interventions, they are compatible with one another without duplicating, and they stay in existence long enough to become well understood in the organization.
(4) Training and orientation are available to all who participate in the intervention.
(5) People who have some responsibility for managing or operating the interventions, including line managers, should be appraised partly on the basis of how well they have discharged that responsibility.
(6) There should be genuine and public top management support. Mayo (1991, pp. 54–5) provides some helpful examples of the distinction between passive and active commitment from top management. The latter includes personal involvement in the interventions and budgeting for them.
(7) Organizations need to convey a clear, careful and honest message about careers to *all* employees. The message may be different for different groups of employees, but some notion of development should be applicable to all. A message which deviates significantly from what staff see happening around them day by day is a kiss of death for career development interventions because there is immediately a credibility problem.
(8) Interventions should be evaluated against their stated goals when they have been in existence long enough to be reasonably expected to have produced results. They should be adjusted or even abandoned in the light of evaluation data. Note that this corresponds to the last two stages of the career management process outlined in the previous chapter.

INTEGRATION OF CAREER MANAGEMENT INTERVENTIONS

Some writers about careers suggest that career management is an important part of the strategy of an organization. Thus, Sonnenfeld and Peiperl (1988, p. 588) have asserted that 'A well-developed career system co-ordinates staffing activities into a process that helps the firm adapt its membership to

Table 3.5 Inputs to organizational career management

The organization	The individual
Strategic plan	Personnel information records
Operating plan	Training records
Organization structure	Appraisal and development
Organization demographics	Reviews
Job grades/categories	CVs
Person specifications	Personal growth profiles
Career structures	Career development plans
Career bridges	Test and assessment results
Development positions	Language capability
Career histories of members	Personal career history

Source: Adapted from Mayo (1991, p. 201)

its environment.' Sonnenfeld and Peiperl suggested that the main distinguishing features of career systems are (1) whether recruitment after entry level is mainly from inside or outside the organization and (2) whether assignment of individuals to jobs is made on the basis of their individual performance or their contribution to their work group.

The notion that career systems are part of organizational strategy is at one level fairly unremarkable. After all, if not, what's the point of having them? But the word strategy suggests that career management permeates the organization and that it is informed by, and informs, many aspects of the organization's functioning. Mayo (1991, Chapter 6) gives particularly thorough attention to this matter. He suggests that a wide range of information about the organization and individuals should feed into organizational career management. Table 3.5 is an adaptation of his list. He places particular emphasis on the organization's strategic plan, which should be helpful in providing information about changes in the numbers of particular kinds of job, new subsets of the organization that will come into being, changes needed in career structures, requirements for joint ventures, and so on.

Mayo (1991) also argues that a person needs to be designated a careers manager. He or she must have some influence within the organization, and must be aware of all the relevant information. Mayo goes as far as suggesting a job description for the careers manager. The following elements adapted from the job description give a good flavour of Mayo's thinking (pp. 301–2):

(1) to prepare from the strategic plan information concerning the capabilities of people, structure and culture that the organization will need;
(2) to define through agreement a common language for describing personal capability that will link people and jobs consistently;
(3) to define populations of special interest;
(4) to prepare and maintain libraries of development positions, career bridges and secondment opportunities;
(5) to recommend candidates for positions who are ready and suitable.

Mayo also points out that the careers manager must be a competent user of IT. He or she needs a database about people with key information, though not too much of it, and not too much overlap with the main personnel information system.

All this has a distinctly organized feel about it. Some would say it is old-fashioned, since now it's self-development all the way. Certainly some of Mayo's ideas do seem most easily implemented in large structured organizations which operate in reasonably predictable environments, which take some responsibility for career management, and which engage in human resource planning. Rothwell (1995) has presented a wide-ranging review of human resource planning in which she argues that although managers in many organizations claim to perform the analyses of staffing profiles, labour market trends, etc. advocated by Mayo, in reality it rarely gets done. This, says Rothwell, is partly because the pace of change makes planning difficult, but also partly because UK managers tend not to be keen on the abstract and hypothetical. She also argues that even minimal planning is better than none because it can avert really avoidable errors such as failing to plan for well-documented demographic changes or one section firing exactly the staff that another section needs. In fact, Rothwell portrays human resource planning as being much less about detailed counting and much more about co-ordination and qualitative overview than was once the case. In large measure this is consistent with the role Mayo sees for the careers manager. Perhaps more problematic is whether hard-pressed organizations will find the necessary staff time to collect and keep up to date the information required for this kind of organizational career management.

This brings us back to the observation that effective self-development does not happen by magic. Individuals need to think strategically about their own development, and organizations need to facilitate and harness self-development to meet their goals. The 'hard' form of human resource management identified by Storey (1995, Chapter 1) and others would favour a heavily organization-focused approach. It can be argued that the Investors in People (IiP) government-backed initiative in the UK is this type. There is great emphasis on identifying and satisfying staff development needs, but needs seem to refer much more to the needs of the organization than those of individual staff. Harking back to the brief discussion of human resource planning, IiP also requires organizations to have a written but flexible staff development plan.

Yet IiP guidelines certainly allow room for some staff development to be driven primarily by staff development needs as defined by the staff themselves. Once again we are back to an old and general issue: how best to balance and reconcile individual and organizational needs, and whether the parties' interests can be in harmony (see for examples Schein, 1978; Herriot, 1992). The last word for now belongs to Andrew Mayo (1991, p. 203), who manages to be balanced and committed at the same time:

Some hold the view that organizations must uncompromisingly reflect the needs of the business and people have to be fitted in afterwards. This may mean there are good people who cannot be accommodated and may be lost, and it limits the opportunities for developing people proactively. The alternative is that organizations should be built around the people available. The optimum is a pragmatic approach between the two, with the needs of the organization predominating. But compromises should be made to provide a good development opportunity for someone ready for a particular type of experience.

SUMMARY

Many organizations have made radical changes which greatly affect the working lives of people in them, often for the worse. Many staff believe they have a poorer deal than before, and are not always inclined to agree that it's all an inevitable consequence of global competition. The notion of a psychological contract is helpful in describing how some staff feel, and in explaining their current work behaviour. However, it has ambiguities and may be unnecessarily complex. It can be argued that the days of an unwritten trust between individual and organization are over for good, and that the most appropriate way to proceed is for both sides to negotiate very explicitly about what they expect to give and receive. In conditions of tight resourcing and frequent organizational change, it is not surprising that many organizations are emphasizing the need for people to engage in self-development. Yet the fact that careers are more difficult to manage than they once were could be taken as a spur to greater effort, not as a cue to give up. Many career management interventions are available to organizations, and a number of them can be considered supports to self-development rather than managing a person's career for him or her. It is important for organizations to send clear, simple messages about careers to employees, and to make sure that their career management interventions have clear objectives and are evaluated against them. This may well mean integration of information arising from career management interventions with other human resource activities such as manpower planning, though there is also a need to retain individuals' ownership of that information and involvement in the process.

4

CAREER MANAGEMENT INTERVENTIONS IN ORGANIZATIONS I

Having set the scene in earlier chapters, it is now time to examine in more detail the specific techniques available to organizations for managing careers. I will discuss the most significant of those listed in Chapter 3. In truth, just about any HR process can influence careers as defined in Chapter 2, but I will focus on those most closely connected with careers. I shall make the admittedly slightly artificial distinction between career management techniques that are not bound up with a person's day-to-day work (this chapter) and those that are (Chapter 5). So in this chapter we will examine succession and succession planning, development centres, career development workshops, outplacement and counselling. These all occur separately from a person's daily work, though of course they affect it. In Chapter 5 attention will focus upon developmental work assignments, performance appraisal, personal development planning/career reviews, career action and resource centres and self-development, networking, and mentoring. This motley collection have in common the fact that they all refer to events that can happen to, and resources and techniques that can be used by, individuals as they go about their day-to-day work.

The career management interventions covered in this chapter are techniques and events that can be not only designed carefully but also delivered in a closely controlled fashion and technically correct manner. On the other hand, those in the next chapter tend to be less amenable to thorough quality control by HR professionals. Indeed, some are career management interventions initiated by individuals without reference to managed processes. In some cases these interventions can be designed carefully and to a high technical specification, but ultimately they depend upon the commitment of people 'on the ground' to make them work.

The interventions discussed in this chapter and the next will receive somewhat different amounts of coverage. This is simply because there is more to say, and more that has been said, about some than about others. For each intervention I will briefly describe the forms it takes, and evaluate its likely impact. Relevant research and observations made by practitioners about the design and operation of the interventions will be reported where appropriate. Usually there is a helpful overlap between these two sets of information. Finally, I will comment on the likely future of each intervention as the 21st century dawns.

SUCCESSION AND SUCCESSION PLANNING

Succession refers to the replacement of one or more people in an organization by new individuals. Succession takes an onlooker's view of such a transition. Much research, theory and speculation has centred upon the succession of chief executive officers (CEOs). In a review of this literature, Kesner and Sebora (1994) have reported a 250% increase in the number of articles on executive succession in management-related journals between the 1970s and the 1990s. They also quoted Vancil's (1987) assertion that average CEO tenure is 14 years. As we will see in Chapter 8, that is much longer than managers in general. It may also be something of a problem if Alexander and Lee's (1996) findings concerning 2,780 community hospitals in the USA can be generalized. Risk of failure increased steadily after the CEO's sixth year of tenure. This might be due to long-serving CEOs tending to become rather out of date about how competitor organizations do things and/or losing interest and motivation in a job that now held few challenges. Some research suggests an additional and less obvious cause: the structures of organizations with long-serving CEOs become increasingly divorced from organizational strategy (Miller, 1991). All this does not of course mean that CEOs should be sacked on the sixth anniversary of taking up the job. But CEOs themselves and those around them should be increasingly vigilant for danger signs as time passes. Vigilance is all the more difficult to achieve because everything may *seem* so well understood and smooth running.

Various hypotheses have been suggested and tested regarding the causes and consequences of CEO succession. Not unnaturally, a prominent issue has been whether CEO succession has the desired effect of improving organizational performance. Related to this is the question whether the incoming CEO is an organizational insider or outsider. At least three possible scenarios have been suggested (Kesner and Dalton, 1994):

(1) CEO succession improves performance because it leads to the introduction of new managerial strategies and techniques in place of the old ones which were clearly not working. This is especially true if the successor is an outsider because he or she is less likely to be tainted with the old way of doing things, and probably more inclined to bring in new people.
(2) CEO succession is in reality little more than ritual scapegoating. An organization happens to be struggling, perhaps for reasons outside the control of management. Circumstances (or luck) may change and make it look as if succession has improved performance but in fact it has had no significant effect either way.
(3) CEO succession sets off a vicious cycle that leads to decreases in organizational performance as a consequence of disrupted relationships, changed systems and uncertain futures for remaining staff. This is particularly the case if the new CEO is an outsider.

Frustratingly, but perhaps predictably, research has not conclusively favoured one of these positions over either of the others. Most of this research has used quite large samples of organizations and archival data about staffing changes and organizational performance. It has been impressive in volume and thoroughness, but has not on the whole examined the particular circumstances and markets of the organizations at the time, nor has it investigated in detail the actions of outgoing and incoming CEOs.

It is important to recognize that succession is not an entirely rational process. It is subject to interpersonal and other social processes. For a start, outgoing CEOs are not necessarily powerless in the succession event. Cannella and Lubatkin (1993) pointed out that it is often suggested that the poorer the organizational performance, the more likely that any subsequent CEO succession will involve an outsider coming in. But in a sample of 472 succession events they found that this trend was *not* observed if there was already an acknowledged 'heir apparent' in the organization, and/or if the outgoing CEO had continuing influence by, for example, being company chairperson or retaining a directorship. Zajac and Westphal (1996) found that boards of directors, if relatively free of influence from the outgoing CEO, tended to choose new CEOs who were dissimilar to the old one in demographic characteristics such as age and education, but similar to the board members themselves. The authors argued that this was due to a tendency to like and value other people similar to ourselves (and know where we stand with them) more readily than those who are less similar. These are not necessarily good bases for the choice of a new CEO.

Sonnenfeld and Ward (1995) among others have strongly urged boards to plan carefully for CEO succession. They also make the case for a sympathetic consideration of internal candidates, for several reasons. First, this sends positive messages to other organizational members. Second, the characteristics and experience of internal candidates are known whereas external candidates are much more able to gloss over the less than triumphant moments in their careers. Third, entering the external labour market is dangerous because it can lead to a neglect of internal talent and relies on the right people being available at the right time.

Sonnenfeld and Ward (1995) counselled that the present CEO should if possible be involved in succession. On the other hand they acknowledged that this might not be easy. They suggested it might be helpful to think in terms of four types of CEO:

(1) Monarchs, who expect to be in charge until retirement or even death. They tend to be autocratic and show little interest in developing their successors. These CEOs leave office only if forced out by (their own) death or a palace revolt.

(2) Generals, who tend to view organizational life as a battle of competing interests with themselves as strong, even heroic, leaders. They may try to return to office after retirement to win old battles and regain old glory.

(3) Ambassadors are CEOs who gradually disengage from office. They are keen to help in the development of a successor and often remain as background advisers after succession.

(4) Governors, who tend to establish effective administrative structures for what they know and accept as a limited term of office. They are usually prepared to exit gracefully, but unlike ambassadors maintain very little contact with the organization subsequently.

Clearly, the first two types of CEO will be harder to involve in a smooth and effective succession than the latter two. Sonnenfeld and Ward argue that boards of directors must know what kind of CEO they are dealing with and plan accordingly. One of several interesting subtexts to the article is how the behaviour of CEOs is influenced by their own personality and personal development needs. Some issues of this kind are discussed in depth in Chapter 7 of this book. The web of succession can be particularly tangled in family businesses (see Ward, 1995/6 for a good example).

The planning for succession urged by Sonnenfeld and Ward has received some attention in management thinking and practice. This has not been confined to CEO level. Succession planning is, however, quite a slippery concept. Hirsh (1990) collected a number of definitions, and it needs just three to make the point:

(1) identifying possible successors for each post on an organization chart;
(2) planning several career steps ahead for senior or fast-track employees;
(3) identifying individuals with high potential.

Underlying these definitions are disagreements about who succession planning is applied to, whether posts or people are the basis for the planning and how far ahead plans are made. More subtly, we can distinguish between, on the one hand, succession planning as a reactive process involving the matching of individual characteristics to job descriptions and, on the other, a strategic development of human resources to meet future organizational needs.

Some of the issues and techniques underlying succession planning have been described in Chapter 3, and will not be repeated in detail here. Perhaps the most important are:

(1) Whether succession planning is desirable or even possible in organizations where both the roles and the people filling them are in a state of flux. As noted in Chapter 3, it can be argued that, even in times of rapid change, organizations should be identifying the competencies required for the future and seeking ways of developing or buying-in those competencies. Nevertheless, succession planning in all its forms is a relatively centralized and 'managed' activity, and it is tempting to take the view that these days organizational life is a case of unsupported self-development and survival of the fittest.
(2) Whether or not to tell individuals who are being 'groomed' that this is the case. Where special development programmes are offered for high fliers there is also the issue of whether it is possible for people to be relegated from the programme or promoted into it. On balance, most managers favour openness for the practical reason that people usually

find out anyway, and for the moral one that withholding information from people about their future is unfair and unhelpful. There are, however, some dissenters from this point of view. For example, for some time one well-known UK retailing organization did not tell people whether or not they were on an accelerated development scheme. One prominent reason was the fear of motivation problems among those who were not in the élite if they knew the truth. Similar fears pertain if a number of people are being developed with a particular role or roles in mind, but the number of people exceeds the number of roles, so that some will be disappointed.

(3) The methods used for assessing phenomena such as performance, competencies and (hardest of all) potential must have some validity, otherwise there is little good information about individuals upon which to base succession plans.

(4) Succession planning is difficult to implement successfully. Somebody (usually HR) has to do the mechanics of it, but ultimately decisions must be made about individuals or groups, sometimes at quite high levels. These decisions sometimes contradict the wishes of local line managers. Particularly in view of trends towards line managers taking more responsibility in decentralized organizations, effective implementation of succession planning will require large doses of top management support. It will also need integration with other HR provision such as training and development centres.

Trends towards project-based work and labour flexibility probably mean that succession planning will (or should) increasingly extend beyond identification of individual people for specific top jobs, and embrace the strategic development of competencies in large numbers of people across the organization. But concerns about the quality and ethics of corporate governance mean that as we enter the 21st century interest in, and planning for, succession among the top people will continue unabated.

DEVELOPMENT CENTRES

The strength of well-designed assessment centres as a means of selecting staff, especially managerial/professional ones, is well documented (e.g. Robertson and Iles, 1988). Assessment centres use group discussions, work simulations, presentations, interviews and psychometric tests to arrive at an overall evaluation of candidates for a job or jobs. These evaluations are made by trained assessors who usually focus, at least initially, on candidates' observable behaviour rather than making generalizations about their personality. The evaluation criteria are often specified in terms of competencies required for the job or jobs in question. Increasingly, however, there is a tendency to specify competencies that reflect the strategic priorities of the organization rather than the requirements of particular jobs. This is in line with the trends as we approach and enter the 21st century described in

Chapters 2 and 3 – especially the move away from static job descriptions towards a more flexible work-force.

Development centres involve the same technologies as assessment centres, but they are used for rather different purposes. It has been recognized that participation in an assessment centre, which might last several days, is likely to have significant impact on assessees (Robertson *et al.*, 1992). Even if there is no formal delivery of feedback on their performance after the event, assessees may well learn quite a lot about themselves and the work of the organization through their participation. From the organization's point of view, a well-run assessment centre is expensive and the selection of one candidate for one job constitutes a serious under-use of the information obtained. So development centres aim to assess the skills and competencies of participants in order to do some or all of the following:

(1) feed back to assessees detailed information on their work behaviour;
(2) encourage assessees to consider how they can develop competencies they currently lack;
(3) encourage discussions between assessees and their line managers about the assessees' future development and the production of a development plan;
(4) review the overall pool of competencies available to the organization;
(5) enable high-level HR or other managers to consider the possible future assignments and training of assessees in the light of the competency profiles derived from development centre activities;
(6) identify high potential staff who might be eligible for future fast-track development.

The last two items in this list imply that many development centres do in fact have more than a hint of selection about them. This may inhibit people's behaviour in the development centre and perhaps their receptiveness to feedback. The perception of 'passing' or 'failing' may erode the motivation of the latter group (Iles and Forster, 1994). Jackson (1993a) has also pointed out a more subtle dilemma here. If development centres are used partly to select better performers for special attention, ironically those with more development needs are unlikely to receive help in addressing them.

A related and more general point made by Jackson is that development centres tend to be strong in terms of quality of assessment carried out, but often much weaker at ensuring that the results of assessment are linked with other career management interventions. This means that participants are unable to translate what they have learned at the development centre into action plans, or to find ways of implementing those plans. In one sense this is understandable if participants in the centres are the sole owners and possessors of the results, for the obvious reason that HR managers do not necessarily find out what their development needs are. But even here the management system needs to be sufficiently flexible to arrange support such as training *ad hoc* for participants who think they need it. Yet again, line manager support is required in, for example, a willingness to discuss development centre feedback with subordinates and to help draw up a personal development plan (see Chapter 5). As an aside, it should also be remembered that although good quality assessment might be common, it cannot be guaranteed. Mabey and Iles (1993) have described an assessor in a development centre run by a UK financial services organization who seemed prone to make a number of negative and very generalized judgements about one particular candidate on the basis of little or no behavioural evidence.

Iles and Forster (1994) have described the implementation of development centres in the Oxford Regional Health Authority (ORHA), UK, in the early 1990s. Development centres were prompted partly by enormous changes in the management and financing of the UK's National Health Service (NHS) consequent upon the 1991 NHS Act of Parliament. New competencies were required in staff, and the use of development centres enabled assessment of whether they possessed them. But development centres also had wider symbolic and organization development significance. They signalled the importance of new competencies and a culture where skill development mattered. One unusual feature was the use of self-assessment by participants. They evaluated themselves on the competencies required by the ORHA. This got round one problem of development centres, which is that assessor and assessee may well already know each other, leading to potential biases in assessments and assessee behaviour. The self-assessments themselves remained confidential to the assessees, but they contributed to a personal development plan, which was a more 'public' document.

Thorough evaluation studies of development centres are quite scarce relative to studies of assessment centres. This is partly because development centres are a more recent invention, and partly because their aims are more varied and sometimes quite long-term. Iles, Robertson and Rout (1989) showed that participant reactions were often but not always quite positive. In one organization, however, participating in a development centre seemed to make people rather *less* sure about their career preferences. This finding has parallels elsewhere – at least in the short term, career interventions may raise more questions for participants than they answer. Jones and Whitmore (1995) have reported a comparison of 113 development centre participants with 167 non-participants. The two groups were both employed in the same US insurance company, and were quite similar in terms of demographic variables such as age. Although the centres were not concerned with immediate selection, they were directed at people thought to be prospects for management in the next 3–5 years. Data over several years showed that development centre participants did *not* obtain managerial posts more often or more quickly than non-participants. But among the participants, those who engaged in the developmental activities recommended by centre assessors were more likely to advance to managerial positions than those who did not. This again suggests the importance of follow-through from development centres to other career-related processes. Nevertheless, the exact reason for this finding is not clear. Perhaps engaging in developmental activity improved people's work performance, which in turn got them promoted. On the other hand, engaging in developmental activity may have been taken by managers making promotion decisions as a sign of employee motivation and commitment deserving of promotion. Indeed, it may truly have been a sign of this motivation and commitment. Jones and Whitmore's data could not rule out any of these possible explanations, though the last looked most plausible.

Engelbrecht and Fischer (1995) have reported another evaluation of development centres, this time in a South African finance company. They too compared participants and non-participants. They found that the work performance of participants as rated by their supervisors three months after the development centre was significantly higher than that of non-participants. Again, this suggests a positive impact of development centres. However, this study had important weaknesses. In particular, participants' bosses knew how their development centre performance had been rated, which may have affected the bosses' ratings of participants' work. Also, there was no measure of pre-development centre work performance, so the participants may have been better workers than non-participants all along.

It looks likely that use of development centres will increase as we enter the 21st century. Although relatively expensive and complex to set up, they can yield a great deal of information to both organization and individual. They have the potential to serve both organizational strategic and personal development needs, thus achieving a balance between centralized organizational planning and individual self-development. But further evaluation studies are needed, and care must always be taken not to treat development centres as sufficient in themselves.

WORKSHOPS AND WORKBOOKS

One way of encouraging people to take responsibility for their own development is to make available exercises and resources which aid career planning and decision-making (see also Chapter 6). Workbooks or computerized equivalents provide a flexible way to take stock of oneself, the opportunities and constraints of the occupational environment, and one's goals and lifestyle preferences. Workshops usually have similar aims and some similar exercises, but also of course involve much more social interaction, support, and usually the guidance of a trained workshop facilitator. They normally take place over several days. These may be consecutive, or they may be spread over several weeks in order to permit reflection and exploration between workshop sessions. Some workshops include participant presentations about their career plans, and feedback on these from other participants. Normally there is a strict rule that what is said and done in the workshops remains confidential to participants. Workshops are often but not always held in work time. This may be a double-edged sword; it demonstrates the organization's commitment to the workshops, but risks attracting participants who are more interested in escaping from their day-to-day work than in career planning.

Workbooks and/or workshops are probably quite commonly used. As usual, however, it is difficult to be precise about just how prevalent they are, and systematic publicly available evaluations of their impact are rare indeed (Russell, 1991). In the UK, the Wellcome pharmaceutical company used workshops for several years, with considerable success in terms of user satisfaction and subsequent involvement in career planning (Jackson and Barltrop, 1994). Computer-assisted self-exploration and information about jobs in the company were provided to complement the workshops. Workshops were used in the software company SCO (Macaulay and Harding, 1996 – see Chapter 3) both to signal a major culture shift toward self-development and to help equip employees to survive and thrive in the new culture. General Electric has long used idea-sharing workshops for engineering and other staff (Jackson and Vitberg, 1987). 3M has run workshops since 1978, and in 1990 these were revamped into a two-day event called Career Directions, with an optional third day on job-seeking skills (Gutteridge, Leibowitz and Shore, 1993). Boeing, Corning, the British Civil Service, Esso, Cable and Wireless and others all use or have used paper workbooks or computerized versions, often with positive reactions from users (Fletcher and Williams, 1985, pp. 54–6; Gutteridge, Leibowitz and Shore, 1993, pp. 153–6).

One recurring issue seems to be a fear on the part of senior managers that staff attending workshops will decide that they want to leave the organization, or that they will develop aspirations that are difficult or impossible to satisfy within the organization. Most of the admittedly sketchy evidence available on this suggests these fears are unfounded. Workshops seem to make attendees more willing and able to discuss their careers with line managers, and to consider how they can develop in their present job. Workshops seem a good way of helping people to clarify which factors they can control and which they cannot, and of fostering a sense of personal responsibility for career management. Another argument vigorously put forward by some (e.g. Knowdell, 1991) is that workshops have no overall effect on employee turnover but make it more likely that the 'right' people (i.e. those who do not fit in the organization) will leave because they see more clearly that they are misfits. This is a neat argument but risks complacency on the part of the organization. The presence of misfits *may* signal an overly narrow and restrictive organizational culture and rejection of alternative perspectives. It is important, then, that data from career workshops are used for organizational development as well as self-development (Granrose and Portwood, 1987).

Another issue concerns the extent to which workbooks and workshops are customized to the organizational context, as opposed to being standard products or services. Most consumers of workbooks and workshops, and managers responsible for their delivery, prefer the former. But of course this tends to be more expensive than a standardized model. Also, if the workbook or workshop is highly specific to the organization, it may fail to help people consider broader options. From an organizational point of view it is important that participants do not erroneously believe that an invitation to participate in a workshop signals that they are being groomed for promotion, or indeed prepared for redundancy (unless they are, of course!). In the latter case the workshop would be part of outplacement provision, which is discussed in the next section of this chapter. A final consideration is that, on the one hand, a workshop which contains people of markedly different status within the organization may be particularly successful in terms of the range of experiences and perspectives available to participants. On the other hand, however, there is also a real risk that there will be some barriers to self-disclosure and openness, even if assurances about confidentiality are given.

As the 21st century unfolds there is little doubt that career workbooks and multimedia career planning exercises will be common and much used. However, their availability on the general market is likely to discourage many organizations from producing their own versions. The future of career workshops is difficult to predict. Increased need for individuals to review and plan their careers may make workshops an attractive part of an employment package. From an organizational point of view they are certainly consistent with self-development. On the other hand workshops are relatively expensive and time-consuming, and some workshop exercises and other experiences can be accessed by other means such as workbooks and networking. There may also be growth in workshops run independently of employing organizations, though this assumes individuals are prepared to pay to attend them.

OUTPLACEMENT

Outplacement (OP) is a collective name given to various career management interventions offered by organizations to employees who are leaving, normally due to redundancy. At its most lavish, OP involves personal counselling from almost the moment of dismissal until re-employment, along with psychometric testing to aid self-assessment, individualized help in dealing with negative emotion, labour market information, training in job search and self-presentation techniques, and use of office facilities. Less comprehensive forms of OP are also available, including a 'base model' of just one or two sessions in which large groups of leaving employees (sometimes referred to as terminatees) receive rudimentary briefing on how to handle job loss and job search.

Predictably, OP is more often made available to higher-level employees than lower-level ones. The use of OP has increased hugely through the 1980s and 1990s. Kirkpatrick (1991) found that more than three-quarters of the largest US corporations offered OP to redundant managers, and Cowden (1992) reckoned that the US outplacement industry had annual earnings of over $650 million, generated by more than 200 firms compared with only a very few two decades earlier.

Why do many organizations offer outplacement? After all, one might think that an organization has no interest in people who are leaving. The answers to this question depend a little on who is providing them, but tend to include:

(1) OP is consistent with a benevolent, employee-centred organizational culture (paradoxically, one might think, given that it is making some of its staff redundant!);
(2) to maintain or enhance the external reputation of the organization as good to work for, with implications for subsequent recruitment and retention;
(3) to reassure the 'survivors' remaining in the organization that there is a concern for its people;
(4) to assuage top managers' guilt about making employees (including perhaps colleagues and friends) redundant;
(5) to reduce the risk of attempts by leaving employees to damage or sabotage the organization, or (especially in the USA) begin litigation against it;
(6) to reduce the compensation demanded by leaving employees, because OP as part of a termination package has value, and may help a person get a new job quickly;
(7) to reflect a humanitarian concern about the well-being of departing employees.

Probably the last of these reasons is the one made most salient to the leaving employees themselves, but there are some tensions inherent in the various aims of the OP provider. Indeed, these tensions may explain why OP is usually provided by an outside consultant. For obvious reasons it is difficult for continuing members of the organization to present themselves as caring OP providers and help terminatees to handle their negative emotions. Those people themselves would feel uncomfortable in the role (Latack and Kaufman, 1988).

Yet the rather blatant contradiction in roles is not entirely solved by hiring an external OP provider. The OP literature has, especially recently, stressed the difficulty and importance of close collaboration between provider and organization so that the OP service is closely tailored to the specific people, their needs and the culture. Summerfield (1996, p. 32) quoted William Grierson of the BBC as saying: 'I am very opposed to the "battery hen" approach that I see in many large outplacement firms. We work hard to create a friendly and welcoming atmosphere.' This of course requires flexibility on the part of the OP provider and probably higher fees than a more standardized approach. But on the other hand it is also thought important that the employer is seen to own and ultimately control the form and quality of the OP process. Simply handing it over to an external OP provider would undermine many of the reasons for offering OP – perhaps all of them.

There is some common-sensish advice available about what to look out for when selecting an OP provider. Dawson and Dawson (1996) have suggested the following, based on their experience of running an outplacement business:

(1) ask applicants to your organization what OP firm, if any, they have experienced, and what they thought of it;
(2) check that the provider's offices are neither too shabby nor too grand, and that they are the right size for the number of people from the organization who will need them;
(3) evaluate the comprehensiveness and appropriateness of the information available in the OP provider's library;
(4) assess whether the programme(s) offered by the provider are designed and staffed in a way that permits goal achievement;
(5) obtain information about how much individuals actually use the provider's facilities and their success rate in job finding, not only in terms of time taken but also quality of job obtained.

Predictably, the outplacement literature has plenty of anecdotes about successes described in articles that are in fact thinly disguised advertising for the author's services. Systematic evaluations are much rarer. One notable exception has been reported by Davy, Anderson and DiMarco (1995). They compared 54 redundant white-collar employees who participated in informal job meeting groups led by a community counsellor with 79 who received a fairly comprehensive OP service. The informal meetings were purely about social support and networking, and did *not* include job search training. Data were collected about three months and six months after job loss. After three months, members of the OP group had more confidence than members of the informal group in their ability to conduct job search effectively. However, the two groups did not differ in the amount of depression and sense of helplessness they reported. After six months, slightly more (34%) of the informal group had found jobs than the OP group (22%). Moreover, these jobs were more comparable to their previous salary and status than was the case for members of the OP group who had found jobs.

These results may of course have been specific to this sample. The two groups may have differed in ways not discovered by the authors, and we do not know their circumstances and psychological states before being made redundant. The OP programme may not have been particularly good, though the authors reported the opinion of OP industry insiders that there was nothing wrong with it. Furthermore, the most informative comparison is impossible to make: how the OP group would have fared had they not received OP. But the Davy, Anderson and DiMarco (1995) case study is a warning that the glowing tributes to OP may be exaggerated.

Miller and Robinson (1994) have produced an article quite critical of the OP industry. They ascribe high importance to the contradictions noted earlier in the role of OP providers, who are in the awkward position of selling their services on the basis of organizational benefits whilst presenting themselves to individuals as sympathetic helpers who are neutral or even on the employees' side. They describe in detail how various OP activities reflect the hypocrisy of the situation, and conclude that the dual role of OP providers should be split. Terminatees should be able to select their own consultant or accept additional severance pay instead of OP. If this is not possible, both organization and OP provider should 'come clean' about what the OP is designed to achieve so that individuals can give informed consent to their own involvement.

One overlooked potential benefit of OP is the increased career management skills it may foster in the work-force as a whole. Given the situation described in Chapters 2 and 3, these skills are increasingly necessary as we enter the 21st century. Employers are making a contribution to this via their use of OP. Whether OP will expand or contract in the future is a difficult question. If the psychological contract has shifted fundamentally away from lifetime employment, so that redundancy and regular changing of employer are the norm, then fewer employers may see any reason to treat termination as an out-of-the-ordinary event requiring consolation prizes. On the other hand, OP may become an increasingly common 'perk' precisely because it caters for an often and widely experienced event of significant concern to many people. The real test here will be whether OP is extended to low-level employees, many of whom are currently excluded from OP provision.

CAREER COUNSELLING

Adapting definitions given by various writers, career counselling may be defined as a set of skills, techniques and attitudes used in an interpersonal communication to help people manage their careers using their own resources. This leads straight away to some observations about what career counselling is or, rather, what it is not:

(1) career counselling is not simply giving advice or telling people what to do;
(2) nor is it sorting out people's problems for them;
(3) career counselling requires not only behavioural skills but also certain underlying attitudes;
(4) career counselling is not necessarily performed only by people called career counsellors.

Following on from this last point counselling is sometimes thought of as a general orientation to interpersonal relationships which can be applied in many situations not labelled a 'counselling session'. Many different people in and outside the work-place may be able to offer a person career counselling. This may occur during day-to-day work or other life domains, and thus, on the basis of the distinction made at the start of this chapter, career counselling would perhaps be equally at home in Chapter 5. However, many individuals do not readily think of themselves as counsellors, and there may be compelling reasons why a person seeking counselling would not wish to receive it informally from work colleagues. When career counselling is available in work organizations, it is often provided by a trained counsellor. This person may not be a member of the organization. His or her only or main role within it is to provide career counselling, perhaps as part of a broader intervention such as outplacement or career planning workshops, or as a free-standing service. Thus the rest of this section will refer to formally provided career counselling.

This is not the place for a detailed analysis of career counselling techniques, skills and attitudes. These are well covered elsewhere (see, for example, Reddy, 1987; Egan, 1990; Nathan and Hill, 1992). Nevertheless, a few words are appropriate here in order to clarify approximately what counselling is, having earlier stated what it is not. Many counsellors see the counselling process as consisting of four more or less distinct phases. These are normally addressed over a perhaps lengthy series of meetings, not just one, and will involve considerable 'homework' for the client.

(1) *Initial contact*. It is important to help the client (or clients in the case of group counselling) to feel at ease, and to agree timescales and style of interaction.
(2) *Understanding the present situation*. Egan (1990) has described this as involving the identification, exploration and clarification of problem situations and unused opportunities. It is crucial that the counsellor avoids premature judgements about the client or his or her situation, and instead concentrates on seeing and feeling how the world seems to the client. This requires warmth, respect, empathy, active listening and tolerance. This highlights the importance of attitude as mentioned earlier – attributes such as tolerance can be signalled via verbal and non-verbal behaviour but are very difficult to fake.
(3) *Clarification of preferred scenarios*. In this phase the counsellor does a little more of the talking, though it should still be less than the client. It may well involve redefinition of the client's current situation in ways which permit constructive action. Whether or not this is the case, the counsellor is likely to pick out themes from the client's account, to summarize and perhaps challenge the client's point of view. All this must be done in a supportive way which does not compromise the primacy of the client's frame of reference over the counsellor's.
(4) *Formulating strategies and plans*. Having defined a potentially achievable situation which is preferable to the present one, the counsellor and client work together in formulating plans of action. The counsellor may be able to coach the client in certain skills such as being interviewed, and give feedback on his or her performance. The counsellor may even give advice at this stage, though normally only about the nuts and bolts of how to implement a plan rather than the advisability of the plan itself. The counsellor may also refer the client on to another individual or agency.

This is of course a very general model, broadly built upon humanist theories within psychology (e.g. Rogers, 1965). The underlying philosophy is that if the counsellor demonstrates acceptance and warmth, the client is more able to acknowledge and deal with issues he or she would be reluctant to broach with others. Within this framework, the counsellor may well use other theoretical ideas concerned with, for example, career decision-making (see Chapter 6) and lifespan development (see Chapter 7). Some counsellors do, however, adopt a significantly different theoretical frame of reference, drawing, for example, on psychoanalytic or behaviourist theory as the source of their understanding of client problems (see, for example, Sharf, 1992, for a review of these). On the whole, though, most counsellors rely more on theories of guidance and counselling than on theories of personality or career development to inform their work (Kidd *et al.*, 1994).

Although the point may be somewhat exaggerated, it is sometimes said that once upon a time counsellors' main involvement with clients was at predictable points of transition, particularly obvious ones such as starting work and retirement (see Chapter 8) but also more subtle ones such as plateauing (see Chapter 5). The issues that arose on each occasion were also relatively predictable. Nowadays people's work lives are less governed by closely age-related phenomena, and more subject to so-called 'non-normative' events such as redundancy and breakdown of relationships that can hit anyone at any time (Vondracek and Schulenberg, 1992). Technological change, intense competition, downsizing and the other phenomena reviewed in Chapters 2 and 3 can also trigger non-normative life events.

A number of practical issues arise in the organization and delivery of career counselling in organizations. The first is that it is very difficult, and perhaps pointless, to draw a boundary around the type of concerns a person is allowed to bring to a career counsellor. In many instances these involve career issues but also others. They may concern relationships with supervisors or family members and other phenomena which do not fall within most definitions of career. Most counsellors are prepared for this, but how they deal with it depends partly upon their relationship with the organization. Their remit may be to deal with certain kinds of problem only, in which case they need to be well acquainted with appropriate referral agencies.

Subtle but important issues surround the question of who is the counsellor's client. Usually the organization pays, so in a sense it is the client. But counsellors will regard the individual they work with as their client. So it must be clearly agreed that the welfare of the individual client is the counsellor's main concern, not any plans the organization might have for the client. Confidentiality is of course a fundamental requirement. As a minimum this means that none of the issues discussed in counselling sessions is revealed to other people unless the client wishes this to happen. Beyond this, it may mean confidentiality about the very fact that the counsellor and client have met. In more 'macho' organizational cultures someone known to be seeing a 'shrink' may be regarded as a lame duck on the edge of a nervous breakdown – grotesque, but true! This 'strong' version of confidentiality requires careful and perhaps rather intricate procedures for arranging and conducting counselling sessions.

A counsellor who works extensively with a specific organization is usually thought to be more effective if some investment is made in familiarizing him or her with the organization at the outset. This is a fair point, but of course this familiarization will probably tend to reflect the 'party line', which may not be the reality experienced by many people in the organization. Over time it may be legitimate for the organization to request, and the counsellor to provide, general feedback concerning what issues have commonly arisen in counselling sessions. This might particularly be the case if the counsellor has been brought in as a support for people during reorganizations. Indeed, there have been calls for career counsellors to recognize that they are inevitably involved in organizational development, not just individual development (Hermansson, 1993). This would mean career counsellors being skilled practitioners in organizational change as well as counselling.

As with most other career management interventions, the benefits of career counselling are often asserted but less often demonstrated (Killeen, White and Watts, 1992). It is very difficult to establish its value because of the long time period needed for thorough evaluation, and also because other things happening in a person's life, and other help that person may have received in the past, both act as 'background noise'. However, Killeen, White and Watts (1992) conducted a careful review of the literature and found clear evidence that recipients of career counselling find jobs more quickly than non-recipients. Furthermore, this speed seems not to be at the expense of the quality of the job.

Career counselling, from whatever source, is likely to be in increasing demand as we enter the 21st century. The increasing diversity and frequency of career-related problems is probably outstripping any increase in people's career management skills. Because counselling does not take responsibility away from the client, it can legitimately be seen as consistent with a spirit of self-development. On the other hand, it is a relatively intensive and expensive career management intervention. As with career development workshops, there must be some doubt about whether many more organizations than at present will be willing to buy in career counselling services. It may be left to line managers to provide whatever counselling is deemed necessary. If individuals do not want that, they may have to pay for their own counselling, though this depends somewhat on governments' decisions about provision of career counselling (Jackson et al., 1996). As for career counsellors themselves, there is no sign of any decrease in the variety of problems they help clients deal with. Their role is a demanding and varied one which increasingly requires knowledge of non-work concerns such as family dynamics.

SUMMARY

Some of the recurring issues concerning career management interventions in organizations are discussed at the end of Chapter 5. So at this point all that need be said is that for several of the techniques discussed in this chapter there is a reasonable amount of literature available. Not much of it reports thorough evaluation, but nevertheless there is some attempt to check on the impact of the interventions. This is commendable given the practical difficulties inherent in the endeavour. Systematic analysis is probably helped by the relatively closely controlled way in which these interventions are delivered – uptake of the interventions and the techniques used can be verified relatively easily. Probably the most unresolved issues concern how these interventions fit with other organizational practices, particularly HR ones. With the possible exception of succession planning, the technical details of how to run the intervention seem to attract relatively little controversy. Perhaps the technical details should attract more attention, and would do so if they were evaluated in the light of the goals of the intervention rather than in terms of their soundness in an abstract, context-free sense.

5

CAREER MANAGEMENT INTERVENTIONS IN ORGANIZATIONS II

Most of the introductory points for this chapter were made at the start of the last one, so only a brief addition is needed here. The focus of this chapter is career management interventions that are part of a person's day-to-day working life. The agenda is much the same as the last chapter: description of the forms the intervention takes, review of relevant research and practice, brief analysis of any evaluation information, and comment on the future prospects of each intervention. As before, my aims are to acquaint readers with the general form of each intervention without getting overly detailed, and to furnish a critical analysis so that the reader is more able to be a discerning user than might otherwise have been the case.

DEVELOPMENTAL WORK ASSIGNMENTS

A rather neglected area has been the deliberate use of jobs themselves in career development. Frequent references to job experiences as key aspects of managers' development in management literature (e.g. Wick, 1989) should not disguise the fact that little systematic thought normally goes into the design of a job as a developmental experience for the person doing it. But developmental work assignments (DWAs) are an important area, for the following reasons:

(1) DWAs permit the expansion of employee skills and experiences whilst still getting a useful job done.
(2) DWAs may keep pressure off training budgets because new skills are being developed on the job.
(3) From the individual's point of view, DWAs help to maintain employability whilst still earning.
(4) DWAs often involve contact between staff who would not otherwise have met, thus opening the way to swapping of ideas, skills and knowledge.

DWAs can take the form of project work within an otherwise unchanged job. They can also be short-term secondments to tackle a specific problem in a setting novel to the individual, with a subsequent return to the original job. Stern (1995) gives a good example of an organized scheme of this kind in the UK's National Health Service. But the most usual form of DWA involves transfer to a new job which is done for a limited time. It may or may not involve promotion. Clearly, DWAs have a key role to play in succession planning (see Chapter 4), both in the strategic development of organizational competencies and in the preparation of individuals for certain key roles. Nevertheless, there are some familiar difficulties with their effective implementation. Perhaps the most pressing is that line managers under pressure to achieve short-term performance targets may not be keen to take on a person who has some learning to do. They might prefer someone who has already proved that he or she can do the job in its entirety, in which case it would not really be a *developmental* assignment for the person concerned. The most effective implementation of DWAs therefore requires not only top management support, but also a culture of learning and the appraisal of line managers on their development of others.

Another often mentioned but rarely addressed issue is getting the right balance between the familiar and unfamiliar in a DWA. Too much to learn might overwhelm the assignee. Too little would undermine the utility of the DWA. Into this equation must also be added the amount of risk of failure the organization can tolerate. The elements of a DWA that are new to an individual probably need to be significant to the organization's performance if they are to be a source of motivation, but on the other hand very high importance could be an unacceptable risk and a source of counterproductive stress in the individual.

Campion, Cheraskin and Stevens (1994) studied the use and impact of non-promotional DWAs (they referred to them as job rotation) among 255 staff in the finance department of a large pharmaceutical company in the USA. The positions were held for between one and five years. Very few involved geographical relocation. Campion, Cheraskin and Stevens found that the impact of job rotation on self-reported skill development and motivation of rotators was generally positive. The perceived benefits generally exceeded the perceived costs, though performance losses in organizational units gaining and losing rotators were seen as significant. Employees in early career were more interested in rotation than were their older colleagues, possibly with reason because a fast rate of rotation was associated with promotion and salary increases. A fast rate of rotation was also associated with greater perceived increases in knowledge and skills, although overly fast rotation was the most common complaint from those involved. Obviously, some of Campion, Cheraskin and Stevens's results may have been specific to the context in which they were obtained, and to managerial populations. Also, as the authors acknowledged, their work did not include objective measures of skill, or an analysis of the cost-effectiveness of rotation relative to other methods of skill development such as formal training. Nevertheless, their research suggests quite wide-ranging benefits from DWAs.

Some important work by Cindy McCauley and colleagues in the USA has produced a way of conceptualizing and measuring the developmental opportunities inherent in managerial jobs. McCauley *et al.* (1994) have reported on the construction of the Developmental Challenge Profile (DCP). The DCP

Table 5.1 The Developmental Challenge Profile

	15 Dimensions of Development
	JOB TRANSITIONS
1. Unfamiliar responsibilities	The manager must handle responsibilities that are new, very different, or much broader than previous ones
2. Proving yourself	The manager has added pressure to show others that he or she can handle the job
	TASK-RELATED CHARACTERISTICS
Creating Change	
3. Developing new directions	The manager is responsible for starting something new, making strategic changes, carrying out a reorganization, or responding to rapid changes in the business environment
4. Inherited problems	The manager has to fix problems created by the former incumbent or take over problem employees
5. Reduction decisions	Decisions about shutting down operations or staff reductions have to be made
6. Problems with employees	Employees lack adequate experience, are incompetent, or are resistant
High Level of Responsibility	
7. High stakes	Clear deadlines, pressure from senior management, high visibility, and responsibility for key decisions make success or failure in this job clearly evident
8. Managing business diversity	The scope of the job is large, with responsibilities for multiple functions, groups, products, customers, or markets
9. Job overload	The sheer size of the job requires a large investment of time and energy
10. Handling external pressure	External factors that impact the business (e.g. negotiating with unions or government agencies, working in a foreign culture, or coping with serious community problems) must be dealt with
Nonauthority Relationships	
11. Influencing without authority	Getting the job done requires influencing peers, higher management, external parties, or other key people over whom the manager has no direct authority
	OBSTACLES
12. Adverse business conditions	The business unit or production line faces financial problems or difficult economic conditions
13. Lack of top management support	Senior management is reluctant to provide direction, support, or resources for current work or new projects
14. Lack of personal support	The manager is excluded from key networks and gets little support and encouragement from others
15. Difficult boss	The manager's opinions or management style differ from those of the boss, or the boss has major shortcomings

Source: Adapted from McCauley *et al.* (1994)

is a questionnaire designed to assess the extent to which a managerial job offers scope for development in the job holder. They construed development as learning, and stated that learning is most likely to occur when managers are faced with challenging job situations which matter. Three general sources of learning were identified: job transitions (see also Chapter 8), task-related characteristics and obstacles. Within each general source, several specific phenomena were identified and measured with the DCP. These are listed and briefly described in Table 5.1.

Table 5.2 Organizational Analysis Survey

Department or unit managers are asked to complete the Organizational Analysis Survey (OAS). It covers seven areas as follows, and also allows the respondent to make additional comments.

1. The tasks and responsibilities of the unit.
2. Which individuals and agencies, inside or outside the organization, produce work for the unit.
3. Which individuals and agencies, inside or outside the organization, use information generated by the unit.
4. What actions members of the unit take.
5. The environmental conditions in which the unit works, and the tools and technology with which it works.
6. The goods or services produced by the unit and who consumes them.
7. The job titles of people working in the unit.

Source: Based on information in Vaughn and Wilson (1994)

Its authors argue that the DCP is a useful method for describing the kind of developmental opportunities offered by any given managerial job (McCauley, Eastman and Ohlott, 1995). This description can then be used to judge whose developmental needs would be best served by this particular job. In their research, they found (as they expected) that managers generally said that they had developed more in jobs with high scores on many of the 15 features shown in Table 5.1 than in jobs with low scores. This was particularly true for the first three and numbers 7 to 9. Bearing in mind the nature of number 9 (job overload), there is the interesting ethical issue of whether people should be overloaded for the good of their development!

McCauley and colleagues admitted that they were surprised by the amount of stress associated with some developmental challenges. For example, the more of items 4 to 6 and 13 to 15 managers experienced (see Table 5.1), the more they reported feelings of being harmed. Given that numbers 13 to 15 are termed obstacles, we should perhaps not be surprised that they were problematic. Again, this cautions against a glib assumption that, for example, having a difficult boss can be called a developmental opportunity.

Another piece of research from the same stable (Ohlott, Ruderman and McCauley, 1994) examined potential gender discrimination in developmental opportunities for managers in a sample of 281 men and 162 women mainly from five large corporations and one government organization. After statistical adjustments for factors like education and age, they found that men tended to experience more high stakes, managing business diversity and handling external pressure than women. On the other hand, women came out higher on two scales. The bad news was that these were influencing without authority and (especially) lack of personal support. In effect, more of men's developmental experiences than women's could be described as opportunities whereas some of women's developmental experiences looked more like threats. The authors suggested that these results indicated subtle but significant discrimination against women. It is difficult to argue with their conclusion.

Of course, one alternative to using the DCP or something similar is to use competency profiling (see Chapter 3). Both of these focus on individuals and jobs. A rather different approach has been suggested by Vaughn and Wilson (1994). They have concentrated on analysing sub-units of organizations in order to establish their degree of similarity. This is done using the Organizational Analysis Survey (OAS – Vaughn, 1988), which is a questionnaire and/ or interview with the leader of a sub-unit. The topics covered in the OAS are shown in Table 5.2.

Vaughn and Wilson asserted that the similarities and differences between organizational sub-units are not necessarily obvious in advance, and do not always reflect the organization chart. Like the DCP, the OAS provides a framework for assessing the degree (and to some extent the type) of novelty for a person in a possible assignment. Again like the DCP, it permits some specific statements about exactly what would be the main sources of learning for a person if he or she worked in a particular assignment – assuming that the person's prior experience is known. The key question then becomes whether this learning would be in areas of strategic value to the organization, or indeed the individual.

These attempts to describe exactly what might be developmental about DWAs are potentially a useful aid to career development, though they are confined largely to managerial occupations in medium-size or large organizations. Whether they are more useful than old-fashioned job descriptions, job analysis, or competency profiling, remains to be seen. Meanwhile, as we enter the 21st century, careers become more fragmented and training may well be seen increasingly as something that individuals arrange and pay for themselves. In this climate it is essential that individuals and organizations make effective use of work assignments for development, particularly development of skills that can transfer to different kinds of work. It seems likely that individuals will be more inclined than organizations to evaluate jobs in terms of their developmental value because their continued employability may depend on it. Thus tools like the DCP may be used more by individuals than by organizations in the early years of the 21st century. Also, they may be used to evaluate projects rather than whole jobs.

PERFORMANCE APPRAISAL

I have chosen not to present a detailed account of performance appraisal techniques and issues. These are well covered elsewhere – see, for example, Fletcher and Williams (1985) and Murphy and Cleveland (1991). Nevertheless, performance appraisal cannot be left out entirely because it often concerns not only the assessment of a person's past performance but also a consideration of his or her future development. As noted in the appropriate sections of this book, data from performance appraisals often feed into career management interventions, especially perhaps development centres (see Chapter 4) and personal development plans (see next section).

Murphy and Cleveland (1991) have argued that it is crucial to get away from the idea that performance appraisal is a measurement device requiring only appropriate design and calibration in order to operate properly. An appraiser may have all sorts of goals in mind when assessing the work performance of an appraisee. These goals may include covering his or her own back, avoidance of confrontation, improving the appraisee's self-confidence, or a hundred and one other things apart from arriving at an accurate performance assessment. Also, performance appraisals are social interactions in which all sorts of things can happen – they are not the equivalent of a tape measure or scales. Thus performance appraisal should be seen as a tool for effective management, and as part of the organization's processes rather than somehow separate.

Unfortunately what Fletcher and Williams (1985) have described as an identikit appraisal system does not make an optimum contribution to *career* management. The appraisee sees and signs much of the form on which the appraisal is recorded. This normally includes numerical ratings of the appraisee's performance and perhaps statements about his or her training needs. The bit the appraisee often does *not* see contains the appraiser's evaluation of his or her potential and appropriate future assignments. Things have changed somewhat towards more openness but many appraisal systems still resemble the identikit one (see Carlton and Sloman, 1992 for an excellent example and account of the politics of appraisal). Further, all of the appraisal process is subject to the various judgement biases that have been such a favourite topic of research for applied psychologists over the years (see, for example, Landy and Farr, 1983). Even worse, several commentators have suggested that appraisal is pretty unpopular – neither party usually looks forward to it, nor do they find it especially satisfactory (Rice, 1985).

Conventional wisdom says that it is best to separate the evaluation of past performance from the review of development needs in performance appraisal (see, for example, Mayo, 1991). If a person's promotion or pay prospects are at stake he or she is unlikely to be candid about weaknesses or errors. The separation might need to be not only in terms of time but also in terms of the person doing the appraising. That person is usually the immediate boss, but other appraisers are often potentially appropriate, particularly perhaps for the review of future development, and particularly where the appraisee is sufficiently reflective not to require an appraiser with close knowledge of the appraisee's job. This separation happens in some places. It is certainly consistent with trends toward self-development, particularly if the performance evaluation element is fed into the HR system but the future development element remains confidential to the appraisee and appraiser. It is, however, rather different from the norm, and would perhaps make it difficult for HR managers to obtain a holistic picture of development needs across the organization.

Murphy and Cleveland (1991, Chapter 13) and Hedge and Borman (1995) have presented analyses of likely and/or desirable changes in performance appraisal in the light of the labour market and organizational changes described in Chapters 2 and 3 of this book. The most significant, some of which are already coming to pass, are:

(1) More disagreements between appraiser and appraisee about what the appraisee's duties are and how well he or she has performed them. This is due to the decline in stable jobs and job descriptions, and more autonomy for many employees.
(2) More use of peer ratings and greater emphasis on general citizenship behaviour, partly as a consequence of (1) above.
(3) (Even) more need for appraisal systems to operate in a way consistent with organizational culture. For example, in an organization with much collaborative project work, an appraisal system with minimal appraisee involvement would not go down well.
(4) A shift to evaluating the relative success of various aspects of a person's performance (i.e. profiling) rather than rank-ordering people in terms of their overall performance.
(5) Due to an increasingly diverse work-force, *either* less bias against members of minority groups as they become more accepted *or* more bias as ethnic majority appraisers feel increasingly threatened. Happily, past research suggests the first possibility is more likely (Kraiger and Ford, 1985).
(6) A decline in staff's willingness to engage in performance appraisal due to its assumed irrelevance to the motivation and development of short-term workers.
(7) Replacement of annual appraisals with appraisals at, for example, the conclusion of project or other assignments, whenever that happens to be.
(8) More feedback to appraisers due to its collection from multiple sources and a corresponding reduction of supervisors' feelings of being put 'on the line'.

On balance these trends suggest that performance appraisal systems will yield more and better information for individuals to use on managing their own careers in the 21st century. But there is a danger that some of the useful information available via, for example, profiling will be neglected in organizations which are concerned solely with immediate performance measurement.

PERSONAL DEVELOPMENT PLANS

If greater emphasis is to be placed on self-development in organizations, then supports are needed to enable people to think about and plan their own development in a structured and purposeful manner. Thus, a personal development plan (PDP) can be defined as a clear development action plan for an individual for which the individual takes primary responsibility. Line managers and the HR function often have a supporting role (Tamkin, Barber and Hirsh, 1994).

Tamkin, Barber and Hirsh's research is one of very few systematic reviews of PDPs. Their findings suggested that the form and organization of PDPs vary quite a lot. Sometimes they are used for all staff; other times just for some groups. The spirit of self-development and current emphasis on using all the skills and knowledge available in an organization would indicate that the former is in principle more appropriate. Some PDPs focus solely on the development needed to perform better in the current job. Others concentrate more on development for the next job, whilst others again take a much broader view of the person's overall personal effectiveness. Again, the spirit of the times would suggest the last of these three is most appropriate, and Tamkin, Barber and Hirsh found that these wide-ranging PDPs tended to be received most positively by the users.

The amount and type of structuring of PDP documents on which people record their development plans appear to vary quite a lot too, though Tamkin, Barber and Hirsh found a strong tendency to use the organization's competency framework. Some PDPs begin very explicitly with the person's current job. A good example is the PDP developed by one region of the Woolwich Building Society in the UK (Higson and Wilson, 1995). Part 1 invited users to specify the tasks their current job required and to decide with their manager how well they were doing them. Apparently for some people this was the first time they had thought in detail about what they actually did in their work. Part 2 of the PDP was a learning plan on which the learner and his or her manager recorded three learning needs in priority order. Also recorded were the means by which learning would occur and deadlines by which the learning specified in the plan would be achieved. Possible methods of learning included coaching from the manager, a job-swap, a training course, visiting another office or a distance learning package. The manager's responsibility was to set up and monitor the learning, and the plan was to be reviewed every three months, or sooner if the learning plan had been completed. Part 3 of the PDP was a learning log completed each week to demonstrate what had been learned. One hour each week was allocated for learning identified in the PDP. When this learning had been completed, the hour could be used to plan the next learning. This explicit allocation of time was seen as an important indicator of management commitment, and necessary for successful implementation of the learning plan. The Woolwich PDP is fairly specific to the person's current job (though with wider implications), and involves line managers more intimately than many PDPs. Presumably a fair degree of trust is required if subordinates are to be willing to discuss their development needs. Higson and Wilson noted that effective implementation required everyone, including line managers, to have their own PDP. This enabled everyone to take PDPs seriously.

This last point was also made by Floodgate and Nixon (1994), who described the introduction and use of PDPs in another UK financial services organization, the TSB. It is worth noting the aims of the TSB PDP in detail because they show the potentially wide impact of PDPs and the extent to which they may reflect a change of organizational culture. The PDP was designed to help individuals to:

(1) adopt a structured way to analyse their strengths and development needs;

(2) articulate this knowledge to managers in a way which resulted in getting the learning activities required;
(3) keep a record of their achievements against learning targets;
(4) describe themselves in terms of skills, knowledge and abilities rather than just their job title and grade;
(5) regard the PDP as a live document for their benefit, not just another bit of form-filling for head office.

Floodgate and Nixon stressed that at first it was 'like pushing water uphill' to promote PDPs into a culture of 'passive compliance' where staff were accustomed to having training done to them. But after careful introduction via supportive managers, PDPs were becoming, at the time of writing their article, more accepted and fairly widely used.

It appears that the most-used source of ideas for inclusion in a person's PDP is performance appraisal, but other inputs such as development centres (see Chapter 4) are also sometimes used. Perhaps more problematic are the outputs from PDPs. In some organizations PDPs are seen as the person's private property and there is no record kept of uptake or continued use (Tamkin, Barber and Hirsh, 1994). But, to repeat a point that recurs in discussion of career management interventions, there needs to be a responsive HR system so that the person can implement his or her plans. Furthermore, the elements of that system into which PDPs feed should not be immediately concerned with succession planning – that could make a person too wary of revealing what he or she saw as weaknesses. In the TSB, PDPs started life as part of the performance management system but after a time they became an independent free-standing intervention consistent with the philosophy that people needed to make independent free-standing judgements about their development.

Whether or not the name 'personal development plan' is retained, it seems clear that the phenomenon it describes is here to stay. Future issues concern the optimal focus of the PDP, design of PDP materials, and the best balance between integration with, and separation from, other HR interventions.

CAREER ACTION AND RESOURCE CENTRES

Another consequence of a shift towards self-development by employees has been growing interest in drop-in centres which individuals are encouraged to use when they feel the need to do so. These centres go by various names: career action centres (CACs), career resource centres and learning centres are perhaps the most common. For the sake of brevity I will refer to them as CACs.

One form of CAC is demonstrated by the British Broadcasting Corporation (BBC). Centres called Career Points were developed at various locations around the BBC (Segall, 1995). Each centre had a variety of careers-related books, magazines and videos, as well as books supporting the BBC's approved MBA programme and a computerized career exploration package

(Career Builder – see Chapter 6). The Career Points were designed to be available to staff on all shifts to use when they wished at their own pace. They were successors to other interventions including secondments and career development workshops, and are seen as flexible, relatively cheap and in line with culture changes in the BBC towards self-reliance.

The reported pros and cons of CACs (Segall, 1995) are perhaps fairly predictable. There is a danger that they will be used principally by people who are already quite career-aware, rather than by people who could most benefit. The informal way of using the CACs means that it is difficult to establish the amount and type of use or user opinion. Linkage with other HR systems such as performance appraisal and on-the-job development is also problematic unless the user and line manager go out of their way to make it happen. Some Career Points have been run down or even discontinued if local management are not interested. But the most common criticism, in the BBC at least, was the absence of support for individual users in the form of professionals to talk to at the Career Points.

Some CACs do, however, have more staff input than the BBC ones. A good example is Cable and Wireless, which employs 60,000 people in over 50 locations across the world, and operates in a competitive and volatile market. The CAC is located in London. Electronic access is possible though many people in the more far-flung corners of the Cable and Wireless empire prefer to call in when on leave or visiting the UK for some other reason. The stated aims of the CAC (Tomlinson, 1996) demonstrate clearly the career culture being fostered in Cable and Wireless:

(1) to provide career planning and development services;
(2) to promote individual career self-reliance;
(3) to support continuous learning;
(4) to encourage and support employee flexibility and mobility;
(5) to help employees manage change in a volatile and highly competitive environment.

The services offered in support of these aims are:

(1) executive career planning;
(2) individual career planning;
(3) graduate development planning;
(4) career review;
(5) international cultural and country briefings;
(6) resource library.

Notice that several of these services involve interaction with professionals such as coaches and counsellors. These people are bought in on an hourly or daily rate, and given a thorough briefing on Cable and Wireless. Notice also that the Cable and Wireless CAC is quite closely aligned with activities that could be the province of a training department. As such it is more integrated with HR systems than is the BBC example described earlier. Careful liaison and division of responsibilities with the training function are required in order to prevent duplication or even incompatibility of services. In some organizations it might be important for CACs to be distanced from the HR department, for example where there have been extensive redundancies. Care might also be needed to ensure that individual confidentiality is maintained – people may be less willing to reveal that they have participated in career counselling than in something labelled a training course run by a training department.

Although based within an organization, the managers of the Cable and Wireless CAC have considered selling their services to other companies. More generally, there is the issue of how CACs are funded. Some are expected to make a profit or at least break even, which means that they have to charge for their services. There are clear problems about confidentiality and ease of success if individuals have to draw upon one of their boss's budgets in order to use a CAC.

US companies such as Sun Microsystems and Raychem have also made use of CACs, but North America has in addition seen a different kind of CAC – one that is independent of any employing organization. These are described in various places, along with the philosophy underlying them (see, for example, Waterman, Waterman and Collard, 1994; Mackenzie Davey and Guest, 1995). Probably the best-known independent CAC is the Career Action Centre in Palo Alto, California, USA. This CAC began in the 1970s as a women's professional support group. It has grown enormously since then, and now has 9,000 members, women and men. It offers a range of services to individuals and organizations, principally in Silicon Valley. Its avowed position is not so much to help people get a job, but to help people develop their career resilience. This is construed as being made up of self-knowledge, flexibility, willingness to move on, knowledge of the labour market and long-term goals independent of the employing organization. Individuals are able to access information and professional help to achieve these things. The CAC also offers training for organizations to promote career resilience in their employees, but will work with organizations only if the culture and top management support their aims. Since some elements of career resilience could heighten willingness to leave an employer, the top managers in some organizations are not keen. Middle managers may be even less so, since they see a danger of losing their best subordinates.

Several trends suggest that CACs in various forms will flourish as the 21st century unfolds. They have greater scope than most interventions for crossing organizational boundaries in an era when inter-organizational co-operation is likely to increase and organizational boundaries are likely to become ever fuzzier. CACs offer opportunities for networking and professional support, both of which are likely to become increasingly prominent elements of career management. CACs can be relatively cheap from an organization's point of view. Because services are offered under the auspices of a CAC, they can be adjusted, discontinued or developed within a stable structure and policy for careers, thus minimizing perceptions of 'here today, gone tomorrow' interventions.

NETWORKING

It is well known, or at least often asserted, that most job opportunities are never formally advertised (see, for example, Bolles, 1993). Vacancies tend to be snapped up or even created by people already acquainted with the recruiter, presumably because this form of recruitment is cheap and it acquires a person whose attributes are already known, at least to some extent. Professionals involved in helping people find jobs consequently tend to endorse the 'it's not what you know, it's who you know' line. Job seekers are encouraged to reactivate existing contacts as well as or instead of perusing the situations vacant sections of newspapers and magazines. The principle of using contacts also extends to other career-related activities such as finding a mentor (see next section), negotiating a developmental work assignment (see earlier in this chapter), obtaining careers advice or updating professional skills.

The effective initiation and maintenance of social relationships for career-related purposes is often termed *networking*. The obvious key idea is that the more people who know and like an individual and respect his or her competence, the more successful that individual's career will be, other things being equal. To start networking after being made redundant is much too late – it will be too obvious that the relationship is based on dire need. So the pre-emptive and proactive use of networking is key. It is vital to establish and maintain one's professional reputation (Arthur, 1994) within and beyond the people with whom one has contact in day-to-day work. Networking can also be used to support people who face obstacles in their careers (see also Chapter 5).

One aspect of networking sometimes forgotten is that it involves giving as well as taking. To be involved in social networks means that one can be expected on occasions to offer help, information, support or advice as well as to receive it. For those who find it difficult to contemplate spending time on entirely altruistic activities, there are two consolations. First, it is possible to learn something useful from other people even if the relationship is more give than take. Second, the social norm of reciprocity means that a favour given now is one that all parties involved can legitimately expect to be repaid at some later date (Gouldner, 1960). Conversely, declining to help a person out now has obvious negative potential consequences in future. One difficulty with both of these encouragements to the reluctant networker is that individuals in low status positions might have little to offer those in much higher and/or much more powerful positions. So to some extent networking appeals beyond simple reciprocity to a wider morality involving perhaps a sense of duty or humanitarian concern. It also tends to involve people of approximately equal status, or at least people who might plausibly be of equal status in the foreseeable future.

One recent analysis has confirmed that people in management roles tend to have larger social networks than others (Carroll and Teo, 1996), which is in line with the picture of managerial work painted by Mintzberg (1973) and others as being dominated by the making and maintenance of contacts outside the formal organizational chain of command. The authors concluded on the basis of survey data from 268 managers and 366 non-managers in the USA that:

> When compared to non-managers, managers show wider organizational membership networks – they belong to more clubs, societies and the like. Managers also have larger core discussion networks, and these contain more co-workers, more strangers, and more people with whom the focal person has close or intimate ties.
>
> (Carroll and Teo, 1996, p. 437)

The last observation in the above passage is perhaps particularly significant. It is sometimes argued that managers' contacts tend to be shallow, confined to the task-related needs of the moment, but Carroll and Teo's findings suggested otherwise.

There is very little scholarly writing about networking, and consequently very little systematic analysis of what networking strategies can be used, and which are most likely to achieve desired results. On the other hand, social psychology boasts an enormous literature on self-presentation, social influence and impression management which is clearly relevant to networking. A detailed review is beyond the scope of this book. Interested readers are referred to Turner (1991) for a scholarly overview, and to Rosenfeld, Giacalone and Riordan (1995) for a very well-written integration of research findings and practical examples of impression management. Feldman and Klich (1991) have analysed the day-to-day impression management techniques and beliefs adopted by what they referred to as 'careerists', hell-bent on increased promotion, status and pay.

Shrewd readers of the above sources would be well equipped with the knowledge (though not necessarily the skill) to present themselves in such a way that those on the receiving end form a favourable impression. It is clear from social psychological research that many, but not all, people are skilled in using varied impression management techniques such as ingratiation, self-promotion, excuses and justifications. Impression management can be designed to enhance one's image over and above a satisfactory level, or it can be a damage limitation exercise when something goes wrong. It seems that people on the receiving end of ingratiation are remarkably poor at spotting that it is happening. On occasions it can be too blatant, but the effective ingratiator will avoid this by taking care to, for example, disagree with the person he or she wishes to impress on just a few matters, probably unimportant ones, or to mix big compliments with just a little mild and peripheral criticism. Non-verbal behaviour such as eye contact and body posture is also very important. Some but by no means all impression management techniques were well described long ago in Dale Carnegie's 1936 book *How to Win Friends and Influence People*, where sincere smiling, honestly meant compliments and avoidance of too much talk about oneself were put forward as the winning formula. The last of these is both important and for some of us not easy: after all, a bore is said to be a person who keeps on talking about him- or herself when you want to talk about yourself.

Impression management is not inherently deceptive or machiavellian, though it can be used for deceptive ends (Weatherly and Beach, 1994). It is not remotely synonymous with lying. It is much closer to marketing, where the good points of a product or service from the point of view of the potential consumer are emphasized. It is important to remember that not only do people's private beliefs about themselves influence their self-presentation, but also their self-presentation can influence their private beliefs. People can indeed end up believing their own story, and perform better in their work as a result (Eden, 1991).

There is little doubt that the 21st century will see high emphasis on networking. Especially with the availability of electronic communication, the scope for self-presentation and the range of skills required to do it well are both increasing. More working at or from home and the blurring of organizational boundaries mean that one's achievements and experiences may be less than obvious to other people. One cannot assume that career-relevant information such as job openings will fall into one's lap. More use of short-term project work and the pace of change require more updating and more frequent work-seeking. These trends do, however, vary somewhat between occupations. In some, a person's work is fairly open to scrutiny and social networks which transcend organizational boundaries are relatively well formed. Academia is a good example. In such cases networking may be much more integral to the nature of the work itself. Also, for some people the formation of close friendships may override the need for impression management. You know you can safely be candid about your weaknesses when you are with your really good friends.

MENTORING

Mentoring has been defined in various ways, sometimes so loosely that it encompasses almost any harmonious relationship between two people. Probably the definition which would command most common assent is that of Kram (1985, p. 2): 'a relationship between a younger adult and an older, more experienced adult that helps the [less experienced] individual learn to navigate in the world of work'. Mentoring as a career management tool has many enthusiasts. There is quite a bit of literature on it, including some systematic evaluation and many case examples. Levinson *et al.* (1978) argued long ago that the mentor relationship is one of the most complex and important a man can have in early adulthood. Clutterbuck (1993) asserted that 'everyone needs a mentor', whilst Collins and Scott (1978) reckoned that 'everyone who makes it has a mentor'. Such bold statements invite a touch of healthy scepticism, but there is no doubt that mentoring has been an important experience for significant numbers of individuals and organizations.

Kram and others have made the important distinction between informal and formal mentoring. The first is where the relationship between mentor and protégé (i.e. person being mentored) springs up naturally, presumably because both parties want it. Levinson *et al.*'s (1978) evaluation of the importance of mentoring was based on informal mentoring. Formal mentoring is where organizations (normally employers or professional bodies) arrange mentoring relationships for all or some members in an attempt to replicate the benefits of informal mentoring in a systematic manner. The word 'planned' is sometimes substituted for formal. Normally the mentor is someone more senior than the protégé, but not his or her supervisor (see, for example, Gibb and Megginson, 1989).

Mentoring is a relationship embedded in the participants' day-by-day work and is therefore likely to be difficult for third parties to arrange or manage. Formal mentoring has in fact been likened to a blind date, where mentor and protégé are brought together and everyone hopes for the best (Chao, Walz and Gardner, 1992). Pairing of mentor and protégé is not necessarily so haphazard in formal schemes, but the point is well made that participants may well construe themselves as being press-ganged rather than volunteering. Hence the width and depth of some informal mentoring relationships may be difficult to replicate through formal ones (Phillips-Jones, 1989). Blunt (1995) and Bennetts (1995) have provided brief case examples of how formal mentoring may fall well short of the mark, partly because many people resist the idea of formalizing something quite personal.

Mayo (1991) made the point that informal relationships that are working well should not be sacrificed in favour of new ones which fit the system. Most students of mentoring would agree with that, but perhaps be less convinced by his relatively *laissez-faire* approach to managing a formal scheme (pp. 189–90): 'No bureaucracy is needed: the career manager needs just to make some matching, choosing those who will be mentors carefully, provide some guidance as to how to manage the relationship, and let it run for as long as it proves to be helpful.'

Before pursuing this further, it is necessary to pause and consider exactly what benefits mentoring is intended to bring. A good general statement of this, together with some cautions, has been provided by W.A. Gray (1989, p. 20):

> [Formal mentoring] is not a band-aid to solve a crisis such as rampant employee turnover, nor should it be implemented as the latest fad. Instead, it provides a proactive means of developing people to do their present job better, to fit into the organizational culture and become loyal to the organization, and to learn new perspectives and skills needed for successful career advancement, etc. Mentoring is a developmental process that takes time; not a quick-fix for endemic problems.

A more detailed list of the potential benefits of mentoring is shown in Table 5.3. Notice that the benefits are thought to accrue to all the parties involved: mentor, protégé and organization. An implicit assumption here is

Table 5.3   Potential benefits of mentoring

For the protégé
Fast and effective learning of work demands, skills, organizational norms and values, career contingencies, and best ways to achieve work goals.
Having an influential person to put him or her forward for desirable assignments, and deflect blame for mistakes.
Having a role model to help clarify own desired future and self-concept.
Having a confidant to talk over issues of personal concern, independent of line management.
A sense of belonging to the organization.
Rapid career advancement.

For the mentor
A sense of a valued role in the organization.
The satisfaction of demonstrating and passing on his or her own know-how and skills.
Use and expansion of interpersonal skills.
Learning new skills and perspectives from the protégé.
Reward for effective mentoring.
Seeing the protégé develop.
A new challenge.

For the organization
High levels of work performance by protégés and perhaps mentors.
Fast progress towards effective performance by the protégé.
Speedy and complete socialization of protégés.
High levels of motivation and commitment by protégés and perhaps mentors.
Good communication and fostering of a culture of collaborative learning.
Low employee turnover.

that the amount of common ground between the parties' interests outweighs any clashes or inconsistencies. In fairness, even the most enthusiastic advocates of mentoring acknowledge that the right conditions are required if formal mentoring is to be successful (see, for example, Clutterbuck, 1993). Case studies, intuition and, to a lesser extent, systematic research have suggested the following ways to ensure that mentoring relationships are initiated, subsequently maintained, and deliver benefits valued by all parties.

(1) The goals of the mentoring scheme should be clearly defined.
(2) So should the behaviours (e.g. frequency and nature of meetings) expected of mentor and protégé.
(3) Both the goals and the behaviours should be consistent with the organizational culture. For example, a mentoring scheme which aimed to establish close, confidential relationships would be difficult to achieve in a formal, status-conscious organization.
(4) Initial training should be provided for mentors and protégés. Alleman (1989) found that this was more important than having 'release time' specifically set aside for mentoring.
(5) Ideally, both mentors and protégés should be volunteers, though this is sometimes difficult to reconcile with the aim of including all employees or all in a certain group.
(6) Performance appraisal and reward for mentors should explicitly include a significant element based on their performance of mentoring duties.
(7) The mentoring should aim to add something not achieved by other interventions such as training schemes or continuing professional

development. As implied by W.A. Gray (1989) in the quotation above, mentoring should not be introduced just because it seems like a good idea and everyone else is doing it.

(8) If mentoring is part of an attempt to change the culture of an organization, care must be taken to select mentors who are experienced and knowledgeable but not too committed to the old ways of doing things.

Some research evaluating mentoring has used a questionnaire called the Mentoring Functions Scale (Noe, 1988a) or an adaptation of it. This assesses the benefits of mentoring as perceived by protégés using a number of questions designed to address various benefits, both psychosocial and career-related. Psychosocial benefits have been defined as those that enhance a protégé's sense of competence, identity and work-role effectiveness, whilst career-related benefits directly concern career advancement (Kram, 1985). There is some evidence that the benefits perceived by protégés tend to be significant but distinctly less enormous than is sometimes claimed, particularly for career-related benefits. Arnold and Johnson (1997) found really quite low perceived benefits among graduates in two UK-based organizations. They suggested that this was due to a lack of training and reward for mentors coupled with an absence of clear 'added value' from mentoring. Ironically, although mentoring is often offered to graduates in early career (Mayo, 1991), these people are often on training schemes which may provide many of the same things as mentoring.

Other research has examined more long-range consequences of mentoring for protégés (see, for example, Whitely, Dougherty and Dreher, 1991; Aryee and Chay, 1994; Pollock, 1995). Often, but not always, having had a mentoring relationship as opposed to not having had one is associated with salary progression and number/speed of promotions. This research is often cited as evidence that mentoring is spectacularly successful, but a careful look suggests caution about this conclusion because much of this research:

(1) does not distinguish between formal and informal mentoring;
(2) does not rule out the possibility that people receiving mentoring were better cut out for success in the first place than those not receiving it, and therefore more likely to attract a mentor. If so, mentoring would not have necessarily been a *cause* of protégés' success;
(3) is not clear whether mentoring came via someone regarded as a mentor, or whether 'bits' of mentoring came from a variety of sources;
(4) relies heavily on people's recollections of mentoring experiences, sometimes over a number of years.

Mentoring is frequently used as a means of fostering the careers of people who are otherwise likely to be disadvantaged. Perhaps the most persuasive example concerns women, since even now in many settings there are few women at or near the top (Segal and Zellner, 1992). Mentoring may be able to help women develop their social networks, skills and knowledge more effectively than other means. There has been a considerable amount of research on gender issues in mentoring, and much of this has focused on potential difficulties experienced by women in obtaining mentoring relationships and then being able to profit from them (e.g. Ragins and Cotton, 1991). Recurring problems include the absence of women in influential positions who can be effective mentors and role models and the possibility of sexual connotations (actual or generated by 'office gossip') in cross-gender mentoring which may constrain the relationship. In fact, however, what evidence there is suggests that once mentoring relationships are established, the benefits experienced by protégés are more or less unaffected by gender (Noe, 1988b; Dreher and Ash, 1990). Perhaps the parties try extra hard to make it work, and the existence of a formal mentoring scheme may well help to legitimize the relationship.

Another avenue for mentoring concerns the careers of members of ethnic minority groups, many of whom have even more difficulty than women in finding influential mentors with whom they can readily identify (Thomas and Kram, 1988). Evans (1995) has provided an example of mentoring for black employees of a London local authority. The local authority served a very ethnically diverse population, and for this reason among many others it was desirable to facilitate the entry and subsequent development of people from ethnic minorities. Various courses had previously been run, but these were seen as too far removed from real developmental opportunities. So a working party was formed, and as a pilot scheme its members were mentored (the term used in the organization was sponsored) by hand-picked influential senior managers. The intention from the outset was to make the relationship worthwhile for all parties (though principally for the protégé) and it was quickly found that mentors (many of whom were white) gained valuable insights into the perspectives of other cultural groups in the organization and the community served by the local authority.

Information and resource packs were made available and clear ground rules and definitions were agreed by the working party. Application forms were devised for both mentors and protégés, on which among other things people stated what they hoped to gain from the scheme. Matching of mentors and protégés was done by a central co-ordinator, and it was quickly learned that effective matching depended more upon congruence of mentor and protégé goals than upon similar personal characteristics. Continuing training and support were available for both parties, and the process was jointly owned by mentor and protégé. The content of conversations was strictly confidential except in cases of very severe misconduct. On the whole the scheme proved successful, with mentors, protégés and organization all reporting many of the benefits described in Table 5.3.

Although I pointed out earlier that HR techniques can encourage mentors to take their role seriously, there are many other relevant factors. An important one is that the organizational culture should support open communication and collaborative relationships. But, just as protégés' needs are considered to underlie their enthusiasm for mentoring, so the same possibility must be considered for mentors themselves (see Table 5.3). Several of the developmental approaches to career management described in Chapter 7 of this book suggest that at certain ages and/or stages people tend to become more open to the importance of bringing on the next generation. This is particularly the case in midlife onward, when a person is said to become more concerned with handing on what he or she knows as an 'antidote to mortality', to maintain his or her position as a useful person, and perhaps to express a deeper concern for and commitment to humanity. Whilst this may sound a little fanciful and does not mean that every 45-year-old should suddenly be required to take on mentoring duties, it reflects the experience of many individuals. A more negative way of putting the same point is that it is no use assigning mentoring duties to people who are still wrapped up with achieving their own successes. Even though they might look like admirable role models for younger colleagues, it is advisable to wait until they are ready to focus on other people rather than on themselves. For some, that time may never come.

Some of the potential benefits to organizations shown or implied in Table 5.3 are quite subtle, and thus very hard to demonstrate conclusively. Effective mentoring means effective relationships and interpersonal communication, including perhaps across intra-organizational boundaries which might normally be significant communication boundaries. If a mentor is outside the protégé's employing organization, he or she may be especially well placed to bring novel perspectives to it. Sometimes tricky situations can arise where a protégé's line manager and mentor may have differing views about the protégé's development, and again if these are handled effectively they may expand the organization's capacity to communicate and deal with conflict. A more measurable benefit of mentoring may be that it helps develop people without raiding the training budget, though of course if a cost was attached to the time spent pursuing their relationship by protégé and mentor it might look less of a bargain.

Mentoring is likely to remain a highly significant aspect of career management into the 21st century. It is very much in line with an emphasis on self-development through interpersonal relationships, and might in a sense be regarded as an extension of networking (see elsewhere in this chapter). The current and future work environment is conducive to the idea that individual aspects of mentoring can be delivered by a number of individuals, not just one who is labelled a mentor. Many or all of these people will be outside the person's employing organization (if any). These possibilities have been discussed before (see, for example, Clawson, 1980) but are now more real as people's attachments to organizations become increasingly short-term, their work more varied, and their career management tasks more complex. For the same reasons it may be that the mentoring relationship is once again seen as essentially a private one, with formal schemes becoming rarer. Finally, the assumption in Kram's (1985) definition of mentoring given at the start of this section that the mentor is necessarily older than the protégé is likely to become less and less tenable. Although that pattern will still be more common than the reverse, the increasing pace of change reduces the 'transfer value' of some aspects of older people's experience.

MANAGING THE CAREER PLATEAU

This section is a little different from the others in this chapter and the last one. It focuses on a career problem or issue rather than a specific career management intervention. But, as we will see, a number of the career management interventions described in Chapters 4 and 5 can be applied to the career plateau.

Although most people probably have a fairly clear intuitive understanding of what the career plateau is, inevitably it has been defined in somewhat different ways. For Ference, Stoner and Warren (1977) it is the point in a career where the likelihood of additional hierarchical promotion is very low. Feldman and Weitz (1988) substituted 'increases in responsibility' for 'additional hierarchical promotion', in recognition of the possibility that increases in responsibility may occur without formal promotion. Of course, there is ambiguity about who can tell for sure whether the probability of promotion/more responsibility for an individual is very low, and about just how low very low is. Nicholson (1993) preferred to use objective information about a person's career progress within an organization, and defined the plateau as a person's standing in a status hierarchy relative to the perceived or actual norms for one's age group. This reflects whether or not a person is 'up to speed' regarding career progress to date. The assumption is that those who have fallen behind are much less likely to move up further than those who have not.

Delayering and downsizing coupled with population trends have meant that in many organizations there are a lot of people seeking very few promotion opportunities. In Chapter 8 we will see that increasing numbers of job moves are level status or even downward. In project-based organizations hierarchical promotion almost ceases to be a relevant concept, though perhaps the same is not true for increases in responsibility. So although the career plateau has always been an inevitable feature of organizational life, it now tends to come sooner and more unexpectedly to more people, and it is often all the more unwelcome for that (Goffee and Scase, 1992).

It is therefore tempting to view the plateau as a problem, and indeed it can be. The career systems in some organizations are akin to a knock-out tournament (Rosenbaum, 1989) where failure to gain promotion in the first round, even if through bad luck or capricious decision-making, essentially rules a person out of later rounds. Only exceptional ability can compensate for an early 'knock-out' (Dreher and Bretz, 1991) in the more rigid tournament systems. So in this situation there will be plenty of people who are plateaued well below their potential. They are likely to experience considerable frustration and motivational problems, at a cost to them and their employer. Less obviously, the tournament model may lead to some not especially able people reaching the level of their incompetence – that is, being promoted one too many times. These individuals are also problematic in that they are likely to be performing badly and know it. Their plateauing is very obvious. Some research that has identified plateaued people (though not usually the causes of their plateauing) has shown that plateauing can have negative consequences for individuals' well-being and motivation (e.g. Veiga, 1981).

On the other hand it would be foolish to conclude that the career plateau is always a major problem. Howard and Bray (1988) have noted that many plateaued people are relatively happy with their lot, and the organization is relatively happy with them. These people may indeed form the majority of staff in an organization, and have been referred to as the 'solid citizens' (Ference, Stoner and Warren, 1977). Nicholson (1993) found that employees of a large corporation who were behind the normal rate of advancement were no less satisfied than those who were around the average rate. People who are plateaued can concentrate more on truly mastering the tasks of their work rather than jockeying for promotion positions. They can also experience more personal growth in and out of work as a consequence of feeling relatively free to pursue their own agendas (Feldman and Weitz, 1988). This optimism needs a little qualification though. Organizations may be delighted to have competent employees who are not seeking promotion, but not necessarily competent employees who want to remain in the same job with the same responsibilities right until retirement. Plateauing is not the same as stagnation, particularly now that skill requirements and job duties change so frequently under people's feet.

So not all plateaued people are the same. For any plateaued individual, how he or she should be managed depends heavily on the extent to which the following reasons for the plateauing apply:

(1) lack of skills and abilities for present job;
(2) lack of skills and abilities for any job of higher responsibility;
(3) lack of information about skills and abilities;
(4) needs and values which lead the person not to seek further advancement;
(5) needs and values which lead the person to seek to stay in exactly the same job;
(6) stress or burnout;
(7) lack of incentives to move up;
(8) absence of promotion opportunities within the organization.

Table 5.4 shows some of the career management interventions most likely to be relevant to each reason for plateauing. Each intervention has potential use for more than one cause of plateauing, and each cause of plateauing can potentially be addressed by more than one intervention. The largest number of interventions are potentially relevant for what is perhaps the most common primary cause of plateauing – the absence of promotion opportunities within the organization. Note also that some of the interventions can be used mainly to meet individuals' needs, some to meet organizational needs, and some both. Further, each intervention may serve a different balance of needs in different circumstances. So, for example, development centres may help

Table 5.4 Career management interventions for plateaued people

Reasons for plateauing	Career management intervention									
	Mentoring role	Developmental assignments	Training/ education	Career counselling	Career workshop	Development centre	Personal development plan	Career action/ resource centre	Revised reward structure	Outplacement
Lack of skills/abilities for present job			✓	✓			✓	✓		✓
Lack of skills/abilities for any job of higher responsibility	✓	✓	✓				✓			
Lack of information about skills/abilities				✓	✓	✓	✓	✓		
Needs and values which lead the person not to seek further advancement	✓	✓			✓	✓		✓	✓	
Needs and values which lead the person to seek to stay in the same job	✓		✓			✓			✓	✓
Stress or burnout	✓		✓	✓	✓					✓
Lack of incentives to move up	✓	✓		✓				✓	✓	✓
Absence of promotion opportunities within the organization	✓	✓	✓	✓	✓	✓	✓	✓	✓	

Note: ticks represent the interventions likely to be most relevant in the first instance for employees in an organization which requires moderate to high levels of change and flexibility from staff.

both individual and organization clarify exactly what the person's skills are. They may help employees to identify non-promotional opportunities even if whether or not they take them has no notable consequences for the organization. Or development centres may obtain information for the organization about exactly where (if anywhere) someone who has proved reluctant to move jobs could be shifted to.

The 21st century will almost certainly see an acceleration of the already evident trend away from construing career success as upward movement in a defined hierarchy. In one sense, therefore, the career plateau is sidelined. But in another sense it is a useful reminder that being plateaued is increasingly a normal state. Career management interventions must be used not to perpetuate the myth that upward movement is likely, but to prevent personal and organizational stagnation in the brave new world.

SUMMARY

This chapter and the last one have shown the variety of career management interventions available to organizations. Similar issues arise with most of them, and include the following.

(1) There is relatively little information available upon which to evaluate the impact of the intervention.
(2) Some interventions have potentially difficult conflicts of interest, or at least differences of emphasis, between individual and organization. Who an intervention is for in practice depends less on the specific techniques used, and more on who pays whom for its provision as well as who has ownership of any information arising from it.
(3) The career management interventions most likely to prosper in the 21st century are those which (a) are cheap to run; (b) take the person away from his or her work as little as possible; (c) give organizations access to information about competencies and development needs without obliging them to take complete responsibility for acting on that information.
(4) Some career management interventions which do not meet the criteria in (3) above may prosper as privately provided services, assuming that individuals can afford to pay for them.

Interventions are definitely not only for the upwardly mobile. Given the likely restrictions on upward mobility in 21st-century organizations, it is ever more important to manage the careers of plateaued employees in order to maintain their motivation and contribution to organizational performance and adaptability.

In the next three chapters the emphasis shifts somewhat towards individuals. We will examine how people make career decisions, how lives develop and how transitions, for example between jobs, can be handled. Although most of the focus is on individuals, there are plenty of implications for organizations too. These will be drawn out.

—— 6 ——

CAREER DECISION-MAKING

Career decisions are often assumed to be decisions about what type of occupation to enter. There are two things wrong with this. The first is that, as we know, careers are not necessarily confined to one field of work. The second (well recognized in the counselling literature) is that there are lots of other decisions people may feel they need to make, such as:

(1) whether to return to employment after childrearing;
(2) whether to continue their education;
(3) whether to apply for a particular job;
(4) whether to accept that job if offered;
(5) whether to become self-employed.

All of these can be considered career decision-making for our purposes. Nevertheless, much of the available literature treats career decisions as decisions about what type of occupation to enter.

As we shall see later, it can be argued that these days one has to do something more than match one's existing characteristics to the requirements of the environment or environments one is considering. Nevertheless, it must be the case that matching is very important. The favourite person to quote on this is Frank Parsons, who right back in 1909 argued that, in order to select a field of work, we should ideally have:

(1) a clear understanding of ourselves, our attitudes, abilities, interests, ambitions, resource limitations and their causes;
(2) a knowledge of the requirements and conditions of success, advantages and disadvantages, compensation, opportunities and prospects in different lines of work;
(3) true reasoning on the relations of these two groups of facts.
(Parsons, 1909, p. 5, described in Sharf, 1992, Chapter 2)

This framework can be broadened to all types of career decisions if we extend the second element beyond 'lines of work'. There is something reassuringly solid about Parsons's formulation. He seemed to assume that there is a relatively stable, certain self waiting to be discovered if only we look carefully enough, and that there is also some stability and certainty about the characteristics of different lines of work. Most of all, though, it is apparently possible to achieve 'true' reasoning about these 'facts'. Again, this implies that there is one correct, or most correct, conclusion to be drawn from our knowledge of self and the world of work.

There are of course alternative ways of seeing things. Most crucially, many social scientists interested in the self would argue that we have a variety of possible selves 'waiting in the wings', to be brought centre stage if and when the situation demands. Therefore career decision-making is a case of deciding which aspects of self to bring to the fore, and why. This lacks the clarity of Parsons, but is perhaps more faithful to our fluctuating self-perceptions day by day, and to our ability to envisage alternative futures for ourselves.

Much of the career counselling literature focuses on how people can make decisions well. In other words, it looks at the *process* of decision-making, and assumes that a well-made decision made in an appropriate manner is likely also to have positive outcomes for the individual concerned (see, for example, Nathan and Hill, 1992). Most self-help careers books adopt a similar line (e.g. Ball, 1996). A key element here is being ready to make a decision. So before we look in more detail at how decisions are made, we will start with what leads up to them. This includes career exploration, career information and self-assessment. Good decision-making may well depend on using appropriate concepts for how people and occupations differ, so we will also examine that in some detail – in particular the widely used model of John Holland (1985). Then, finally, attention will turn to the process of making decisions, including the role of computers.

READINESS FOR CAREER DECISION-MAKING

We have already seen that Parsons (1909) put his cards on the table. To be ready for decision-making is to know about self, know about the world of work, and be able to put the two sets of information together. Stated at that level of generality, it is hard to argue. The developmental approaches to careers described in Chapter 7 also have quite a lot to say on this – particularly those of Erikson and Super. Effective decisions require a well-founded sense of personal identity and understanding of the world. Although now less popular than it was, the notion of *career maturity* is relevant here. In its most general sense, career maturity is defined as a person's readiness to tackle the career management tasks that face him or her. In practice, it has usually been interpreted as meaning readiness for career decision-making. So, for example, Super's measure of career maturity, the Career Development Inventory (CDI) (Super *et al.*, 1979), includes questions asking about the extent to which the person has engaged in career planning, career exploration and decision-making, and the extent of his or her knowledge of the world of work, including of a preferred occupation, if any. The knowledge of the world of work section of the CDI is interesting because it includes multiple-choice questions in which it is possible to give correct or incorrect answers. This is unusual in career development measures, but consistent with the notion that career maturity is based partly on attitudes and partly on ability. This distinction can also be seen in the Career Maturity Inventory (CMI) developed by John Crites (1978). This has an attitude scale consisting of questions assessing among other things a person's decisiveness, involvement in the decision-making task, and willingness to compromise. It also includes a competence test designed to assess a person's abilities to appraise self, select goals and solve problems.

There have been some heated academic debates – or, rather, squabbles – about which measures and ways of looking at career maturity are best (see, for example, Westbrook, 1985). It is also possible to question whether it is helpful to think in terms of career maturity at all. The word maturity seems to imply something that seems increasingly unrealistic these days, namely an orderly unfolding of personal capacity to meet predictable environmental demands. The measures seem to have dubious psychometric properties, and possibly reflect a middle-class perspective on careers.

Even if the notion of maturity is not viable in this context, exploration (i.e. collecting information about oneself and the world of work) before decision-making is normally necessary.

Exploration can take many forms, including:

(1) finding printed, videotape or computerized information about occupations, educational opportunities, etc.;
(2) trying out a particular activity (for example via voluntary work or a college access course) to see if one likes it and/or is good at it;
(3) talking to one or more individuals about the work they do, what they think of it, and how they got to where they are now;
(4) filling in some psychometric tests and questionnaires (such as those mentioned in this book) in order to gain self-insight;
(5) 'shadowing' somebody at work for a day or two, in order to observe what he or she does;
(6) looking at job advertisements to see what sorts of work are available and what personal characteristics are required;
(7) looking over possibilities with a careers adviser or counsellor;
(8) participating in a career planning workshop.

In fact, when you think about it, there are many activities that could involve career exploration. To some extent, career exploration is a purpose one can bring to bear in a wide range of activities rather than activities themselves.

Here too, diagnostic questionnaire measures have been developed to assess the extent to which a person is engaging in exploration. For example, Stumpf, Colarelli and Hartman (1983) produced the Career Exploration Survey (CES), which includes questions assessing among other things the amount of occupational information the person has obtained and the extent to which he or she intends to engage in systematic exploration. More detail is shown in Table 6.1.

Note that the CES is not only about how much information a person has, but also about his or her satisfaction with the information, how confident he or she is that future exploration will help, and how much stress he or she is

Table 6.1 Aspects of career exploration

Some (slightly adapted) questions from the CES are as follows:

To what extent have you done the following over the last three months?
Obtained information on specific jobs or companies.
Obtained information on the labour market and general job opportunities in your career area.
Reflected on how your past integrates with your future career.

How satisfied are you with the amount of information you have on:
Jobs that are congruent with your interests and abilities?
The types of organizations that will meet your personal needs?

How much undesirable stress have the following caused you *relative* to other significant issues
with which you have had to contend?
Exploring specific jobs.
Deciding what you want to do.

What is the probability that each of the following activities will result in obtaining your career
goals?
Initiating conversations with friends and relatives about careers.
Learning more about yourself.
Planning your job search in detail.

Source: Stumpf, Colarelli and Hartman (1983)

experiencing. This comprehensiveness is useful in picking out people who might require counselling help, and in identifying their problem areas.

Perhaps not surprisingly, there is good research evidence that the extent to which persons have engaged in exploration affects their progress in decision-making, at least among college students (Blustein *et al.*, 1994). However, one distinction which gets rather lost in considerations of career exploration is that between doing exploratory things and finding useful information. Just going through the motions does not necessarily yield useful results. Greenhaus and Callanan (1994, Chapter 3) have pointed out that people's career exploration can be incomplete, perhaps because work is not very important to them or because they do not see any worthwhile choices open to them. Exploration can also be coerced rather than voluntary. For example, several times when I have engaged in career counselling with people in their late teens it has quickly become apparent that it was their parents who wanted the counselling to happen. Exploration can also be random – dotting about here and there, not really building upon prior learning. Most fundamentally of all, perhaps, exploration may be defensive. That is, the person doesn't confront the difficult things. So, for example, he or she may maintain a view of self that ignores important aspects of reality. Some people avoid seeking out a key piece of information for fear that it will not be what they want to hear.

INFORMATION ABOUT THE SELF AND THE WORLD OF WORK

Parsons (1909) reminds us that it is necessary to relate information about oneself to information about the world of work. Probably the simplest way of doing this is to describe people and environments in the same language and with the same conceptual frameworks. To think of oneself as an assertive yet sensitive individual may be a valid self-insight, but it will only be useful in career decision-making if possible future environments can be described in similar language, either in terms of the activities required or in terms of the kind of people who tend to inhabit those environments.

Personality

It is debatable whether general personality constructs are very useful in choosing a type of work. Attempts have been made to relate general personality characteristics to occupations. For example, on the basis of personality test data from a large sample, Bartram (1992) found that, relative to the general population, managers tend to be:

(1) considerably more uninhibited and spontaneous;
(2) considerably more self-confident;
(3) somewhat more experimenting and free-thinking;
(4) somewhat more self-reliant and realistic;
(5) somewhat more forthright.

Bartram and others acknowledge that any given type of work tolerates different personality characteristics. In line with this observation, personality assessments at work are often used to review how people tackle their work and how they might do it differently, rather than to select them into or out of particular kinds of work. Nevertheless, general personality assessments do sometimes give some broad indications. A person who is submissive rather than dominant, anxious rather than emotionally stable, would probably not be well advised to enter general management, though this does not in itself offer any insight about what kind of work such an individual should go into. A person who is dominant and emotionally stable *might* be suited to general management (depending on other factors such as ability and career goals), but equally might also be suited to other things. And what about a person who is neither submissive nor dominant, anxious nor stable – in other words, in the middle? Perhaps such a person would find it easier than people nearer the extremes to demonstrate, for example, either submissiveness or dominance in his or her behaviour. The notion briefly described earlier that decisions involve choices between alternative selves might be particularly applicable to 'in the middle' people.

But we should not get too carried away with personality. Other aspects of self (some of which are related to but not the same as personality) are more applicable to career decisions. One of these is *values*, which can be loosely defined as abstract outcomes a person wishes to attain. Super (1973) suggested that 14 values are most readily applicable to work, including altruism, autonomy, prestige, risk and variety. The extent to which a person regards each of the 14 values as being important in his or her life is highly relevant information for decisions such as what type of work to enter, whether to go for a particular job, what sort of course to enrol upon, or whether to work at all. There are some obvious similarities between values and career anchors (see Chapter 7).

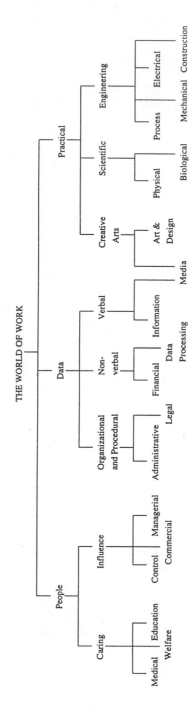

Figure 6.1 A hierarchichal model of vocational interests

Source: Reproduced from *Occupational Interest Inventories: Manual and User's Guide* with permission of SHL. ©Saville and Holdsworth Ltd: not to be reproduced without permission

Interests

Interests are another category of relevant information about the self. Interests are activities and/or subjects to which one feels drawn. They are a product, at least in part, of personality and values, though probably our accumulated experiences of success and failure, reward and punishment (particularly in childhood) also play a part. It is relatively easy to map interests on to types of work, because interests refer to fairly specific activities or bodies of knowledge, unlike personality and values. Therefore it is not surprising that many psychometric tests devised to assist vocational choices focus on interests. An early example from the USA was Strong's (1943) Strong Vocational Interest Blank, which has since then been through a number of revisions and is now called the Strong–Campbell Interest Inventory (SCII) (Hansen and Campbell, 1985). The SCII assesses 23 'basic interest areas' such as agriculture, medical services, writing, public speaking, teaching, and office practices. The 23 are grouped under John Holland's (1985a) sixfold classification (see later in this chapter).

One other of the many interest tests available is produced by the UK occupational psychology consultancy company Saville and Holdsworth Ltd. In its General Occupational Interest Inventory (GOII) and Advanced Occupational Interest Inventory (AOII), the company divides interests and occupations into groups based initially on a long-established 3-fold distinction between data, people and things derived from functional job analysis (Fine and Wiley, 1971). The Saville and Holdsworth structure of interests is shown in Figure 6.1. The questions on the GOII and AOII ask people about their level of interest in activities relating to each of the areas shown on the bottom line of Figure 6.1.

Interest inventories are likely to be most helpful for people who are uncertain about what type of work they should enter. For more fine-grained decisions such as whether to take one secretarial job or another secretarial job, or whether to go on a 3-month IT training course, interest inventories are probably of very limited use. In my experience some people really warm to interest inventories, and learn a lot from completing them – not only about themselves, but also about how to understand the similarities and differences between different kinds of work. Other people simply do not find them helpful. This is sometimes because they feel the test tells them nothing new, and sometimes because they object in principle to having their individuality squeezed into categories.

Perhaps the most important things to remember about interest inventories are:

(1) They can only be as good as the conceptual structure on which they are based and the care with which the questions are formulated and tested.
(2) They can only reflect how the person has responded to the questions, albeit in a structured way.
(3) They rarely if ever point to one single option that is clearly better for the person than all others.

(4) Sometimes they are better at clarifying a problem than solving it. For example, a person may be interested in just about everything, or conversely hardly anything.

(5) They are often the basis for a discussion. So, if a person says that none of the occupations apparently most consistent with his or her interests feels quite right to him or her, careful discussion of why this is could lead to valuable new insights.

Although interests derive partly from values, they can be in conflict. I have worked with a number of employees of a charity with a very explicit ethical stance. Some said that although they were fully behind the charity's values, they found their jobs paralysingly boring. This was particularly the case for those in lower-level administrative positions. They could see that their work was important and contributed to achieving the goals of the charity, but after a time this alone was not enough. They needed to be interested in what they were doing. This was a surprise to some.

Talents

Other aspects of self relevant to career decisions are what Greenhaus and Callanan (1994) refer to as *talents*. Some examples they list are manual dexterity, verbal reasoning, interpersonal skills, precision of movement, creativity and speed of response. Some, but not all, of these talents align quite closely to many psychometric tests of ability/intelligence that are commercially available. Talents are more general than specific skills, but they undoubtedly contribute to them. Driving a racing car might be considered a skill. That skill is easier to develop, and probably develops more fully, if the budding Damon Hill has talents such as high response speed and precision of movement. But simply having those talents does not permit a person to jump into a racing car and establish a new lap record.

Rather like interests, talents are probably at their most useful when a person is considering what type of work he or she wishes to enter. More detailed decisions such as between two alternative jobs may rest more on specific skills such as whether one is proficient with a particular spreadsheet. Certainly some employers see it that way, since for some jobs (for example secretarial or other IT-based) familiarity with specific tools or techniques is required. They may not be willing to employ someone who clearly has relevant talents but not yet the specific skills because of training time and costs, even if there is little doubt the person could quickly acquire the required skills.

Talents are obviously important. They dictate whether it is worth trying to learn a specific skill. A consideration of one's specific skills (or competencies, see Chapter 3) is also clearly relevant to effective career decision-making. These often form the core of a person's curriculum vitae. It is important to remember that whilst most people tend to become interested in things they are good at, and become good at the things which interest them, this is not always the case. Some people who seek a change to a different type of work do so because although they are competent at what they currently do they do not enjoy it. Also, what interests some people may reflect what they see others doing, for example on television, rather than what they can do themselves. That is one reason why the instructions on most interest inventories emphasize that the questions should be answered strictly on the basis of what the respondent him- or herself would be interested in doing.

ACCURACY OF SELF-ASSESSMENT

Some people are not good at, or perhaps simply not accustomed to, identifying their skills and talents. Indeed, being guided through one's achievements and the reasons for them can produce some surprising results. But, even after we have identified a list of talents or skills relevant to our personal circumstances, how good are we at knowing how good we are at them? Presumably effective career decisions rely on accurate self-assessment, or at least self-assessment which other people such as potential employers are prepared to believe. With personality, values and interests it is difficult to find indicators other than what the person says about him- or herself, so it may not be very useful to speak of accuracy. But by using various psychometric and practical tests, it is possible to obtain relatively objective information about the extent to which we possess some skills and talents. It is also often possible to ask observers what they think of a person's skills and talents. This opportunity has been used by some researchers to address a question of practical significance: just how accurate, or at least supportable, are our estimates of our talents and skills, and indeed of our performance?

The short answer is not very accurate, but not as inaccurate as cynics might think. There are two ways of looking at accuracy. One is whether the overall level of ratings people give themselves is comparable with assessments obtained from other sources such as test scores, academic or work performance ratings, or ratings of them made by their supervisors. The other is whether, regardless of overall scores, the rank-ordering of a set of people is similar for self-rating and for the other more objective form of assessment. So if persons 1 to 8 rate their mathematical ability out of 20 they might give themselves 18, 17, 16, 15, 14, 13, 12 and 11. A test of their mathematical performance might reveal the following scores for the same eight people listed in the same order: 12, 11, 10, 10, 7, 6, 6, 5. Assuming the two sets of scores were genuinely comparable, we would have a substantial over-rating of self, but high accuracy in terms of the eight people relative to one another; since the rank-order of self-ratings is almost the same as the rank-order of test scores.

Regarding comparison of mean levels, most research finds that people over-rate themselves (Mabe and West, 1982), especially in comparison with how their supervisors rate them. This over-rating of self does not always occur (Farh, Dobbins and Cheng, 1991), and it is not clear why over-rating occurs on some occasions, under-rating on some others, and neither over-rating nor under-rating on others again (Somers and Birnbaum, 1991). It could reflect cultural differences, though Yu and Murphy (1993) failed to find any. Regarding similarity of rank-ordering, an old review of research by Mabe and West (1982) even now represents a good summary. They examined the results of 55 studies comparing self-evaluation of ability or performance with other evaluations such as tests, course grades and supervisory ratings. The mean correlation between self-rating and other evaluation was 0.29. If you are not familiar with correlation, in English this can be translated as meaning some similarity but not very much. However, when the data were corrected to allow for the less than perfect reliability of measures used in the 55 studies, the mean correlation rose to 0.42. This can be considered significant though still far from perfect agreement.

Of perhaps even more interest was Mabe and West's finding that the extent of agreement between self-ratings and other assessments varied a lot between studies. Closer scrutiny showed that the following factors seemed conducive to agreement, at least in terms of rank-order (i.e. the second form of agreement identified earlier):

(1) expecting that self-evaluations will be compared with other measures of ability or performance;
(2) having instructions for how to do the self-evaluation which emphasize comparison with other people;
(3) knowing that self-evaluations would remain anonymous;
(4) having had previous experience of self-evaluation.

Broadly speaking, the first two of these are about avoiding *incentives* to distort one's self-evaluation whilst the last two may reflect the circumstances in which a person is *capable* of accurate self-evaluation. Most of the research studies reviewed by Mabe and West did not include many of these features, so perhaps the overall lowish level of agreement they found is not surprising. On the other hand some subsequent research has failed to replicate the apparently beneficial effects of the four factors (Fox and Dinur, 1988).

A study by Lowman and Williams (1987) is of particular interest because they compared students' self-rated competencies on a vocational guidance questionnaire (John Holland's Self-Directed Search (SDS) – see later in this chapter) with scores on intelligence-type tests, of aspects of intelligence most closely related to the competencies on the SDS. They found correlations around 0.2 and lower, which really does suggest substantial inaccuracy of self-evaluations. There was, however, significant variation in level of agreement between different competencies/areas of intelligence. It was highest in artistic areas, and the authors suggested (pp. 9–10) that 'Perhaps it is easier to self-rate oneself accurately in an area perceived to be narrowly distributed within the population and in which having the ability is not tied to self-esteem.' Paradoxically, then, we may be able to assess ourselves more accurately in areas we don't care about than in those we do! As you may have noticed, the concept of accuracy is problematic. Even where a test of someone's ability is apparently objective and thorough, for example a carefully validated intelligence test, who is to say that it is 'correct'? Where the comparison point is ratings made by a supervisor it might be better to think in terms of agreement (a word I have used at times in the last few paragraphs) rather than accuracy.

Finally, perhaps we shouldn't be surprised at the lowish correlations between self-ratings and other assessments. When we rate ourselves we are likely to be influenced by at least two factors which could reduce the level of agreement. The first is our own relative abilities. So if I am very good at everything except art, at which I am still fairly good relative to most people, I am likely to be highly influenced by the contrast between my different abilities and rate my artistic ability lower than I otherwise would. In other words, my reference point may be my other abilities, not other people's abilities. Second, to the extent that I do compare myself with other people, I may confine the comparison to people rather similar to myself. This may be why, in my experience, many business and social science students rate their mathematical ability as average or even lower, even though their GCSE grades in maths indicate that they are in the top 20% of the population. They may compare themselves with other students, some of whom are highly numerate, rather than with people as a whole. These psychological processes may be inconvenient for research, but equally they may make practical sense. If I am trying to make effective choices for myself, it makes sense to be clear about my own relative strengths and about my standing relative to people who might be applying for the same jobs as I am.

SELF-EFFICACY

At least some research and theory suggests that some degree of over-optimism about one's abilities is good for mental health (Taylor and Brown, 1988 – though see also the debate initiated by Colvin and Block, 1994). The related concept of self-efficacy (Bandura, 1977) has been defined as the extent to which a person believes that he or she can perform the behaviour required in any given situation. It has been shown to influence people's willingness to tackle tasks and their performance in them. Although the extent of this is not yet certain, self-belief may even influence a person's performance quite independently of actual ability. So whilst gross overestimation of one's ability is probably not healthy, mild overestimation may be.

Some but not all research suggests that women tend to rate their abilities lower than men rate theirs. It seems that, on average, women have less sense of self-efficacy across a range of tasks. Likely causes revolve around sex-role stereotyping such that women have less opportunity to accomplish things, less chance to learn from successful people and less encouragement to be successful than men (Hackett and Betz, 1981). This may be particularly marked for stereotypically masculine attributes, since some research suggests that whilst men rate their ability to do traditionally feminine activities fairly high, women do not pay themselves the same compliment for traditionally masculine ones

(Clement, 1987). There is also some suggestion that women are actually more realistic though perhaps it doesn't do them much good. An anecdotal illustration of the difference in self-efficacy of males and females is provided by the following extract from a research interview with a woman in a large company (Mackenzie Davey, 1993, pp. 306–7):

Interviewee: I . . . I'd probably be able to cope with the job. That's the other thing, being a woman . . . I can only do nine-tenths of a job description and therefore I won't be able to cope with it. . .

Researcher: Is that what you thought?

Interviewee: Well every woman does, don't they? They, you know, not like a man 'Gosh I can do ten percent of this job, I can do it I'm all right.' I thought I'm going to struggle, I'm never going to be able to cope.

The concept of self-efficacy has been applied to career decision-making. Taylor and Betz (1983) produced a questionnaire designed to assess people's confidence in their ability to make career decisions, including five aspects of decision-making that should by now sound rather familiar: occupational information, self-appraisal, planning, problem-solving and goal selection. In reality, all five have a strong tendency to go together so it is legitimate to think of career decision-making self-efficacy (CDMSE) as a single phenomenon. Interestingly, it seems that on the whole males and females differ very little in their levels of CDMSE (e.g. Arnold and Bye, 1989).

JOHN HOLLAND'S TYPOLOGY OF PEOPLE AND OCCUPATIONS

Earlier in this chapter I said that having a single way of describing both people and occupations would be a great help in decision-making about the type of work to enter – though, as also noted earlier, this is just one of many different career decisions. Most career guidance techniques, however rudimentary, make some attempt to achieve this unified form of description. Probably the best-researched and validated conceptual structure is, however, that of John Holland. Holland's work has been based in the USA, and whilst his theory is dominant there, it seems not to be in the UK and the rest of Europe. Certain aspects of Holland's theory and resulting practical tools do not travel well, but nevertheless the relative neglect of his work in Europe has probably been Europe's loss.

John Holland worked for many years as a careers counsellor in the USA. He felt that he could discern various personality types among his clients, and in the 1960s he began to research this in earnest. This led to a refinement of his ideas, a book (Holland, 1973), subsequent revision of the book (Holland, 1985), numerous research papers and the production of several tests and questionnaires to aid decision-making (more about these below).

Holland reckons it is possible to discern six pure personality types. He acknowledges straight away that nobody exactly resembles any one type, but asserts that people resemble each type to different degrees. Most of us

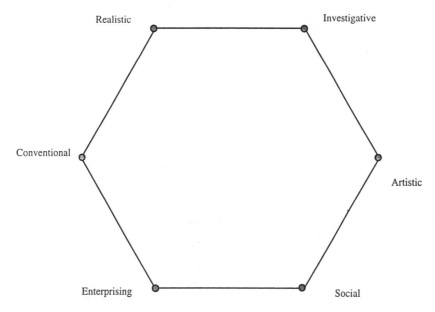

Figure 6.2 John Holland's six types of vocational personality
Source: Holland (1985b)

resemble one type more than the rest. The six types have varying degrees of similarity with each other, as expressed in their distances from each other in the hexagonal structure which has become Holland's trademark (see Figure 6.2). The six types are as follows:

(1) *Realistic* people like practical and/or physical activities requiring strength or co-ordination as opposed to abstract, theoretical thinking. They are not particularly interested in social interaction and may be resistant to expressing feelings.

(2) *Investigative* people are interested in concepts, logic and abstract problem-solving. They tend to be logical, critical and cautious. They put a low emphasis on human relations and like to tackle problems in a rational, impersonal way.

(3) *Artistic* people like to use their imagination and self-expression. They enjoy environments with few rules, where they can use their creativity and be in touch with their feelings. They tend to dislike rules and regulations.

(4) *Social* people tend to enjoy working together to help others and solve problems. They are often quite idealistic and altruistic. They usually come across to others as quite warm and caring.

(5) *Enterprising* people, like social ones, enjoy contact with people. But unlike social types, they are interested in managing, persuading and getting their own way in an assertive manner. They enjoy action rather than thought and tend to seek leadership roles.

(6) *Conventional* people tend to emphasize organization and planning. They

like structured environments such as administrative offices, and they value security and dependability. They enjoy clarity and being in control, but are less comfortable using their imagination.

In many senses, the types at opposite corners of the hexagon are the opposite of each other. You probably noticed this, in reading the above descriptions of types and cross-referencing them to Figure 6.2. It is perhaps particularly obvious for artistic and conventional. Individual people may resemble both of two opposite types quite strongly, though it is more common to resemble adjacent types. So, for example, if I resemble the enterprising type most closely, it is likely that the type I am next most similar to will be either conventional or social. In passing, one may note that the greatly increased emphasis in many universities on teaching and entrepreneurial/consultancy activities since the mid-1980s creates something of a problem for staff originally hired for being abstract critical thinkers and researchers. Holland's typology helps us to see why. Investigative types (research) are not very similar to social types (teaching), and pretty dissimilar to enterprising types (entrepreneurial activity/consultancy). It is relatively unusual to find people who resemble quite closely all three of these types. Holland suggests that it is most useful to describe people in terms of the three types they resemble most closely, in descending order. So an SAE isn't a self-addressed envelope, but a person who is most similar to the social type, next most similar to artistic, and next most similar to enterprising.

How does Holland describe occupations? He argues that occupational environments (as he calls them) have their force through the people who inhabit them. So for any given occupation (or, more rarely, organization) if we collect data about the personality types of the people, then we can discern the type of occupation or organization it is. So, describing the environment of, say, dieticians, would mean surveying a representative or random sample of dieticians and noting their most common personality types. Holland and colleagues have indeed done this for a variety of occupations in the USA. Over and above that, other classifications such as the Strong–Campbell Interest Inventory (SCII) mentioned earlier and the US Department of Labor Dictionary of Occupational Titles (DOT) have been tied in with Holland's types. This means that data about occupations collected over the years by researchers working on SCII and DOT can be 'converted' to Holland's language. The upshot of all this is that a huge range of occupations is now described in terms of their three-letter code. A small selection is shown in Table 6.2. Just to illustrate the rarity of opposite types appearing together, only two of 12,099 occupations coded have A and C as their two dominant types.

The Self-Directed Search

John Holland has produced several structured questionnaires in order to help researchers research and, more importantly, individuals to make career choices. His best known questionnaires are the Vocational Preference

Table 6.2 Selected occupations and their Holland codes

Occupation	Code
Petroleum engineer	RIE
Bridge inspector	RSI
Animal breeder	RES
Actuary	ISE
Marine surveyor	IER
Market-research analyst	IAS
Playwright	ASE
Sculptor	AER
Architect	AIR
Department store manager	SER
Career counsellor	SAE
Medical record clerk	SCI
Tax accountant	ECS
Foreign exchange trader	EIR
Sales engineer	ERI
Book-keeper	CIS
Medical secretary	CES
Building inspector	CIE

Source: Holland (1985b)

Inventory (VPI) and the Self-Directed Search (SDS). The former is based exclusively upon interests. The latter also includes self-estimates of competencies, and is worth examining in a little more detail because it illustrates a number of important points.

In the SDS Manual, Holland (1987) states that the SDS is designed to be a simulation of a counselling experience, not just a test. Although he is sometimes accused of being too rigid, in fact Holland (1987, p. 36) acknowledges that 'people, in fact, are suited to broad categories of jobs; occupational titles do not reveal the duties, and most people have considerable flexibility for adaptation to different jobs'. He also asserts that most people do not need expensive and time-consuming counselling. They want reassurance that they are thinking along the right lines, and perhaps a few suggestions about occupations to which they might be suited but which they haven't yet considered. That is why the SDS is designed so that people can work through it themselves, see for themselves what it is getting at, and score it for themselves. They can also look up suggested occupations for which they might be suitable on the basis of their SDS scores in the Occupations Finder which accompanies the SDS. The Occupations Finder lists occupations according to their three-letter code, together with an indication of the required level of educational attainment. There is also a Leisure Activities Finder if you wish to apply Holland's ideas to your spare time. All this is a little unusual (though not quite as revolutionary as Holland makes it sound) since many psychometric tests can be scored and interpreted only by qualified experts and the questions in the tests are sometimes designed so that the person taking the test cannot easily tell what they are getting at.

The Self-Directed Search contains sections asking people to indicate their:

(1) occupational daydreams;

(2) interest in performing specific activities;

(3) interest in a range of occupations;

(4) competence in performing specific activities;

(5) self-estimates of competence in general areas.

Questions are grouped into Holland's six types in every section except the first. Respondents are shown how to calculate their overall score for each type. They are then instructed to write their three-letter code on the basis of their SDS scores. But, in line with Holland's attempts to make his ideas flexible, he suggests a 'rule of 8', whereby if the difference between two type scores is less than 8, the two scores can be considered reversible. If that sounds a bit confusing, perhaps an example will help. Supposing a person scores as follows: realistic 23, investigative 18, artistic 12, social 19, enterprising 28 and conventional 33. Taking the scores at face value, this person's three-letter code is CER, and he or she would indeed be encouraged to look up occupations with that code in the Occupations Finder. But on the basis of the rule of 8, this person would also be encouraged to check out ECR, CRE, CEI, CES, ECI and ECS. No shortage of suggested occupations here – in fact, perhaps too many.

Holland's research indicates that most people can indeed use the SDS effectively without help. For example, they usually score it correctly and look up occupations in the appropriate section(s) of the Occupations Finder given their SDS scores. User satisfaction is apparently quite high, and from the point of view of organizations, it is a low-cost career management tool. On the other hand, there are dangers that, in common with many vocational guidance questionnaires, the SDS may produce too many or too few suggested occupations, and that people's self-rated competencies may not be accurate (see earlier in this chapter). In my experience there is also a risk of tautology: people are not necessarily impressed if they tick elementary school teacher as an occupation that interests them, and later find that one of the occupations suggested by the Occupations Finder is elementary school teacher!

Many of the SDS questions force the respondent into a yes or no response – there are no shades of grey. Some people do not like that, and prefer the chance to say 'maybe' or 'somewhat'. There are, however, some good psychometric reasons for the yes/no format. For example, if someone really feels moderately attracted to most of the occupations, activities and competencies listed in the SDS under, for example, realistic, he or she will probably tick 'yes, I'm interested' to about half of them, and 'no, I'm not interested' to the other half. The individual will then come out with a middling score on R, which faithfully reflects his or her moderate level of interest. So although the user of the SDS may feel uncomfortable about coming down on one side or the other for each question, it all 'comes out in the wash' in the overall type scores. Also, self-scoring of the SDS would be much more difficult if there were more response options to each question.

Another potential problem, particularly for people who have considerable occupational experience, is that the sections on competencies can have too much influence on their overall type scores relative to the sections on interests. This means that the suggested occupations reflect what they *can* do (but may be seeking to escape from) rather than what they *want* to do.

The simplicity of the SDS scoring is also seen by some as a disadvantage. It means, for example, that people's scores are not adjusted to reflect their sex. You probably will not be surprised to learn that, on average, males score higher than females on the realistic type, whereas the reverse is true for the social type. So if a woman scores, say, 25 on the realistic type, that score is not exceptionally high in the great way of things, but is nevertheless higher than most women. If her score was adjusted to reflect its magnitude *relative to other women*, it is more likely that realistic occupations would be in her suggested list. Holland, however, prefers not to make such adjustments. On a practical level, it would make self-scoring much more difficult. More fundamentally, he takes the line that it is not his responsibility to undo any sex-role stereotyping that may occur. Raw, i.e. unadjusted, scores have an authenticity for the users. They reflect how they feel about themselves, and how they relate to real occupational environments rather than those that might occur in an ideal world.

Tests of Holland's theory

You will not be surprised to find that Holland's key prediction is that people who experience congruence (that is, they are in an occupation and/or organization which matches their personality) will, other things being equal, enjoy more satisfaction and more success, and stay in the occupation or organization longer than those who experience incongruence. He also makes other predictions. One is that people in an incongruent environment will over time tend to change towards congruence – assuming they remain in the environment of course. Another is that highly differentiated people (that is, those who are *much* more similar to one personality type than any other) should experience even more satisfaction and success in a congruent environment than less differentiated people.

A review by Spokane (1985) of research testing Holland's predictions was cautiously positive. Across about 60 studies (many based on students rather than people in employment) there was a discernible tendency for congruence to be associated with job satisfaction, stability of job or course choice and academic performance. There wasn't much evidence either way about job performance. People did indeed tend to increase in congruence over time, and this was more often by changing self than by changing occupation or course. But Holland's prediction concerning differentiation was not generally borne out. Spokane also pointed out a number of weaknesses of the research, which meant that conclusions about Holland's theory could be only tentative. One of these was that because Holland makes quite a few predictions, only a few studies provide tests of any single one, so the available evidence was limited. Another problem was that only about a third of the research studies were longitudinal (i.e. followed people over time), so it was often difficult to draw conclusions about cause and effect.

A review of more recent research on Holland's predictions (Tranberg, Slane and Ekeberg, 1993) is less optimistic than Spokane's. They reviewed 27 research studies and found little evidence that congruence is associated with satisfaction outcomes. Tranberg, Slane and Ekeberg point out that the problem may be more to do with the limitations of the research than with Holland's theory. After all, Holland does make the point that greater congruence should produce greater satisfaction, *other things being equal*. It is known that many factors can affect, for example, job satisfaction, so probably all other things are not equal in the research. Also, in most of the studies the congruence investigated was to do solely with interests (e.g. as measured by Holland's Vocational Preference Inventory), which might be too narrow a form of congruence. All this may help to explain why the overall correlation between job satisfaction and congruence was only 0.20. But ominously for Holland, research studies which *did* find such an association paradoxically tended to be those which used the least thorough measures of the concepts in question.

If we make the assumption that *some* kind of match between person and environment is a good thing, one possible conclusion is that Holland has not hit on the best way of describing people and environments, at least for career purposes. Perhaps something like Schein's career anchors (see Chapter 7) might do a better job. Nordvik (1991) found that people's scores on a career anchors measure are only slightly correlated with those on Holland's personality measures, so perhaps career anchors are picking up different aspects of the person.

If Holland is indeed studying vocational personality in his work, we would expect people's scores on his personality measures to correspond well with their scores on other well-established and more generalized personality (and ability) measures. Holland supplied some evidence to this effect in 1985. So, for example, people's extraversion scores on the NEO Inventory (Costa and McCrae, 1992) are positively correlated with their scores on Holland's social and enterprising types (a high score indicates high resemblance of person to type). Investigative types scored higher on average than realistic types on measures of verbal and numerical aptitude. Tokar and Swanson (1995) have found that people's scores on Holland types correlate in predicted ways with some but not all parts of the currently fashionable five-factor model of personality (Goldberg, 1990).

Overall, the evidence is reasonably encouraging that Holland's types do link with general personality theory. But strangely that may be part of the problem for Holland. Although he is inclined to assume that values, interests and competencies are parts of vocational personality, I argued earlier that this could not be taken for granted. Although Holland's Self-Directed Search asks questions about interests and competencies, perhaps Holland's tendency to combine these into overall personality type scores leads to the

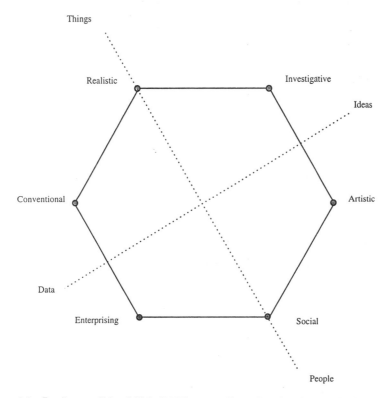

Figure 6.3 Prediger and Vansickle's (1992) career dimensions in relation to Holland's types
Source: Adapted from Prediger and Vansickle (1992)

loss of useful information. Another possibility is suggested by Rounds and Tracey (1993). They conducted a detailed and complex statistical analysis of data on John Holland's theory and concluded that it might be helpful to draw an imaginary circle rather than a hexagon through the six Holland types (this is possible – try it on Figure 6.2!). It would then be possible to locate six types at rather different points on the circle from those chosen by Holland. In other words, Holland may have the *structure* of vocational personality correct, but have chosen sub-optimal points on the circle for the location of his types. Dawis (1992) has made a rather similar point in suggesting that the choice of six types is itself an arbitrary decision, and other numbers are possible (e.g. 8 – see Roe, 1956). Prediger and Vansickle (1992) preferred to describe people and occupations in two-dimensional space, using axes of things v. people and data v. ideas, as shown in Figure 6.3.

Thus every person and every occupation could be summed up as a point on a graph, according to their relative emphasis on data as opposed to ideas, and things as opposed to people. Indeed, Prediger and Vansickle (1992) showed how this could be done using scores for individuals and occupations on Holland's measures.

So Holland is under some attack at present, but nearly all his assailants are seeking to build upon his work rather than demolish it. His categorizations of people and occupations have a relatively well-grounded foundation which helps people think about their occupational options in a structured way which reflects reality. These last three words are important. It is all very well for the producers of less well-thought-out vocational guidance tools to say they provide a stimulus and basis for thinking, but if that basis does not reflect the real structure of personalities and occupations it will be hard to use effectively, and risks the building of castles upon sand.

THE PROCESS OF DECISION-MAKING

One might think that if appropriate preparation and exploration are undertaken, decisions will look after themselves. Up to a point that is indeed the case, but of course sometimes two or more options are quite closely matched. On other occasions it may not be easy even to identify what the options are. Studies of decision-making processes are therefore not redundant. As we will shortly see, they tend to focus on different styles of decision-making.

We must first remember, however, that doing exploration before decision-making is not enough in itself. It is necessary to draw valid conclusions from the exploration. Career counsellors (e.g. Nathan and Hill, 1992) spend a considerable amount of time with clients trying to arrive at key statements concerning the client's goals, needs and values, and concerning what each client is looking for in jobs. Different writers have different ways of describing this. London and Stumpf (1982) refer to identity statements, which are general and relatively all-embracing descriptions of self. John Krumboltz (see, for example, Mitchell and Krumboltz, 1990) has coined the term Self Observation Generalization, which also refers to general statements about the self. According to Krumboltz, these are derived from accumulated learning experiences involving success and failure, pleasure and pain. Some barriers to decision-making are a product of incomplete or shallow exploration – or maybe simply an absence of opportunity to obtain relevant information. Research (e.g. Vondracek et al., 1990; Callanan and Greenhaus, 1992) suggests the following as a reasonable list to be going on with. Much of this should look pretty familiar by now:

(1) lack of knowledge of one's own abilities;
(2) lack of knowledge on one's own interests;
(3) conflict between two or more attractive possibilities;
(4) conflict between two or more unattractive possibilities, not all of which can be avoided;
(5) conflict due to a potential solution having both attractive and unattractive features;
(6) lack of general labour market information;
(7) lack of specific, e.g. within-company, labour market information;

(8) lack of confidence or familiarity with decision-making;

(9) lack of knowledge about what people in a particular occupation actually *do*.

The general point is that we need to get behind surface statements about the self. If I say that I like to work alone, it is necessary to discover why. It could be because I am afraid of competing with other people. Or it might be due to my preference for personal rather than team goals. Alternatively, I might be aware that I find it difficult to stand up to others, and be worried that working with others would mean being (metaphorically!) trodden-on. No doubt there are also many other possible explanations. The point is that it is necessary to combine several or many self-perceptions in order to arrive at something deeper and with more general applicability.

Not that this process is always so neutral. We are easily deflected by, for example, the expectations other people have of us. Sometimes these are so deeply ingrained that we see them as our own opinions. On other occasions we are aware of a discrepancy between how we see ourselves and the expectations other people have of us, but we nevertheless feel that somehow we ought to be different from what we are. Our feelings matter and are a legitimate input to our decision-making, but they can also block a good solution by clouding our judgement. We need to recognize also that our feelings can be contradictory – for example, we might view a particular course of action with a mixture of excitement and fear.

Some people with low self-esteem find it difficult to trust their own judgement, or to believe that they can make and implement an effective decision. In these cases it might be important to bolster self-belief by going out of their way to think of times when they succeeded at something. For other people a better technique for clarifying values and preferences may be asking difficult questions such as what is the work activity they would least like to give up. Everyone has their own way of seeing the world and drawing inferences from information. Sometimes this can simply be an expression of a person's individualism, to be honoured in decision-making. But it may also be faulty or self-defeating – as, for example, when a person sees everything as a sign that life is unfair to him or her.

A three-way distinction much used by some careers counsellors is that between people who are already decided about what they want to do vs. those who are currently undecided vs. those who are habitually undecided. It can be quite difficult to tell whether a person is undecided or indecisive, but it is important to do so. A person who is indecisive needs help to overcome possibly serious blocks and to develop decision-making skills. Someone who is simply undecided may need less intensive help in order to clarify his or her opinions and options.

Another three-way distinction has been described by Phillips and colleagues (Phillips *et al.*, 1985), who drew upon the earlier work of Harren (1979) in describing three decision-making styles.

(1) *Rational*   This involves systematic appraisal and logical deliberation using a long-term time perspective. The person weighs up information carefully, accepts responsibility for decision-making, and anticipates consequences of previous decisions.

(2) *Intuitive*   The emphasis here is on emotional factors. There is heavy reliance on attention to feelings and on fantasy and imagination. Responsibility is accepted for decision-making, which is often based upon 'gut feeling'.

(3) *Dependent*   Here the person does *not* accept responsibility for decision-making. Instead, other people or random events are seen as responsible and capable of acting in either a benign or malevolent way. The person tends to be passive and compliant, heavily influenced by the expectations of others.

It doesn't take a genius to figure out that the dependent style is the least likely of the three to produce successful outcomes. But is either of the other two superior? There isn't very much evidence on this, but it appears that they are both equally good at least in terms of progress in career decision-making, though not necessarily subsequent satisfaction with the decision. Note, however, that each of these two styles is not necessarily equally effective for any individual. Across a large number of people they may be equally effective, but that could be because each person uses the style that works for him or her personally. It might be interesting to ask people who normally prefer one style to use the other, and then see if they looked equally effective!

It is important to remember here that the intuitive style does *not* mean making decisions in the absence of information relevant to the decision. Intuition is what a person uses to evaluate the information. In my experience, most managers say they prefer the intuitive style whereas most technical specialists tend to go for the rational style. Those who use the rational style tend to like drawing up 'balance sheets' of pros and cons for each possible option, and may even go as far as assigning importance weightings to each one. Intuitive decision-makers may also draw up balance sheets to help them, but are much more likely to find themselves 'fixing' the outcome to match what they know deep down they already want, or tearing up the paper because it doesn't seem to help.

Another analysis of decision-making styles was presented long ago by Dinklage (1968). This involves no less than eight styles, and what I particularly like about it is that four of the eight are about how we *avoid* making decisions:

(1) delaying – putting it off;
(2) fatalistic – do nothing, and wait for luck or circumstances to strike;
(3) compliant – let someone else decide for us;
(4) paralytic – inability to make a decision due to fear and anxiety.

Luckily, there are also four ways of actually making decisions:

(1) intuitive – based on 'gut feeling', as described earlier;

(2) impulsive – sudden, quick decision, perhaps made mainly to 'get it over';
(3) agonizing – much thought and emotion are invested in every facet of the decision;
(4) planful – equivalent to the rational approach described earlier.

As with the earlier simpler threefold classification, it is important to realize that these styles are not necessarily deeply ingrained features of personality. They may be quite situation-specific and/or open to change through learning and training.

One decision-making strategy that would appeal to most rational decision-makers is Gati's (1986) sequential elimination approach. This is shown in diagrammatic form in Figure 6.4.

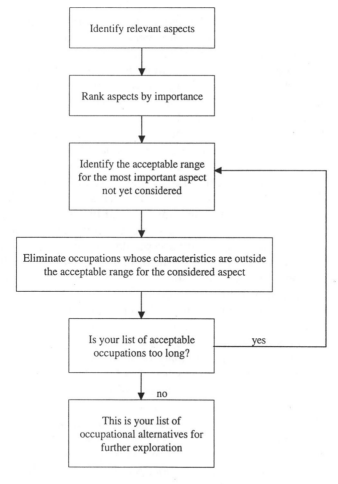

Figure 6.4 A schematic diagram of the sequential elimination model
Source: Gati (1986)

This approach can be described as *prescriptive*, because Gati suggests that this is the best way to make decisions. Applying it to choice of occupation, we would start by identifying features of occupations relevant to our choice, and then ranking the features in order of importance to us. Then, taking the most important feature first, we would decide what was acceptable. So, for example, we might decide that salary was the most important factor, and that an expected salary of £30,000 by the age of 35 would be acceptable. We would then strike off our list of possible occupations any which did not meet this criterion. If too many possible occupations remained we would then take the next most important feature and do the same again until the remaining list of occupations was sufficiently short for further exploration.

Note the sequential elimination approach as described by Gati does not take us right the way to a solution, only to the point where we can consider other factors (for example, likelihood of being able to implement the choice). This suggests some flexibility to his model. On the other hand it is a very fragmented way of tackling decisions. It treats relevant aspects in isolation from each other. So if one option scores very well on the second, third and fourth most important aspects but not so well on the most important aspect, it might fall at the first hurdle even though its cumulative virtues might outweigh its shortcomings on the single most important factor. More subtly, the importance of some features of occupations may vary according to other factors. So I might consider that, if I had to work in expensive London, salary would be most important to me, but otherwise less so. So there would be no easy way of making absolute statements about importance of features.

There might be a tendency to over-complicate the whole thing. Particularly if a person does not regard his or her work life as very important, it may be that he or she chooses the first option that seems acceptable – a sort of bypassed sequential elimination approach that produces a 'good enough' outcome as opposed to the best possible one. In group decision-making this has been referred to as a minimally acceptable solution, and in some other contexts as satisficing (as opposed to maximizing benefits). So, either deliberately or subconsciously, people sometimes do not maximize their gains. Perhaps they cannot be bothered to do so, or perhaps they are more concerned with making sure they do not make a bad mistake than with striving for the best possible outcome (see Kahneman and Tversky (1984) for an analysis of how people think about gains and losses).

Irving Janis is well known for his analyses of group decision-making, including disastrous government foreign policy decisions. He has coined the term 'groupthink' to describe the situation where members of a group value each other's esteem more than they value making the best possible decision. This reminds us that as individuals we can also fail to evaluate options fully because of our wish to conform to the opinions of people we value. Janis (1982) also suggested 'second chance' meetings where group members voice any lingering doubts, and the assignment of one or more people as 'devil's advocate', whose job it is to put alternative points of view. An individual can take these lessons to heart by, for example, checking that yesterday's decision still seems appropriate this morning, and by quite deliberately trying to think of problems with the currently preferred option during the decision-making process.

All this could be rather tedious and painful for the person, but can be considered part of what Janis and Mann (1977) called *vigilance*, where the decision-maker searches carefully for relevant information and evaluates it in an unbiased fashion. This can be contrasted with various other ways of going about decision-making, mostly less effective. One of these is hyper-vigilance, which is where the decision-maker is desperate for a solution, and seizes upon the first one that seems to offer quick relief (a kind of satisficing strategy caused by impulsivity). But probably the most common poor strategy is what Janis and Mann called defensive avoidance, which is where the decision-maker avoids the problem by delaying a decision or denying responsibility for it. This resembles the dependent style described earlier. People are most likely to use a vigilant style if:

(1) they are aware of, but not obsessed by, the risks attached to any given decision;
(2) they are optimistic about finding a solution;
(3) they believe they have sufficient time to make a decision.

Finally, Janis and Mann point out that nearly every decision has some negative features. It is important that a person prepares for these, and does not misinterpret them as a sign that he or she has done the wrong thing. We look again at some post-decisional phenomena in Chapter 8 on work-role transitions.

Table 6.3   Some computer packages for career management

DISCOVER (USA – American College Testing). USA package now available in various forms. It includes elements on self-awareness, opportunity awareness, decision skills, action planning, CV writing.

CAREERBUILDER 3 (UK – Stuart Mitchell Associates). Based on Hopson and Scally's career planning book *Build Your Own Rainbow*, and with some reference to John Holland's theory. It includes information on jobs and courses developed by the UK Department for Education and Employment. A company-specific version is called Corporate Horizons.

ADULT DIRECTIONS (UK – CASCAID). Intended for career changers, this system was developed from one for school and college students. It includes opportunities for self-analysis and exploration of new career ideas. It makes some use of personal construct theory.

PROSPECT (UK – AGCAS). System for assisting occupational choices of undergraduate university students. It includes some of the same elements as DISCOVER, and uses UK universities' career services information about occupations.

ACHIEVING YOUR CAREER and JOB SEARCH FOUNDATION (USA-Upsoftware Inc.). Developed in California, these packages are training programs designed to assist in the writing of CVs and letters of application, and in preparing for interviews and negotiations.

ECCTIS (UK Department for Education and Employment). Database of available courses in UK colleges and universities. Updated quarterly.

MICRODOORS (UK Department for Education and Employment). Database of information about occupations. All occupations are reviewed over a two-year cycle.

TAP (UK – Training and Enterprise Councils). Each of the 56 TECs produces its own database of local courses and learning opportunities.

PICKUP (UK – Guildford Educational Services). National version of TAP, but less comprehensive than all 56 TAPs combined.

NVQ DATABASE (UK – National Council for Vocational Qualifications). Listing of all available National Vocational Qualifications.

Source: Adapted from information presented at Career Development Network seminar, 'Computer Support for Career Management', London, May 1996

COMPUTERS AND CAREER DECISION-MAKING

There are quite a few software packages available to help people make career decisions. Again, most are first and foremost about choosing types of employment and/or types of educational course. Table 6.3 shows a few of those available. A number are based on development work carried out as long ago as the 1970s, though they have of course been updated a number of times since then. The most common pattern is for users to be invited to input information about themselves which is then matched against information about occupations held in the package's database. In the 'old days' people completed paper questionnaires which were then sent for analysis on a mainframe computer, with a printout of the results being sent to the user a week or two later. I can recall completing one of these (GRADSCOPE) in 1979. One of the occupations it suggested for me was minister of religion, which seemed absurd at the time but strangely prescient now.

These days of course most careers guidance packages are on PCs, so no sending away is required. Nevertheless some teachers and careers advisers still prefer mainframe analysis so that they can discuss with a young person his or her printout which will be in a known format. The packages have also become much more flexible, so that it is possible, for example, to change one's responses to the questions, perhaps because of a change of mind or simply to check the effect on suggested occupations. It is also possible to start at different points, and obtain occupational information on-screen. On some it is also possible to specify your own questions rather than simply responding to those the computer throws at you. Indeed, in one or two it is even possible to construct your own problem, list of potential solutions, and criteria for evaluating them using repertory grids (see, for example, Wooler, 1985). Most packages aim to help the user learn career management skills rather than being passive matching fodder. To some extent, of course, learning can occur simply through answering the computer's questions, but it is likely to be deeper if the user is taken through exercises in decision-making.

Some packages (for example CASCAID/Adult Directions) are supported by enormous amounts of regularly updated occupational information, and at the time of writing, Stuart Mitchell Associates had succeeded in tying in the UK government's occupational information database (MicroDOORS) with CareerBuilder 3. There are also examples of large companies having certain packages customized so that their own employees can use them. In the UK, Wellcome adapted CareerBuilder for this purpose, whilst in the USA AT&T commissioned Tom Jackson to produce a version of his package called Taking Charge of your Future. Customizing in this way may involve altering the questions, but more often concerns producing organization-specific job information, and company-specific algorithms for linking person data with job information. Updating is clearly crucial, as is some degree of constancy in the organization's language for describing jobs. Bearing in mind changes outlined in Chapters 2 and 3, there must be doubts whether there is sufficient continuity in many organizations to make the exercise worthwhile.

There is nothing magical about computerized aids to career decision-making. As Jackson (1993b) has pointed out, they are for the most part self-assessment exercises rather than psychometric instruments. Adding to Jackson's observations, we can say that these packages are only as good as:

(1) the conceptual structure underlying the questions the user is asked to answer;
(2) the reliability and validity of the questions, including the extent to which they reflect the underlying conceptual structure;
(3) the algorithms for matching person to occupation (many packages use rather scanty and/or subjective data about what kinds of people are best fitted to what kinds of jobs);
(4) the ease of understanding instructions;
(5) the suitability of the package for diverse users (e.g. different ages, ethnic groups, genders);
(6) the flexibility with which users can use the package to meet their own needs at the time;
(7) the extent to which they are evaluated and adapted in response to evaluation (see, for example, Watts, Kidd and Knasel, 1991).

For the most part, these packages are not marketed to individuals, but to organizations such as schools, colleges, universities, local careers services and (in the UK) Training and Enterprise Councils, and to a much lesser extent public libraries. Some packages are produced by not-for-profit organizations such as (in the USA) the American College Testing Program, and (in the UK) the Association of Graduate Careers Advisory Services. Watts (1993) has noted that public funding has often been required for the initial development of careers guidance packages, and that the political and economic pressures this brings can have a dramatic impact on the speed of development and nature of the eventual product. As Jackson (1993b) has noted, the advent of interactive CD-ROM greatly increases the possibilities for computer-assisted career management. For example, it might be possible to simulate a work-shadowing experience through video extracts showing occupations the user chooses to explore. The development costs relative to market size may mean this is a long time coming, but nevertheless in many respects most of the packages available at the time of writing are relatively crude given the technology now available.

SUMMARY

Good career decisions rest upon good knowledge. Exploring self and the world of work, and drawing appropriate conclusions from one's experiences, are not optional – unless, of course, one is in the happy position of being able to tolerate making a poor career decision without serious consequences. Interests are probably the aspect of self most central to career decisions, but values, talents, competencies and general personality characteristics also have relevance. A number of paper and computerized exercises, tests and questionnaires are available to help clarify aspects of self. Research has tended to find that people's estimates of their own abilities are not in particularly close agreement with other assessments, so it may be useful to get a 'second opinion'. A good understanding of self and the occupational world is much easier if valid ways of describing people and occupational environments are used. John Holland's typology of vocational personalities and environments is helpful here, though it may not reflect all the most significant aspects of self in career choice. Holland has developed easy-to-use materials to help people select appropriate occupations. Even so, styles of decision-making may matter – there are many ways of making decisions (and indeed of avoiding them). For some people, blocks to career decision-making lie in a lack of self-confidence and self-esteem.

7

DEVELOPMENTAL APPROACHES TO CAREER MANAGEMENT

Quite a lot of psychological research suggests that our *personality*, in the sense of our habitual tendency to behave, think and feel in certain ways, is quite stable during adulthood (Furnham, 1992). In other words, the kind of person we are does not change very much. Our *attitudes*, that is, the things we like and dislike, may be more changeable, particularly in early adulthood (Alwin, 1994), but our preferred personal style remains pretty constant. Costa and McCrae (1980) summed it up nicely in the wording of the title of their article 'Still stable after all these years' – with apologies to songwriter Paul Simon, for those readers old enough to have heard of him.

But that is only part of the story. Personality research, along with much developmental psychology, tends to concentrate on the *structure* and *content* of our psychological make-up. It focuses on the key elements of our behaviour, thoughts and feelings, and on how these fit together. But there is another tradition too: one that is particularly evident in lifespan developmental psychology. This views development in terms of the *tasks* we face as we progress through life. So whether we are extrovert or introvert, neurotic or stable, we are brought face to face with dilemmas, contradictions and tensions as we encounter certain ages or phases of life. Perhaps this is what gives us a sense that we and our lives are constantly changing, no matter what the personality theorists might say.

In this chapter we will examine some of the better-known theories of lifespan development, and then some related material on career development, ageing and wisdom. If this material has validity, it should offer insights into the following issues pertinent to this book:

(1) What key developmental tasks affecting their careers and lives do people encounter?
(2) Do they encounter these at specific ages, and why (or why not)?
(3) What are the implications for how individuals manage their own careers?
(4) What are the implications for how organizations manage people's careers?

ERIK ERIKSON

Like several influential post World-War II psychologists, Erik Erikson was a refugee from Nazi-occupied Europe. He had been schooled in the psychoanalytic psychology founded by Sigmund Freud. This tradition in psychology emphasized the power of the unconscious, irrational drives, and conflict between different parts of the human psyche. In common with some other psychologists of his time, Erikson rejected certain aspects of Freudian orthodoxy. In particular, he argued that the conscious, rational self (the ego) was more dominant than Freud gave it credit for, and that development and change routinely occur in adulthood rather than ceasing in middle childhood. On the other hand, he retained a key Freudian concept of tension between opposing forces. Erikson (1959, 1980) attempted to map out eight stages of psychosocial development. The first four stages refer primarily to childhood and are not discussed here, though it should be noted that 'hangovers' from unresolved dilemmas at those stages may affect adult life. The latter four stages are now described.

Life stages and developmental tasks

Identity v. role confusion
This is the stage for which Erikson's work is best known, and it concerns the adolescent identity crisis. The onset of puberty leads to physical changes and a growing awareness of future adult life. Childhood certainties and continuities fly out of the window, and there is a strong need to establish a clear sense of who one is and what one is like in order to cope with this. Success in establishing an identity leads to a perception that one is taking successful steps towards the future, and this in turn bolsters one's sense of self-esteem and self-confidence. Erikson said that an identity disapproved of by society may be more desired than no identity at all. It might be added that such an identity could even be more desired than an approved one, because it is more distinctive, more clearly recognizable. Like several of Erikson's stages, this one is like walking across a narrow bridge – it's possible to fall off either side. So, on the one hand, there is the danger of being unable to establish an identity. Perhaps one's environment is too confusing, or one's experience too contradictory. On the other hand there is the danger of rushing too eagerly to a rigid and inflexible self-identity which is not capable of sustaining the young person in the future, and/or insufficiently accurate to do justice to how that person really experiences his or her life.

Intimacy v. isolation
This stage typically occurs during a person's 20s and early 30s, though Erikson emphasized that there was no close link between ages and stages: a person in their 80s could in principle still be seeking an identity. The theme of this stage is that if a person has developed an authentic sense of identity, he or she should be able metaphorically to reach out to others with it. The

person should be able to form relationships with other people, organizations, or causes, without losing his or her own sense of self. The potential gain here is love: a capacity to value others deeply without entirely sacrificing oneself to them. Again the dangers are twofold. On the one hand is the possibility already described that a person will so immerse him- or herself in relationships that his or her sense of self is lost. Such relationships are likely to be very one-sided and to end in tears. The opposite danger is that a person will remain self-absorbed. If someone fears too much a loss of identity that might occur in relationships, he or she may remain isolated, his or her behaviour governed almost entirely by expressing and reinforcing his or her own very individual identity.

Generativity v. stagnation
This stage typically occupies much of a person's adulthood. Generativity might tritely be called the 'antidote to mortality'. More precisely, it concerns the bringing on of the next generation: handing on one's knowledge and experience and accomplishments to younger people. In one sense this is to do with oneself: how will one be remembered? Will one be remembered at all? This would imply the preservation of oneself – a sort of immortality so that after one's death people will say that you accomplished some important things, were a wise counsellor or whatever. Perhaps this book is my bid for immortality! However, Erikson also placed emphasis on the notion of care at this stage: that is, care for others, altruism. Handing on what you have learned is achieved through genuine care as well as a need to be needed. One obvious possible route to generativity is parenthood, but this is by no means the only one. Failure to achieve generativity means that one stagnates and becomes self-centred by caring about oneself rather than others.

Ego integrity v. despair
This eighth and final stage concerns the extent to which a person is able to accept him- or herself and his or her life without undue regret, and also to feel a sense of community with people in other cultures and even other eras. Along with this goes an acceptance that one is just a tiny, tiny speck in the universe. Failure to achieve ego integrity leads to despair over one's lack of time to put things right. This despair sometimes shows itself as disgust and contempt for others: a turning outward of the hostility one feels inside.

Critique and practical applications
It is possible to criticize Erikson's work on a number of counts, but equally it is important to remember that any analysis of the whole lifespan is bound to have some omissions or imperfections. Some commentators argue that, given his early life, Erikson had a strangely benevolent view of society. Healthy development was seen rather readily by Erikson in terms of integration between individual and society. Yet if society is dominated by evil, this integration should not be thought of as healthy or appropriate for develop-

ment. Perhaps more central to our concern with careers and their management, it is interesting that Erikson tended to play down achievement for achievement's sake, especially in early and middle adulthood. Our achievements probably assist us in forming a secure identity, in being able to relate to others, and in having something worthwhile to pass on to the next generation, but that seems to be only background in Erikson's writings. Vaillant (1977, p. 202, quoted in Sugarman, 1986, p. 90) among others has pointed out that in their early thirties his highly educated sample were 'too busy becoming, too busy mastering crafts; too busy ascending prescribed ladders to reflect upon their own vicissitudes of living'. So, if you or I, or our employer, were to try to manage careers in ways consistent with Erikson, we might overemphasize opportunities to establish and maintain work relationships at the expense of achievement. That said, there are several pointers here to effective career management. During adolescence and early adulthood it is important to explore different activities, interests and experiences in order to see how they fit with one's sense of self (see also Chapter 6). This exploration should ideally be done with some restraint and from a secure base. A rapid succession of unconnected and diverse experiences with little opportunity to 'take them home' and think about them might do more damage than good. On the other hand, people who restrict themselves to what they already know well may fail to develop important aspects of their potential, and thus saddle themselves with an unduly narrow identity.

However, let us pause for a moment. Just as Freud's ideas were partly a product of a society in which sex was almost a taboo subject, so Erikson's ideas are characteristic of a place and era (America in the 1950s and 1960s) where questions like 'who am I?' and 'how can I express myself?' were very salient. Perhaps now it is more a case of 'what can I do?' and 'what could I be?' The more turbulent world described in Chapter 2 perhaps offers less opportunity to establish a lifelong sense of identity, or to find work which exactly matches one's identity. Indeed, it could be argued that a key aspect of remaining employable is to take on tasks which challenge one's weak or unexplored areas and have the potential for personal growth (or failure of course). Erikson probably wouldn't have argued with the idea of personal growth, but taken at face value his work can be taken to suggest that you establish your identity through exploration and then express it. The occupational world of the 21st century will probably demand more flexibility than that.

Erikson's ideas on intimacy v. isolation may indeed underplay achievement, but in my opinion these days there is a tendency to underestimate the importance of relationships at work, except to the extent that they facilitate access to work opportunities, as in networking (see Chapter 9 for coverage of networking). Close relationships between people at work can foster personal development through sharing of tasks, insights and information. This may also improve organizational performance. Hall and Mirvis (1995a) argue that 'relational' work such as helping and supporting others often goes unnoticed and unrewarded, but might be crucial to organizational performance. They surmise that older people may be better than younger ones at this relational work.

The generativity v. stagnation stage contains some important insights, again all too easily overlooked in eras of rapid change. People in mid-career and beyond often have a deep understanding of the world of work to pass on: they can also learn a lot from the younger generation. This should encourage individuals to seek, and organizations to offer, opportunities for older people to act as mentors or coaches to younger ones. It is important too to remember the 'antidote to mortality' aspect here. As individuals, we need to think about which achievements, characteristics or creations we want to be remembered for. Since this is likely to be a major motivator in mid or late career, organizations might be well advised to seek and accommodate employees' wishes as far as practicable. An additional benefit is that doing so should make the ego integrity v. despair stage easier to handle by minimizing the number of regrets and unfulfilled ambitions.

DONALD SUPER

Beginning around the 1940s, Donald Super embarked upon half a century of work which aimed to apply ideas from developmental and humanistic psychology to careers and their management. One of his original concerns was to supply an alternative perspective to the then dominant approach to careers. This dominant approach arose from what is sometimes called differential psychology – i.e. the branch of psychology concerned with measuring individual differences. So, people's intellect, personality and interests were measured using tests and matched against the requirements of occupations. This was very much a 'square pegs in square holes' approach. What was more, the person was quite passive in the process – people were told what they were like and told what occupations they would be best suited to.

Super acknowledged that the concept of matching person to occupation is a helpful one (and it is still heavily used today, see Chapter 6). However, he argued that it took an unduly static view of the person, ignoring how one has changed in the past, how one might change again in the future, and why one is as one is right now. It also took no account of how the person saw him- or herself: that is, his or her self-concept.

Super spelt out some of his key propositions in his early work (Super, 1953, reproduced in Super, 1990, pp. 194–6). Here are adaptations of four of his 12 propositions. They show how he accepted the notion of matching but also went well beyond it.

(1) People differ in their abilities, interests, and personalities.
(2) Occupations require a characteristic pattern of abilities, interests and personality traits, with tolerances wide enough to allow both some variety of occupations for each individual and some variety of individuals in each occupation.

(3) The process of career development is essentially that of developing and implementing self-concepts; it is a synthesizing and compromising process in which the self-concept is a product of the interaction of inherited aptitudes, physical make-up, opportunity to play various roles, and evaluations of the extent to which the results of role-playing meet with the approval of superiors and fellows.

(4) Change may be summed up in a series of life stages of growth, exploration, establishment, maintenance and decline. A short-term cycle takes place in transitions between jobs, involving growth, re-exploration and re-establishment.

The first two propositions are consistent with differentialist views of career choice. The last two are not exactly inconsistent with it but, in choosing to place emphasis on them, Super made his work distinctively developmental. This is particularly noticeable in his fourth proposition listed above.

Life stages, roles and concerns

Originally (Super, 1957) it was suggested that a person's career typically had five stages, as follows:

(1) *Growth* – Expansion of a person's capabilities and interests, especially in areas related to his or her life situation. Typical ages: 0–14.
(2) *Exploration* – of both self and the world of work in order to clarify the self-concept and identify roles which could be consistent with it. Typical ages: 15–24.
(3) *Establishment* – Perhaps after one or two false starts, the person finds a career field which suits him or her, and makes efforts to prove his or her worth in it. Typical ages: 25–44.
(4) *Maintenance* – The person seeks to hold on to his or her position in the face of work-place change and competition from younger people. Typical ages: 45–64.
(5) *Decline* – Decreasing capacities and involvement in work. Typical ages: 65+.

Even at the time, Super acknowledged that this might not represent the careers of everyone. Indeed, he was subsequently irritated by the extent to which people seemed to assume he was saying that all careers did, or at least ought to, conform to this pattern. So he set out to make his ideas more obviously flexible and applicable to all people, not just men in middle-class occupations. In doing so his aim was not primarily to produce an integrated testable theory, but to suggest concepts that would help people understand and manage their own careers. In passing, though, it is notable that some research has tested hypotheses derived from his early work where stages were quite closely linked with ages (e.g. Isabella, 1988).

One development of Super's early ideas has been further elaboration of the career stages, together with more explicit recognition that nowadays

Table 7.1 Super's adult career concerns

Exploration	
Crystallization.	Developing ideas about the general field of work one would like to be in.
Specification.	Turning the general preference into a specific choice of occupation.
Implementation.	Making plans to enter the occupation, and carrying them out.
Establishment	
Stabilizing.	Settling into an occupation, including supporting and developing self, and adopting a lifestyle consistent with it.
Consolidating.	Making self secure in occupation, and demonstrating one's value in it.
Advancing.	Increasing earnings and level of responsibility.
Maintenance	
Holding.	Retaining one's position in the face of changing technology, competition from younger employees, and other pressures.
Updating.	A more proactive version of holding – keeping abreast of changes in one's work demands and personal goals.
Innovating.	Finding new perspectives on familiar tasks, and new ways of doing them.
Disengagement	
Decelerating.	Reducing load and pace of work, perhaps by delegation if work circumstances permit.
Retirement planning.	In terms of finance and lifestyle.
Retirement living.	Learning to live without work.

Source: Adapted from Super, Thompson and Lindeman (1985)

people's careers are quite varied so that particular stages can be encountered at a variety of ages. More prominence has also been given to the notion of short-term cycles mentioned in proposition 4: that is, that people cycle through the stages whenever they change jobs or type of work. Table 7.1 gives brief descriptions of the substages within each stage, derived from a questionnaire called the Adult Career Concerns Inventory (ACCI) devised by Super, Thompson and Lindeman (1985). Notice that the word 'stage' is no longer prominent – the emphasis is on assessing the extent to which the concerns associated with each substage preoccupy a person at any given time.

One might argue a little with the allocation of some of the substages shown in Table 7.1, even though Super collected some research data which supported the structure shown. In particular, especially these days, one might expect updating or innovating not to be confined to the maintenance stage of any given job or career. But in a sense it doesn't matter: part of Super's point is that any person can have his or her own unique set of career concerns at any given moment, though each concern tends to be most salient at certain times.

Super's flexibility goes further. He identifies a number of life-roles in addition to worker. These are homemaker, citizen, leisurite, student and child (including as a grown-up child of one's parents). Any of these roles may occupy the majority of a person's day-to-day life at any given time. And yes, you might have guessed: a person might be at the growth, exploration, establishment, maintenance or disengagement stage within each role at any time. Note also that the rather depressing word 'decline' has been replaced by the more neutral 'disengagement'. So what is being built up here is a framework within which a person can consider his or her allocation of time between different roles in life, and his or her current dominant stage or concern within each one.

In a retrospective account of his work, Super (1990) re-emphasized some points he considered important. First, he had some regrets about using the term *self-concept* so freely. He said that *personal construct* would have been better because it includes a person's perception of his or her environment or situation as well as of him- or herself. Second, and connected to the first point, he emphasized that his perspective on career development is not confined to middle-class males. He stressed that he did take into account how people's opportunities in life are influenced by factors such as their gender and socioeconomic status. But he also emphasized that such factors affect a person's self-concept, and that the careers people experience are heavily influenced by features of their self-concept as well as societal structures. By self-concept he meant not only the content (e.g. I am gentle, patient, serious, etc.) but also more general features such as self-esteem and clarity of self-concept. Finally, and perhaps most controversially, Super asserted that his approach is equally valid for women and men. Of course, one of the obvious criticisms of his stages and their original link with age is that they imply a career involving unbroken employment probably in one kind of work with no significant conflicts between family and work roles. Super's later work (e.g. Super, Thompson and Lindeman, 1985) fairly obviously tried to rectify this, but his statement about equal applicability for both sexes refers more generally to the development of the self-concept and expression through work.

Critique and practical applications

So what can we make of Super? The flexibility of his later ideas is both a strength and a weakness. The strength that it helps applicability to diverse groups in diverse circumstances has already been mentioned. The weakness in some people's eyes is that it offers few clear or straightforward prescriptions for action in career management. Super's ideas are often said to be best used in counselling or career development workshops where one or more people are reviewing their current work and life situations and comparing the actuality with their preferred state of affairs. But even then, activities such as completing and scoring the ACCI risk a response of 'So what? I knew that already. I didn't have to fill in a questionnaire to find out.'

On the other hand a tool like the ACCI might be used by an organization to conduct a census of employee career concerns. The results of this might be less predictable than an individual's scores are to him- or herself, and perhaps more informative. Dominant employee concerns with, for example, updating or retirement planning would lead to different career management interventions than if, for example, advancing had been the highest scorer. In a more abstract sense, Super's work also reminds us just how personal careers are. His emphasis on personal experiences and their uniqueness presents a strong challenge to those who think they know 'by osmosis' what people make of their careers in the organization.

Finally, although Super's exploration stage is similar to Erikson's identity v. confusion, his establishment stage places more emphasis on task achievement than any of Erikson's. Super's analysis (along with some others described in Chapter 8) reminds us that people need challenges in their early stages in a new job or line of work, so that they can develop a competent identity and prove their worth to themselves and others. It is important not to start with a lot of easy work (Schein, 1978). Often there is more risk of doing that than of over-stretching newcomers. Although Super asserts that his maintenance stage is not a static preservation of the status quo, it does have less flavour of striving for something lasting than Erikson's generativity v. stagnation. Even acknowledging Super's point that maintenance can involve quite creative activities doesn't get round the fact that the concept of maintenance probably underestimates people's desire to 'hand the torch' to the next generation. On the other hand one could also suggest that Erikson downplayed the extent to which that requires up-to-date skills.

DANIEL LEVINSON

Levinson and colleagues (Levinson *et al.*, 1978) produced a very detailed and rich account of the development up to midlife of 40 men living in the USA. There were ten each of business executives, authors, industrial workers and biologists. Each man was aged between 35 and 45, and each was interviewed 5 to 10 times for a total of 10–20 hours over 2–3 months. Most of the men were interviewed again about two years later. A mind-boggling 300 pages per man of interview transcripts were produced.

Levinson's model of adult development is based on these interviews, plus analyses of published biographies. He also later conducted a study of women in which he claims to have replicated his findings with men, but as far as I am aware this has not been published in much detail. Levinson's model has aroused controversy for two main reasons: (1) it may be specific to men in the USA around 1970 and (2) unlike Super and Erikson, quite precise ages are attached to each phase. Levinson preferred to avoid the word 'stage' because he felt that it implied progression to better things, whereas he felt that the phases of life were simply different from each other, not better or worse – hence the title of his book *The Seasons of a Man's Life* (Levinson *et al.*, 1978).

Phases of life

Levinson divided adulthood into three eras. With regrettable lack of imagination but commendable avoidance of jargon, he named the eras early, middle and late. Transition periods between the eras are included in both the era that is ending and the one beginning. More generally, adulthood is composed of alternating stable and transitional periods which occur at

Table 7.2   Levinson *et al.*'s (1978) phases of adult life development

Early adult transition (age 17–22)	Financial and emotional separation from parents, trying out adult roles.
Entering the adult world (age 22–28)	A relatively stable period when the person needs to get the right balance between exploring possibilities and creating a stable life structure.
Age 30 transition (age 28–33)	Reappraisal of life circumstances, spurred on by knowledge that if any long-term changes are to be made, it will need to be soon.
Settling down (age 33–40)	The person clarifies a 'dream' of how he or she wants to live his or her life and to become a 'fully fledged' adult, and sets about making the dream a reality.
Midlife transition (age 40–45)	Reappraisal often stimulated by bodily changes, ailing parents and growing children, and the fact that it is now possible to see whether the dream will be achieved. May be experienced as a crisis, and may lead person to make dramatic life changes.
Entering middle adulthood (age 45–50)	Implementing whatever life structure and lifestyle are appropriate given decisions made in midlife transition.

After 'entering middle adulthood': Levinson *et al.* (1978) also identified further stages: age 50 transition, culmination of middle adulthood, late adult transition, and late adulthood. These are only sketchily and speculatively described, however, since the men he studied had not reached those ages.

predictable ages with a 'margin for error' of only two or three years. Figure 7.1 shows the theory in schematic form and Table 7.2 adds a brief description of each phase.

In another description of his ideas, Levinson (1986) emphasized several points made in his 1978 book. He stressed that even a successful early adult transition means that a person is at best off to a shaky start in adult life. One can sense the real involvement and excitement Levinson felt about this work in the way he reported it. In describing the nature of the early adulthood era, he wrote (1986, p. 5):

> Early adulthood is the era in which we are most buffeted by our own passions and ambitions from within and by the demands of family, community and society from without. Under reasonably favorable conditions, the rewards of living in this era are enormous, but the costs often equal or exceed the benefits.

Early adulthood sees the formation of what Levinson called 'the dream' – at first poorly defined but later more so and with efforts devoted to making the dream a reality. The dream represents the person's preferred way of life, encompassing occupation, relationships, leisure activities and their integration. The late 30s were described by Levinson as BOOM time – Becoming One's Own Man – characterized by particularly strenuous efforts to achieve the dream (so *that's* why I'm writing this book at the age of 37), only to be followed soon after by doubt and reappraisal in midlife (so I'll soon be wondering why I bothered!).

Levinson *et al.* (1978) devoted a great deal of attention to the midlife transition, which they said was experienced as a crisis by 32 of the 40 men. They defined crisis as realizing that the current situation was untenable but being unable readily to see anything better. Levinson acknowledged a debt to Erikson in describing the midlife transition as being concerned with

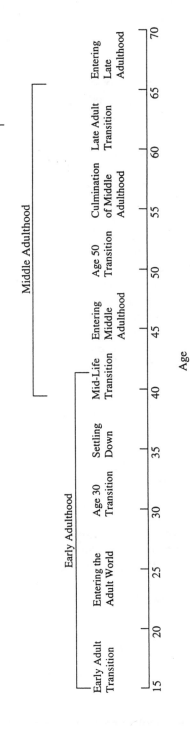

Figure 7.1 Model of development in adulthood
Source: Adapted from Levinson, *et al.* (1978)

generativity v. stagnation. It is brought on by realization that one is probably at least halfway through one's life. Children may be growing up, making it harder for a person in midlife to see him- or herself as young. In occupational terms it is probably now obvious whether or not earlier ambitions are going to be achieved. Levinson sees middle adulthood as distinctly different from early adulthood, with great opportunities to be more genuinely oneself and to express previously suppressed aspects of identity. But it isn't easy, or at least it wasn't for the men in Levinson's study, because in the midlife transition:

> Every aspect of their lives comes into question, and they are horrified by much that is revealed. They are full of recriminations against themselves and others. They cannot go on as before, but need time to choose a new path or modify the old one.
>
> (Levinson *et al.*, 1978, p. 199)

The midlife crisis was to a large extent made fashionable by Levinson. There is now even a board game of that name. Some argue that it is absolute nonsense to say that most people feel a sense of crisis at that time, just as in some societies adolescence seems not to be experienced as a crisis. But the concept of the midlife crisis has entered popular culture – as Gail Sheehy (1974) put it in her book *Passages*, if I'm late for the crisis, please start without me!

It is important to be clear on a couple of points where misunderstandings of Levinson often arise. First, the phases he refers to concern the internal, psychological issues facing people, *not* the observable events which happen to them. Thus he claims that his theory is not confined to lives where everything happens right on cue. Indeed that was not the case for all of his 40 men. To illustrate the point, Levinson *et al.* (1978, p. 52) wrote:

> A transitional period comes to an end not when a particular event occurs or when a sequence is completed in one aspect of life. It ends when the tasks of questioning and exploring have lost their urgency, when a man . . . is ready to start on the tasks of . . . a new life structure.

The second and related point concerns the distinction between stable and transitional phases. The former refer to times when a person knows what life structure (that is, pattern of relationships and activities) he or she is trying to build, and the latter to times when the life structure is being reviewed and questioned. But importantly, structure-building phases are not necessarily more tranquil than transitional ones. A person who is trying and failing to create a preferred life structure is unlikely to experience tranquillity.

Critique and practical applications

Perhaps Levinson and his research colleagues saw what they expected to see, though he vigorously and repeatedly claimed that the regularity of the phases came as a great surprise to them. More subtly, perhaps the findings reflected how the 40 men looked back on their own lives. Perhaps they were simply explaining their development in ways which fitted the culture and pattern of life of that era in that place. Levinson acknowledges that the course of human development must be somewhat dependent upon societal structures, but, on the basis of his analysis of various biographies spanning many centuries, he stated:

> I agree that neither individual personality nor social roles evolve through a standard sequence of age-linked stages in adulthood. . .. I agree further, that major life events occur at varying ages. . .. It is my hypothesis, however, that the basic nature and timing of life structure development are given in the life cycle at this time in human evolution.
> (Levinson, 1986, p. 11)

Some interesting implications for careers follow if Levinson is correct. First, attempts to manage careers should be very closely linked to age. Opportunities to achieve should be available in 'stable' periods, and opportunities to review and rethink should be targeted at 'transitional' periods. Thus it might be that, in terms of the interventions listed in Table 3.3, counselling is provided primarily for people in the early adult, age 30, midlife, age 50 and late adult transitions, whilst developmental work assignments are geared to those in structure-building phases. But things aren't quite that simple, even in Levinson's strictly age-related theory. People struggling to build a stable life structure may be as much in need of counselling as those in transition, and the life structure a person is seeking to build may not include occupational achievement, thus rendering developmental work assignments unhelpful and perhaps unwelcome.

Perhaps the most concrete implication of Levinson's theory is that optimal matches between individuals and labour markets can be achieved only if there are opportunities for people to change direction at midlife and perhaps later too. This may be somewhat unpalatable in organizations because considerable retraining hassle and costs are implied. It is easier and perhaps cheaper to make a person redundant and find someone else who wants to do what the organization wants him or her to do. That may be all right as long as redundancy payoffs or other financial supports are sufficient for a person to take his or her career in a new direction, and as long as opportunities for individuals to retrain are offered by educational and other establishments.

Levinson also has something to say to individuals. We should not be surprised or disturbed that periodically we question the directions our lives are taking. What's more, we can be ready for it at certain ages as well as being ready for concerted action to implement a certain lifestyle at other ages. We must not allow ourselves to shelve developmental tasks associated with certain ages because this only stores up trouble later. You might find it interesting to try to interpret your life so far in terms of Levinson's model. You might find that it is possible to fit your life to Levinson, but still be left with a nagging feeling that it would also have been possible to fit it with other quite different theories if challenged to do so. Part of the reason is that word 'life'. Although Levinson wrote a lot about the work of the men he studied, he was interested in all aspects of their lives. This makes it more difficult to apply his ideas to careers, because people's efforts to review their lives may focus on, for example, their marital relationship, and not be very evident in the work sphere.

Levinson's research sometimes provokes opposition bordering on outrage – more so even than Erikson and Super. This is probably because Levinson is very specific about ages, which gives people plenty of opportunity to find examples of lives which don't fit his predictions. It is also because his theory, as well as the other two, is vulnerable to accusations that it applies only to men, however much he protests otherwise. We now turn to this issue in more detail, as well as some more points evaluating the three developmental approaches.

WOMEN, MEN AND PHASES

Examination of Erikson, Super and Levinson shows that they all tend to view people as developing a sense of individuality before then relating more intimately to others. In addition, Super and Levinson in particular portray people as using their sense of individuality to achieve personal goals. This is often referred to as agency. This general line of reasoning has been criticized for being too male-orientated. Some critiques seem to take the view that the phases or stages proposed may also apply to women but because of societal opportunity structures and childbearing it is much more difficult for women to navigate the phases/stages successfully. For example, Franz and White (1985), in a discussion of Levinson's theory, have argued that societal norms about the timing of marriage put women more at risk than men of making a premature step to intimacy.

Gallos (1989) and Gilligan (1982) among others have argued that women's development is quite different from men's. Young males are encouraged to develop independence and autonomy through separation from the mother, whereas young females are encouraged to identify with a caring role through continuing attachment to the mother. This means that women tend to emphasize relationships and common interest (often referred to collectively as communion) more than men. Gilligan argued that female development proceeds through three stages: (1) caring for the self; (2) caring for others; and (3) recognition of one's own capacity for independent action and others' responsibilities for themselves. Given that men's development is thought to involve decreasing agency and increasing communion in midlife and beyond, this suggests the interesting possibility that men and women develop in opposite directions. The cross-over where they may fleetingly have similar developmental concerns happens sometime in midlife. But at other times the developmental needs of the two sexes are different. Within any given marital or other relationship, these different needs may be complementary, or they may be in direct conflict.

Of course, one obvious objection to Levinson is that for women particularly the phases of development may be more tied to the family life cycle than to their age (Reinke, Holmes and Harris, 1985). One can extend this specific point to the more general one that there is perhaps a less close link between age and life circumstances than was once the case. Neugarten and Neugarten (1987) have illustrated this with research findings that in the 1960s most people said that they would expect a man described as 'young' to be between 20 and 25 years of age. A quarter of a century later, expectations seem much more fluid: 20–40 was the most commonly stated age range. Of course, part of the reason for greater flexibility in age perceptions is that life expectancy has increased greatly through the latter part of the 20th century in most industrialized countries. Through accident or design, people may enter and leave particular roles at varying ages, and fulfil more roles simultaneously than used to be the case. Neugarten and Neugarten, for example, are greatly taken with the observation that nowadays it is not uncommon for a person to be simultaneously a grandchild and a grandparent. Other reasons to expect only loose links between age and life and career concerns have been described at length in earlier chapters: people have fewer expectations of staying in the same line of work with preordained sequences of jobs than was once the case.

On the other hand not everything changes very readily. Virginia Schein (Schein, Mueller and Jacobson, 1989) studied the beliefs of male and female managers about the sort of person a successful manager would be. Most of the personal characteristics nominated were stereotypically male, such as emotional stability and self-reliance. There was a shift in perceptions between 1975 and 1989 toward recognition of stereotypically feminine characteristics as being appropriate for successful managers, but this shift was small and largely confined to the female respondents. In spite of this, in an era of uncertainty and changing gender it might be suggested that people with so-called androgynous self-concepts, i.e. those which include both stereotypically feminine and masculine characteristics, will be the most psychologically healthy and adaptable.

Everyone recognizes that it is dangerous to generalize about differences between men and women, and even more so about why those differences occur. Whilst the 'on average' differences should not be ignored, it is important to remember that individual men and women may develop in ways not typical of their gender. Also, societal and/or organizational intervention may serve to change typical patterns of development by, for example, rewarding co-operative empathic behaviour. Indeed it could be that the increasing emphasis on teamwork in the work-place is encouraging exactly that. On the other hand, consider the following extract from an article entitled 'Men Behaving Better' by Peter Baker in the *Observer* newspaper, 9 June 1996:

> current expectations of men at work are contradictory and not just about them becoming less traditionally masculine. . . . Alongside the demands for more flexibility and empathy, men are required to work

more intensively and competitively. . . . men could start competing about their ability to be co-operative.

Whether or not real changes in sex-role behaviour are happening, developmental theorists need to create frameworks which are sufficiently flexible to account for varied patterns of development of both men and women. Powell and Mainiero (1992) have had a stab at this. They have suggested that careers should be construed in terms of (1) emphasis on career versus relationships with others; (2) success in career; (3) success in relationships with others and (4) time. The degree to which a person emphasizes different elements of (1), (2) and (3) may change over time. It is perhaps significant that Powell and Mainiero seem to see emphasis on or success in relationships as being distinctly different from emphasis on or success in career, and perhaps even contradictory to them. Powell and Mainiero's model is quite flexible in that it permits success to be construed in a number of alternative ways, according to what the person values. It also explicitly includes personal relationships. But in a sense it runs the risk of perpetuating the separateness of achievement and relationship concerns that has, according to some observers, contributed to the neglect of women's perspectives. Marshall (1984) among others has tried to tackle this by suggesting that women should follow a path of 'communion enhanced by agency'. This quite deliberately places high value on communion whilst also recognizing that many work-places are dominated by agency, and that in any case women's success and their personal development may be well served by some emphasis on it. Whether it is possible to adjust one's behaviour and thinking in this way is, however, far from certain.

Perhaps rather against the odds, some empirical research has suggested that Levinson's phases are evident in the lives of women as well as those of men. Roberts and Newton (1987) studied the biographies of 39 women and discerned stable and transitional periods of the kind proposed by Levinson. Of particular interest was the age 30 transition, which was difficult for some women because of dilemmas about relative emphasis on work and relationships. The Roberts and Newton study clearly suggests that developmental theory does indeed apply to both sexes, but that the specific issues that life throws up tend to be different for women than for men. This is in line with the first position identified at the start of this section. On the other hand, Roberts and Newton were familiar with Levinson's theory so again perhaps they simply saw what they expected to see.

More generally, some research has examined whether Super's and Levinson's theories seem to be valid in the work-place, in terms of people's attitudes and work behaviour (e.g. Ornstein, Cron and Slocum, 1989; Smart and Peterson, 1994). On the whole, support for the stages has been limited. But this may not be because the theories are wrong. The research has not really provided a fair test. In terms of Super's ideas, some research has tested the early formulation of his theory, thus tying his stages to ages in a way which he later revised. Ornstein, Cron and Slocum (1989) avoided this by using

Table 7.3 Coping responses and behaviours in the establishment stage

Developmental task	Sample coping response	Sample behaviours
Adapting to the organization	Establish self as a team player	Do not rock the boat Try to be on the same wavelength
Good performance in the job	Get feedback from multiple sources	Solicit feedback from peers Do frequent self-evaluations
Maintaining performance	Be organized	Leave little to chance Use time-management techniques
Good relationships with colleagues	Take time to listen	Listen more than you talk Focus on non-verbal communications
Advancement	Keep up to date in field	Learn about new developments Set annual goals for self-development
Future career plans	Set specific career goals	Orientate self to the future Set a time line for goal attainment

Source: Adapted from Dix and Savickas (1995)

Super's Adult Career Concerns Inventory rather than age to assess the stage people were at, but then related the stages people were at to variables for which there was no obvious reason to expect differences between stages. For example, it is hard to see why levels of work satisfaction, supervisor satisfaction and pay satisfaction might vary between Super's stages. Rather similar objections apply to Smart and Peterson's examination of Levinson's theory with a sample of 498 Australian professional women. I would say that Levinson's ideas can only really be tested using detailed case material.

Research which looks at how people handle the developmental tasks that face them is perhaps most useful from a practical point of view. A good example is work by Dix and Savickas (1995). They identified six tasks associated with Super's establishment stage, namely adapting to the organization; achieving good performance in the job; maintaining that performance; having good relationships with colleagues; advancing in the field or organization; and making future career plans. Interviews were conducted with 50 men nominated by colleagues as showing 'high practical intelligence in dealing with the tasks of career establishment'. The idea was to tap their tacit knowledge about how to get established. So each of the six areas was broken down into coping responses, and each of these into a number of sample behaviours. Examples are shown in Table 7.3. Probably the sample behaviours form the basis of a good 'manage your own career guide', albeit in fairly traditional organizational settings. But further research to include women and to see if certain coping behaviours differentiate between people who are successfully and unsuccessfully tackling the establishment stage would clearly do a lot to build upon Dix and Savickas's findings.

Table 7.4 Schein's (1993) career anchors

(1) **Technical/functional competence.** This anchor concerns the development and use of particular skills and expertise in a particular kind of work. This is not necessarily technical or scientific. People with this anchor value above all using their expertise in challenging tasks. They expect to be rewarded for their expertise, and do not want to be promoted into general management tasks. They value recognition from their professional peers rather than from members of management.

(2) **General managerial competence**. People who adhere to this anchor value management for its own sake. They tend to be ambitious and seek status, income and responsibility. The anchor involves analytical competence, interpersonal and intergrouping competence, and emotional resilience. The recognition sought by people with this anchor is usually promotion to higher levels of responsibility. Specialization is to be avoided.

(3) **Autonomy/independence.** The need to do things one's own way to one's own standards unrestricted by formal and informal rules is at the heart of this anchor. A person who subscribes to this anchor will often be happy with contract work on a project, as long as he or she is left to achieve the project goals in his or her own way. The most desired form of recognition is being granted more autonomy, and/or portable things such as prizes or letters of commendation.

(4) **Security/stability.** This anchor has two closely related but not identical variants: security of tenure and security of location. The personal motive here is safety and security in the form of a predictable future. Obviously, long-term employment preferably with good pay and pension provision is a priority. Job challenge is less vital. Preferred recognition is for loyalty and steady performance within a system with published grades and ranks.

(5) **Entrepreneurial creativity.** The central concern here is to create new organizations, products or services which can be clearly linked with the entrepreneur's own efforts. Income and profitability are the key signals that this is being done successfully. People with this anchor tend to become bored easily. They also tend to seek the limelight.

(6) **Service/dedication.** This anchor is apparent when people enter work which upholds values that are important to them. The specific skills and activities required may be less important. Obvious examples of occupations which attract some people with this anchor are the helping professions, but not everyone in those professions has this anchor, and some people elsewhere also have it. Money is not central; the chance to reflect the organization's mission, and influence it if necessary, is.

(7) **Pure challenge.** This anchor expresses a desire to overcome the odds by winning against apparently invincible opponents or solving difficult problems. The exact nature of the challenge is less important than its level of difficulty. Some athletes may show this anchor, as may some managers, for example those who relish turning around ailing enterprises.

(8) **Lifestyle.** People with this anchor are centrally concerned with integrating the requirements of self, family, other interested parties and careers. They want flexibility in employment relationships, but unlike a person with an autonomy career anchor, are happy to work for a long period in an organization which offers flexibility of the kind desired. Examples might be paternity leave, variable hours or opportunities to work at home.

Source: Drawn from information presented in Schein (1993)

ANCHORS AND THEMES

The developmental theories described in this chapter are clearly designed to encompass the whole of adult life. They map out the tasks that people face and the psychological processes involved in dealing with them. A different approach is to concentrate less on the stages, and more on the content of the career and lifestyle preferences people develop.

Schein's career anchors

A popular example of this alternative perspective is Edgar Schein's work on career anchors (Schein 1985a, 1985b, 1993). Schein's ideas were derived from some research he did way back in the early 1960s with 44 graduates from the Master's programme at the Sloan School of Management at the Massachusetts Institute of Technology, USA. The graduates participated in research interviews and completed questionnaires at intervals during the first twelve years of their careers. Schein (1993, pp. 25–6) wrote:

> The actual events of the career histories proved to be highly varied, but the reasons that respondents gave for their choices and the pattern of their feelings about events proved to be surprisingly consistent. For each individual, underlying themes – of which he or she often had been unaware – reflected a growing sense of self, based on the learnings of the early years. When these people tried jobs that did not feel right to them, they referred to the image of being pulled back to something that fitted better, hence the metaphor of an anchor.

Of course, the original 44 constituted a somewhat restricted sample, being managerially orientated graduates of an elite American management school. So Schein and colleagues conducted additional career history interviews with 'several hundred people in various career stages' (p. 26), though details of how these were conducted are not given. It was concluded that eight distinct career anchors exist, and a questionnaire (the Career Orientations Inventory) and workbook have been developed so that a person can assess which is most important to him or her. Career anchors consist of a mixture of interests, skills, needs and values. The anchors and brief descriptions are shown in Table 7.4

Schein (1993) makes some interesting claims about career anchors. He suggests that ultimately people are wedded to one and only one anchor, and that it guides their career decisions and attitudes to their work. He also suggests that these eight are the lot: possible competitors such as variety and power are in fact parts of other anchors. After five to ten years' work experience, he says, people quite readily become aware of their hierarchy. Anchors may appear to change, but in fact this is merely activation of something that was already there. This is an interesting proposition which probably cannot be proved or disproved.

There has been remarkably little research using the concept and measure of career anchors. This may be because the Career Orientations Inventory is seen more as a consultancy tool than a formal psychometric instrument. Be that as it may, some interesting questions revolve around whether anchors do indeed remain unchanged after the first few years of work, and if so what implications this has in an increasingly turbulent world of work. Perhaps there is an optimal mix of career anchors for organizations in particular environmental conditions.

Schein (1993) points out that people with different career anchors need to be managed in different ways. They are motivated by different things. They will seek different rewards, work styles and features of their work. Even within the same sub-unit or the same job title, different individuals may have different anchors. The danger of course is that because of their apparent similarity from the point of view of an observer, they will be treated in the same way. Hence perhaps the best use of career anchors is rather similar to Super's Adult Career Concerns Inventory (Super, Thompson and Lindeman, 1985) – to conduct a survey of staff needs and preferences. This may find particular favour now that there is supposed to be more emphasis on managing people as individuals rather than on the basis of their job title.

Some anchors fit better than others with current employment trends described in Chapters 2 and 3. People with a security/stability anchor are likely to have a rough time. So, to a lesser extent, are some with general managerial competence and technical/functional competence anchors, though there are undoubtedly plenty of niches for members of these two groups. Lifestyle concerns seem to be on the increase but they are difficult to satisfy in many demanding employment situations (see also Chapter 9). Perhaps autonomy/independence, entrepreneurial creativity and pure challenge are the anchors which best enable people to prosper in turbulent work environments.

Life themes

Schein's isn't the only attempt to describe the evolving focus of people's lives. A lesser known but in some ways better researched analysis was generated by Douglas Bray and colleagues (see Howard and Bray, 1988) in an enormous long-term study of 274 male entrants to the giant American telecommunications company AT&T in the 1950s. The researchers used a mixture of interviews, tests and questionnaires in a very wide-ranging investigation. They discerned nine of what they called life themes, which had differing levels of significance in the lives of the men. The themes were:

(1)	Marital–familial	the man's spouse (if any) and children (if any)
(2)	Parental–familial	the man's parents and siblings
(3)	Occupational	the demands and opportunities presented by work
(4)	Financial–acquisitive	the pursuit of material rewards
(5)	Ego–functional	development of skills and interests
(6)	Locale–residential	the man's home and neighbourhood
(7)	Recreational–social	leisure and friendships
(8)	Religious–humanism	spiritual and ethical concerns
(9)	Service	voluntary and other activities on behalf of those in need

The marital–familial theme was highly important to most of those who were married, and increasingly so over the first 20 years of the men's working lives. Over the same period the financial–acquisitive theme also increased in importance, rising from sixth to second out of the nine. The occupational theme dropped slightly in importance in the men's lives over the twenty years. Naturally, these average patterns did not apply to all the men: their individual life circumstances as well as their personalities caused variation. Some aspects of the findings may also have been somewhat history-specific: that is, a product of the era and events of the time. Also, the researchers did not develop a relatively quick and easy measure of life themes in the way that Schein did for career anchors, and the themes more explicitly refer to people's lives as a whole, not just their careers. This makes the life themes more difficult to use than career anchors, but nevertheless they may be useful in helping individuals to understand, review and plan their careers.

AGEING

Ageing is not a simple phenomenon. It is the subject of many jokes and anxieties. Nobody quite knows why it happens, though apparently all animals which reproduce more than once show some of the well-known characteristics of ageing, including skin wrinkling and hair loss. But ageing isn't only biological. It is also about social roles sometimes thrust upon us such as the wise elder or the helpless pensioner. And the saying 'you're as old as you feel' also has some insight – two people of the same chronological age may answer the question 'would you say you were an old person?' quite differently. We should also remember that at any given time older people have had a different set of life experiences from younger ones, and not just because they have lived longer. They have grown up in different eras with different cultural norms, technology, and so on. It may be that differences between old and young are more to do with that than with biological changes. This is an important observation which is often overlooked in discussions of lifespan development.

There can be little doubt that in Western societies most though not all age-related stereotypes favour the young against the old. One in-depth study of 20 companies (Institute of Manpower Studies, 1990) found that although responsibility, reliability, work commitment and likelihood of staying with the employer were all seen as increasing with age, the reverse was the case for ambition, trainability (especially for IT), flexibility, mobility and adaptability to change. Bearing in mind that eight of the 20 companies surveyed were deliberately targeting recruitment at older workers, this is not a particularly optimistic picture, especially given the frequent need for retraining, using IT and adaptability at work. Warr and Pennington (1994) studied perceptions of suitability for various non-managerial jobs among a sample of 1,140 personnel managers. Jobs seen as suitable for older workers were also perceived to make relatively few cognitive demands, be slower paced, and less demanding of energy than jobs deemed appropriate for younger workers. Heise (1987, p. 247) was not wrong when he wrote:

> The typical trajectory in Western industrialized nations aligns adulthood with productive mental activity, childhood with impractical thinking, and old age with enfeeblement. However, trajectories in some other societies give more potential to the elderly, suggesting that Western stereotypes are not grounded in human biology.

This insight seems not to have reached many recruitment advertisers. A number of research studies have shown that age restrictions are common even when the rationale for them is not obvious. Usually, but not always, it is middle-aged or older people who are ruled out. For example, Cagnoni (1988) found that nearly a thousand vacancies for clerical, administrative and secretarial jobs in one week in June 1988 in three publications specified an age requirement. Many of these specified preferred age ranges of 20 or 25 to 35, and such age bars were most common where training was being offered. In many countries such apparently indiscriminate use of age barriers would be illegal, but not (at the time of writing) in the UK. Worsley (1996) has wryly observed that the prevalence of age discrimination is strange given that so many people stand eventually to lose from it. But Worsley detected a shift in attitude from many recruiters. About 80% of the large UK employers he contacted stated that they either had, or were going to have, equal opportunities policies which addressed discrimination on the basis of age.

Of course, we cannot be sure whether policies will translate into practice, or whether restricting use of age barriers in job advertisements will prevent selection on the basis of age. There are well-documented cases of some organizations positively favouring older people for their steadiness and sensitivity to customer needs. This seems to have been particularly the case in the retail sector (especially DIY chains), but is not confined to it. The UK high street newsagent and stationer W. H. Smith among others has responded to business arguments for employing older people. If the tendency for older people to stay longer is borne out, W. H. Smith should save money since it reckons each sales assistant who leaves costs about £2,500. Whilst reliance on known 'on average' differences between age groups is welcome, it must also be acknowledged that, as with any general trend, there are plenty of exceptions. Also, some perceptions which favour older people may be based purely upon stereotypes with no real foundation, which seems no better and no worse than other stereotypes favouring the young.

So what are the facts about ageing and work performance and attitudes? I suppose I have rather set myself up here, because as usual there is no simple or entirely agreed answer. Experimental psychologists have conducted a great deal of laboratory research examining performance in various artificial tasks requiring memory, attention and information-processing. These tend to show that older adults do less well than younger ones, especially when the tasks are complex and require switching of attention from one thing to another (see Davies, Matthews and Wong, 1991 for a summary of this and other relevant research). At least one researcher (Cerella, 1990) has argued that the decline in performance with age is best explained by simple decay of neurons in the brain which occurs with chronological age.

There is some dispute about how seriously to take these laboratory findings. To some extent, it appears that training in how to tackle them can reduce or even eliminate age differences in performance. This suggests that it is habitual ways of behaving rather than lack of ability which handicap older people relative to younger ones. Many would argue that they have little applicability because the tasks are divorced from day-to-day life, performance decrements with age are too small to affect work performance, and in day-to-day life our behaviour relies more on our accumulated knowledge and understanding (so-called crystallized intelligence) than on speedy information-processing. Salthouse (1987) has carried out some interesting work with typists which shows that older learners make more use than younger ones of strategies, such as looking ahead to what they will soon be typing, which help to compensate for any slower speed of thought and finger movement. Schaie (1983) has conducted much interesting work with intelligence tests which shows that declines in many facets of intelligence occur much later in life (e.g. 60s or 70s) than was once thought, or perhaps I should say later than used to be the case. Thirty or forty years ago perhaps intellectual functioning did indeed start to decline in midlife but in the meantime improvements in education, standard of living and nutrition may have changed all that. Again, then, an age difference may be a consequence of societal change rather than an immutable law of human development.

Research linking age with job performance is inevitably hampered by the likelihood that age is mixed up with all sorts of other factors such as the kind of job one has. But on the whole it seems that there is no decline in job performance with age, and possibly a slight improvement (McEvoy and Cascio, 1989). Warr (1993) has made a distinction between types of work tasks which may aid our understanding in this area. On the one hand is whether or not a task exceeds a person's basic cognitive capacities. On the other is whether performance benefits from experience. This is shown in Figure 7.2. Warr suggests that performance should improve with age in tasks of type A, deteriorate in tasks of type D, and neither improve nor decline in B and C where the two factors cancel each other out.

		Exceeds basic cognitive capacities?	
		No	Yes
Benefits from experience?	Yes	A	B
	No	C	D

Figure 7.2 Warr's (1993) classification of work tasks
Source: Adapted from Warr (1993)

Research does fairly clearly show that on average older workers do exhibit more job involvement and organizational commitment, and less voluntary turnover, than younger ones (Davies, Matthews and Wong, 1991). The evidence for job satisfaction is less clear, with some suggestion of a dip in satisfaction during one's thirties (Clark, Oswald and Warr, 1996). Whatever the truth of that, it is clear that older people are not more prone to dissatisfaction than others.

Overall, then, it seems that whilst negative perceptions of older people are not entirely without foundation, they tend to be greatly exaggerated. They ignore older people's capabilities to use their superior experience and their capacity to relearn if given the opportunity to do so. Most of all, as with all stereotypes, there are very many individuals who defy the generalization. This means of course that individuals should be assessed on the basis of their individual merits rather than their group membership.

From the point of view of career management, perhaps the most crucial question for present purposes is whether managing careers (including one's own) exceeds basic cognitive capacity, and whether it benefits from experience. My best guess answer would be yes and yes, which in Warr's (1993) terms would mean career management is a type C task, uncorrelated with age. On the other hand, if an older person has not been accustomed to managing his or her own career, age might not translate into experience. More generally, given that the laboratory research tends to suggest that older people are at a disadvantage relative to younger ones in unfamiliar situations, another possibility is that the pace of change nowadays is such that some of the negative age-related stereotypes do after all have some truth.

WISDOM

The phrase 'older and wiser' is often heard: indeed I believe I have used it in this chapter. But what is wisdom? Answers to this question are many and varied. They vary from the intensely mystical and spiritual to the practical. Inclining towards the latter are many analyses rooted in social sciences. Some of these refer explicitly to the word wisdom. Others use rather different terms and concepts such as expertise and post-formal logic. This is not the place to get too immersed in the finer conceptual points of this field, so what follows is a summary drawing on sources such as Sternberg (1990) and Ericsson and Smith (1991).

The long and the short of it is that thinking that can be described as wise, advanced or expert exhibits the following features:

(1) appreciation of alternative points of view;
(2) tolerance of contradiction (for example between two or more beliefs one holds, or between one's beliefs and emotions);
(3) an attempt to resolve such contradictions, not by denying they exist, but by finding new ways of seeing the world which reflect both (or all) elements of the contradiction;
(4) recognition that 'facts' are normally filtered through the expectations and perspectives of people, so that little or no knowledge is truly objective;
(5) recognition that no solution to a problem is a sure-fire winner;
(6) recognition that not all points of view are as good as each other, but that their relative merits depend not on their objective truth but on how well they reflect one's own values;
(7) classification of problems in terms of their underlying features, not the obvious surface ones;
(8) lots of knowledge relevant to the problem at hand.

This list can of course be criticized on various grounds. These include possible culture-specificity, an overly slavish adherence to postmodernist thought and, more mundanely, incompleteness. But if we take them seriously they have some implications for what characterizes someone who thinks effectively about his or her career. Such a person is likely to recognize that there is no single career perfectly suited to him or her, but on the other hand be clear that not all possible options have equal value. Such an individual will appreciate that advice and information received may come from sources which do not share his or her values. He or she will attempt to reflect apparently contradictory aspects of self in career choices and behaviour; will be well informed about the world of work; will have an established but flexible way of going about solving career problems.

Such characteristics are unlikely to be acquired on a short training course or series of counselling interviews. They take years to build up, and even then it doesn't happen automatically. Baltes and Smith (1990) have argued that people who have a lot of contact with a variety of other people, who have experienced both success and failure, and who have experienced periods of structured study and mentoring are most likely to display wisdom. Whilst acknowledging that these predictions are speculative, it is notable that trends described in Chapters 2 and 3 probably increase the extent to which many people have experiences which could foster wisdom. As in all learning, the key thing is that people don't feel so threatened by an experience, for example of failure, that they freeze and fail to learn anything useful.

SUMMARY

Several well-established theories of lifespan development can be applied to careers. All suggest that sequences of concerns, themes or developmental tasks confront a person as he or she travels through life. There is some, but not complete, overlap between the theories regarding the nature of these concerns, etc., and some disagreement about whether they necessarily occur at certain ages or in a certain order. Even so, the theories do suggest a number of practical applications. One criticism of many theories of lifespan development is that they reflect male patterns of life, and probably middle-class male patterns at that. Women's lives and careers may unfold in quite different ways from men's. Another perspective on lifespan development is provided by the literature on ageing. There is clearly age discrimination in the employment market. Some of it is based on stereotypes of older and younger people which have only very limited truth. Older people are perhaps slower to assimilate new information but can use their experience and knowledge of how to learn to compensate for that. Successful performance of some tasks may depend more on those factors than on mental agility. It is as yet not clear whether this can be said about the tasks of career management.

8

WORK-ROLE TRANSITIONS

Back in 1982, Meryl Reis Louis lamented the lack of attention paid to managing the process of changing jobs. All the effort seemed to go into mapping out long-term career paths (an activity Louis suggested was rather unrealistic) and very short-term efforts to obtain a job. She went on (1982, p. 69):

> I believe that the critical middle range between finding a job and moving along a career path has not been adequately addressed in career development – especially lacking is guidance in adapting to the new job and the organization. Inattention to such middle-range activities has resulted in serious limitations in the practice of career planning and development.

Since 1982 there has been considerable progress towards rectifying the blind spot identified by Louis. In this chapter we will examine transitions between, into and out of jobs, and how these transitions can be managed by individuals and organizations. This will include an analysis of different types of transition as well as the various stages of the transition process. Socialization is a key aspect of the transition process. It refers to attempts made in organizations to influence the behaviour, attitudes and values of newcomers, whilst commitment to the organization is often one outcome of socialization. Towards the end of this chapter these two phenomena will receive attention. We will also take a brief look at certain specific transitions, including those at each end of working life – starting work and retirement, as well as domestic and international relocation. Some other transitions such as into and out of unemployment, and returning to work after childbirth, receive attention in Chapter 9.

DEFINITIONS AND TYPES OF WORK-ROLE TRANSITIONS

I suppose 'work-role transition' is a rather jargonized term in itself, but if you think that's bad, feast your eyes upon this definition of a transition, drawn from a leading writer in the field (Schlossberg, 1981, p. 5): 'An event or non-event resulting in a change in assumptions about oneself and the world, thus requiring corresponding changes in one's behavior and relationships.' Obviously, I haven't chosen this definition just to denigrate its language. It points out rather nicely that transitions necessarily involve several changes in:

(1) how a person understands the world;
(2) where he or she locates him- or herself within it;
(3) what he or she does day by day;
(4) how he or she relates to other people.

So, transition is all about change. Notice also that Schlossberg allowed non-events to count as transitions. For example, if someone fails to achieve an expected promotion, that is a non-event requiring changes in relationships and understandings about self and the world. Such changes will probably be quite painful for the person concerned, and perhaps for those around him or her too.

Most of the literature on work-role transitions concentrates on events rather than non-events, significant though the latter may be, as Schlossberg (1981) noted. The following definition, drawn from Nicholson and West (1988, p. 48), probably strikes the best balance between being specific enough to get hold of, but also general enough to encompass a range of transitions experienced in the work-place: 'Any move into and/or out of a job, any move between jobs, or any major alteration in the content of work duties and activities.' So this definition includes starting work, retirement, moving from one job to another for whatever reason, being made redundant, and returning to work after, for example, unemployment or raising a family. It also allows the possibility of a job changing 'under a person's feet' as it were. Sometimes reorganizations or technological change can mean that a person's job title remains the same but his or her activities, responsibilities and perhaps status change considerably. This is likely to become increasingly common.

The value of Schlossberg's (1981) definition given earlier lies partly in the fact that it identifies the changes common to all or nearly all transitions. But beyond this we need to be clear about the unique meaning of any specific work-role transition for any particular person. This means paying attention both to the 'objective', observable features of that transition and to the individual's expectations and prior experiences.

Several writers on life events and lifespan development (e.g. Brim and Ryff, 1980) have identified differences between transitions which are likely to affect how they are experienced and how they should be managed. So, transitions vary in the extent to which they are:

(1) anticipatable ⎫
(2) desirable ⎬ from the individual's point of view;
(3) controllable ⎭
(4) experienced by a group of people together;
(5) experienced by many people;
(6) experienced more than once by the same person;
(7) 'on time' or 'off time';
(8) taboo;
(9) novel to the individual.

Perhaps this list needs a little explanation. Anticipatability, desirability and controllability can all be taken to refer either to the occurrence of the transition itself or to the specific form the transition takes. So, for example, a person may be able to anticipate when his or her full-time education will end, may feel that this transition is desirable, and might even be able to control to some extent when it happens. On the other hand, the same person may be less able to foresee exactly what he or she will do day by day once his or her education is complete, and the labour market may make this difficult to control. In retrospect the transition might seem less desirable than it had seemed earlier. We often fail to use the anticipatability of a transition to exert control and make it as desirable as possible, or even to collect information about it. We also sometimes misinterpret the amount of control we have over the form it takes. So the first rule of managing transitions is to be proactive: if you know a transition is coming, attempt to find out how much you can influence it.

The next three items in the list all concern the availability of people (including oneself) from whom information can be obtained and with whom experiences can be shared. Again, it is important for an individual to be clear about how many people, and which people, he or she can consult in order to manage a particular transition as well as possible. Some work-role transitions, such as management trainee to first management position, are widely experienced and may indeed be experienced by a group of people who are in contact with each other. Other work-role transitions might be more isolated. On time vs. off time refers to whether or not a transition happens when it is supposed to, according to some predefined timetable. That timetable may be derived from societal norms, organizational norms, individual expectations or some combination of these factors. Thus it might be considered 'on time' to have children in one's late 20s or early 30s, but 'off time' to have them at 18 or 40. That said, as we move into the 21st century, the increasing diversity of people and career patterns in the work-place make it ever more difficult to think in terms of generally accepted timetables. You may have thought that my assumption above concerning the 'right' age to have children was a little restrictive – if so, you prove my point!

If a transition is 'taboo', people are unwilling to talk about it openly, or even to refer to it at all. Think, for example, of the number of euphemisms for death, and the difficulty many of us have in discussing it. For the most part, work-role transitions are openly discussed. They are not on the whole a taboo subject. Nevertheless, there may be difficulty in speaking about some transitions – for example redundancy or demotion. Unfortunately exactly those work-role transitions which approach taboo status are the ones which tend to be hardest to cope with. It may be the 'tabooness' of redundancy which leads to incidents like the following, described in the *Observer* newspaper, 10 March 1996:

> Last month, for example, 32 people were laid off in the London office of [X Co.] on instructions from senior management in New York. All 150 staff were told to wait by their desks one morning. Those facing redun-

dancy got a telephone call, asking them for a brief interview. The process took three hours. It was only at lunchtime that the calls stopped, and the staff who were being kept on knew where they stood.

Novelty refers to the extent to which the activities, status, responsibilities and relationships a person experiences after a transition are (1) different from immediately before the transition and (2) different from anything the person has experienced before. The pace of change as we enter the 21st century is likely to mean increasing novelty in work-role transitions. The more novel in this sense a transition is, the more the individual is well advised to use any anticipatability to find out as much as possible, and to use other people as sources of information about what to expect. More about novelty shortly.

Notice that the above discussion was framed largely in terms of individuals experiencing transitions. It is also possible to look at things from the perspective of organizations through which individuals flow. A particular transition for any individual or group may or may not be desirable, controllable, on time, openly discussable or novel (in terms of the issues it throws up) to the organization. Other things being equal, we would expect transitions to be easiest to manage from both sides of the fence when they are anticipatable, desirable, controllable, commonly experienced, on time, openly discussed and not novel. But of course, other things are not always equal. For example, novelty may be sought by an individual. But using this list of features is an important first step in identifying the likely problems in managing any given work-role transition.

Nevertheless, these features of transitions are relatively abstract. We can also examine more specifically work-related distinctions between different transitions. This was done by Nicholson and West (1988), who reported a survey of 2,304 managers and professionals in the UK. The survey focused on the last five job changes experienced by the respondents, and used questions similar to those used in earlier surveys of UK managers in order to facilitate comparison. Nicholson and West found that on average the managers were changing jobs every three years, which represented greater frequency than had been found in the earlier surveys. There was, however, a long tail to the distribution: some managers had not changed jobs for years, whilst on the other hand most were changing about once every two years. This is a good example of how the median can differ significantly from the mean. About 40% of job changes were between different industry types.

Regarding types of job change, Nicholson and West (1988) identified a total of twelve types, representing all possible combinations of:

(1) Change of employer?   Yes/No
(2) Change of function?   Yes/No
     (e.g. sales, line management, finance)
(3) Change of status?   Up/No/Down

You might like to pause here for a moment and consider which combinations would have been the most common types of job change. I can give you a clue: two of the 12 possible combinations accounted for over half the total number of job changes. In fact the two most common job changes were what Nicholson and West referred to as in-spiralling and out-spiralling. The former involves an upward status move and change of function, but no change of employer. The latter includes a change of employer as well as the other two. In-spiralling accounted for 27.6% of most recent job changes, and out-spiralling for 24.6%. The picture was very similar for earlier job changes. Straightforward promotion accounted for just one in twelve job changes.

The picture here is therefore one of quite frequent and radical job change for managers and professionals, involving considerable novelty and new learning. This impression is further reinforced by another finding. In a follow-up of 1,100 of the original respondents one year later, fewer than half of those who had predicted at time 1 that they would change jobs in the next year actually did so, whilst 26% of those who experienced job change of some kind had not been expecting it. Furthermore, one third of job changes in the intervening year were into newly created jobs, for which presumably there would often be relatively little information about what the role was and how it should be carried out.

Nicholson, West and Cawsey (1985) used some of these data to argue that the notion of career is something we construct after the event in order to make sense of chaos. Given the relatively poor performance of the managers at predicting their own jobs changes, how could we sustain the notion of a planned, coherent career? Their point is well made but rather overdone. You or I might have general or specific plans, but whether opportunities will arise to pursue them this year, next year or the year after is hard to predict. The managers' mistakes in predicting their immediate future do not mean that they were without implementable plans. In support of this, the most common reasons given for job changes were 'to do something more challenging and fulfilling' and 'a step towards my career objectives', though circumstantial reasons such as company reorganization were often present as a secondary factor.

A more recent study of UK managers has been reported by Inkson (1995). He looked at the incidence and reasons for job change between 1980 and 1992 amongst 828 managers in mid-career, which Inkson defined as being between 35 and 55 years of age at the time of the job change. Inkson was also interested in the potential impact of economic conditions on job change, and divided the period 1980 to 1992 into: 1980–2 – Recession; 1983–5 – Greater stability; 1986–8 – Growth; 1989–92 – Recession. He found that the rate of job change increased apparently independent of economic conditions, from 20.7 changes per 100 respondents per year in 1980–2 to 29.6 in 1992. But he also found significant changes over time in the nature of the job changes and the reasons for them. There was an increase in the number of downward status and equal status moves. Proactive reasons for job change such as career development or personal reasons were among those given for about 90% of job changes until 1989, but by 1992 this was down to 61%. During the same time period reactive reasons such as redundancy and reorganization increased from 30–40 mentions per 100 jobs to 74 in 1992. Clearly, a greater proportion of moves were undesired and unsought by the person in the early 1990s than had been the case earlier (including when Nicholson and West (1988) collected their data). Cawsey and Inkson (1992) found quite similar patterns in New Zealand.

Although all these findings are based upon relatively narrow (though large) samples, they strongly suggest an increasing incidence of job change as we approach and enter the 21st century. Moreover, the job changes people experience can be unexpected (at least in their timing), undesired (especially in recession) and require substantial new learning. All these factors raise the stakes for managing work-role transitions. It is becoming ever more important to manage them well. The picture is further complicated by the questionable future of the notion of a job (Lawler, 1994), which is central to the studies described above. As some people's work becomes more project-based, their activities and relationships may change even more frequently than suggested by Nicholson and West and by Inkson. On the other hand, changes may be less all-encompassing. If a person is working on several projects simultaneously, the ending of one and starting of another represents only part of his or her working life. So transitions may more often be tackled with more background stability in a person's life than has hitherto been the case.

STAGES

One line of thought about transitions has borrowed from literature on difficult life changes, particularly bereavement. This portrays all transitions, even those welcomed by a person, as essentially traumatic and stressful. For example, Adams, Hayes and Hopson (1976) suggested seven stages a person passes through in any transition:

(1) Immobilization. The person is unable to make any plans, to reason, or to understand what is happening. Everything is problematic.
(2) Minimization. The person denies that change is happening, or at least attempts to make it seem as small as possible.
(3) Depression. The reality of change is now acknowledged, but the person feels powerless to do anything about it, and is uncertain about how to cope.
(4) Letting go. The person fully accepts that his or her old situation really is a thing of the past, and cannot be re-created.
(5) Testing. The person starts trying out new ways of coping; new patterns of living. At first he or she may need to see things in overly simplistic ways in order to make them understandable.
(6) Searching for meaning. The person tries to understand how and why things are the way they are.
(7) Internalization. The person now takes on the new reality as his or her own. Self is seen more in terms of his or her new role.

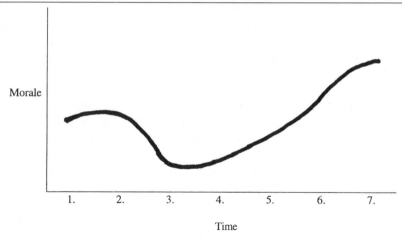

Stages of transition
1. Immobilization
2. Minimization
3. Depression
4. Acceptance of reality and letting go
5. Testing
6. Search for meaning
7. Internalization

Figure 8.1   Self-esteem changes during transition
Source: Hopson (1984)

The typical level of morale or well-being a person is said to experience through these stages is shown in Figure 8.1.

As you can see, transitions appear to be quite an emotional rollercoaster. However, it is assumed that a person eventually reaches a satisfactory (to him or her) adjustment to the new situation. This model and others like it provide some helpful insights into how transitions are sometimes experienced. Many people are reassured to hear that even welcome transitions often evoke some confusion and regret. Failure to appreciate this could lead a person to conclude that he or she is doing the wrong thing, when in fact he or she is not. Second, the model is realistic in suggesting that real letting go of one's old situation is not immediate. Every transition is about the situation a person is leaving as well as the one being entered. It is not normally possible to parcel up one's old way of being in a box and put it in the loft. Just as it takes time to become fully integrated with the new situation, so it also takes time fully to detach from the old one.

On the other hand, most people presented with this model quickly ask some questions about it. Do we necessarily go through all the stages, and in the order suggested? Can we recycle through them? Can stages be tackled successfully even if one or more earlier ones have not been? These are all sensible questions. Those who ask them usually do so because they can think of examples which contradict the model, and therefore they are inclined to reject it. In my view the model does betray its origins in traumatic life events, and although all transitions carry some confusion and regret, the amount of stress implied is probably overdone for many work-role transitions. The strength and the weakness of the model are that it focuses on people's emotions and reactions. These are very difficult to generalize about, since, as we have already seen, both transitions and the people who encounter them differ considerably one from another.

On the other hand, treating transitions as potential traumata has led to some helpful hints for people who are experiencing a difficult transition. Hamburg, Coelho and Adams (1974) and Hopson (1984), among others, have suggested the following:

(1) Handle one crisis at a time – don't try to deal with everything at once.
(2) Seek information from multiple sources.
(3) Formulate specific, attainable goals.
(4) Rehearse new behaviours in 'safe' situations.
(5) Monitor your own reactions – feelings as well as thoughts.
(6) Have contingency plans.
(7) Look after yourself – give yourself treats now and then.
(8) Get reasonable amounts of sleep and exercise.
(9) Look out for gains made, things that are going well.
(10) Reflect on past experiences of transitions and learn from them.

A cynical reaction might be 'easier said than done', which of course is true enough, but that doesn't invalidate the advice.

THE TRANSITION CYCLE

A rather more flexible approach to stages of work-role transitions has been proposed by Nigel Nicholson (1990). He argues that too much theory and practice assume a 'steady state' work-place where roles and the people filling them are largely constant and long established. We have already seen that work-places tend not to be like that these days. Nicholson proposes a *transition cycle* with four phases:

(1) *Preparation*: The period before starting a new job, when the fact that it is going to happen is known or at least expected.
(2) *Encounter*: The early days and weeks in a new job. The task for both newcomer and organization here is to develop a basic understanding of the roles, relationships, expectations and behaviours associated with the new situation.
(3) *Adjustment*: The period during which newcomer and organization, having established an understanding of the situation, seek and implement ways of handling it to mutual satisfaction.
(4) *Stabilization*: The period during which a stable adjustment has been reached, when each side has a fairly constant and rarely disconfirmed experience of the other. The pace of change for some people in some jobs is such that this stage is never reached.

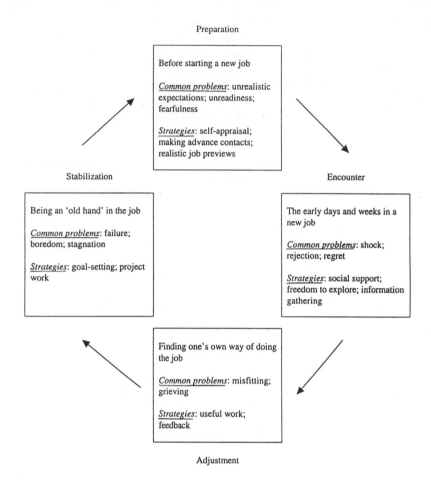

Preparation

Before starting a new job

Common problems: unrealistic expectations; unreadiness; fearfulness

Strategies: self-appraisal; making advance contacts; realistic job previews

Stabilization

Being an 'old hand' in the job

Common problems: failure; boredom; stagnation

Strategies: goal-setting; project work

Encounter

The early days and weeks in a new job

Common problems: shock; rejection; regret

Strategies: social support; freedom to explore; information gathering

Finding one's own way of doing the job

Common problems: misfitting; grieving

Strategies: useful work; feedback

Adjustment

Figure 8.2   The transition cycle
Source: Based on Nicholson (1990)

The transition cycle and some of the potential issues associated with each stage are shown in Figure 8.2. Although the stages are not so separate that people wake up one morning knowing that they have passed to the next one, Nicholson does argue that there are real distinctions between them. Preparation is principally about expectations and motives. Encounter is characterized by emotions and perceptions, whilst adjustment concerns the changes newcomer and organization attempt to make in themselves and the other party. During the stabilization stage both sides are free to concentrate on performance (though this of course is also a significant concern at earlier stages too). The stages are described by Nicholson as interdependent, which means that what happens during one stage influences what happens during the next. For example, if a person arrives at an accurate view of how things work in his or her new environment (encounter), he or she stands a much better chance of finding a successful and mutually acceptable way of doing his or her work (adjustment) than if the encounter is unsatisfactory and/or incomplete.

The transition cycle is first and foremost a framework for analysing work-role transitions. Indeed, I will shortly use it in exactly that way when describing some key phenomena. But it also offers a few insights in its own right. The first is that transitions do not begin on the first day a person is in a new environment. The preparation stage shows very clearly that important things can happen (or fail to happen) before then. Second, both a newcomer and the employing organization can benefit from appreciating that at first it is most important to establish the 'lie of the land' before figuring out how you are going to handle it, and well before actually implementing that way of handling it. As Nicholson (1990, p. 93) put it:

> At the encounter stage, to minimize the impact of negative emotions and to avoid defensive coping, the individual needs a map, a bicycle and good weather. The good weather is a climate of psychological safety and supports, the bicycle is the psychological freedom to explore and pathfind in the new environment; but the maps which organizations usually give to people are totally inadequate.

So encounter is a real task requiring real supports; supports which are not always available.

A third insight is that in an era when performance right now is valued most highly, it will be tempting to try to perform optimally and fully before completing encounter and adjustment. But this is likely to be unsuccessful. If a person has not understood roles and relationships, and/or has not established his or her own '*modus vivendi*', then he or she is likely to make mistakes, duplicate or accidentally subvert other people's efforts, or commit to a way of working which turns out to be inappropriate. Successful transition management involves effective tackling of each stage, not bypassing them.

PREPARATION

No doubt we have all heard anecdotal accounts of people who arrive in a new workplace only to find that nobody is expecting them, and that nobody knows what the newcomer's role is supposed to be. Similarly, there is no shortage of stories about newcomers (particularly young people fresh from full-time education) who seem to have little idea of what they will be expected to do, or absurdly optimistic expectations, even though the reality was explained to them in some detail during the selection process. Whilst the real frequency of such incidents is unknown, it is clear that the anticipation stage is often not used to good advantage by the newcomer-to-be, or by the future employing organization. Some aspects of the anticipation stage have been examined under other names in other chapters. Career exploration (see Chapter 6) could be considered an aspect of anticipation, as could the exploration and identity formation stages in developmental theories (see Chapter 7). But they aren't the whole story. We must bear in mind that recruitment and selection usually take place in a 'climate of mutual selling' (Schein, 1978), where both sides attempt to portray themselves in the best possible light. Many writers have warned against this, not least because it sets up unrealistic expectations on both sides, which in turn leads inevitably to the broken psychological contracts discussed at some length in Chapter 3. But still the selling happens, not least because both sides are afraid of being disadvantaged if they decide to be brutally frank but their competitors do not.

At least, the selling *usually* happens. Some organizations, however, use what has come to be called a realistic job preview (RJP). This term and techniques associated with it were developed by the American psychologist John Wanous (e.g. Wanous, 1980). As the term suggests, RJPs attempt to present a realistic view of a job and the organization to applicants. The realism normally comes from present and/or past incumbents, who describe their experience of the job 'warts and all'. This description is reflected in literature, videos and briefings presented to candidates for the job. The key idea is that the person or persons appointed to the job will have less inflated expectations than would otherwise have been the case. This in turn will reduce the likelihood of them leaving the organization – an expensive occurrence for the employer (and also perhaps for the individual, though that is less often acknowledged).

The 1980s saw quite a lot of interest in and research on RJPs. Premack and Wanous (1985) reviewed much of it and concluded that RJPs do indeed reduce the expectations of newcomers and increase job survival. They estimated that 12% of the recruitment and induction budget could be saved in an organization with a 50% survival rate of newcomers – a significant saving indeed. Premack and Wanous also found that RJPs increase self-selection on the part of the candidates – that is, more people voluntarily drop out of the selection process. An unexpected finding was that using audio-visual RJPs also seemed to be associated with better work performance, perhaps because they demonstrated effective work behaviour. It seems a little strange to me that increased work performance was not originally expected to be one outcome of using RJPs. One might reasonably assume that an RJP would set people thinking about how they would handle the job if they got it, leading perhaps to quicker passage through the encounter and adjustment stages, as well as better considered strategies for work performance from day 1.

There are no doubt some circumstances in which RJPs do not have an effect (Breaugh, 1983). If the nature of the job and/or organization is already well known to applicants, there is little sense in trying to change expectations. If jobs are very hard to obtain, we should not expect people to leave if their expectations are unmet, thus again perhaps rendering an RJP redundant. There is also some doubt about exactly *why* RJPs have an effect, when they do. It could be because:

(1) people are less disappointed by the reality of the job and therefore more motivated and less inclined to leave;

(2) different people get selected for the job than if an RJP had not been used (indeed, one concern for HR managers is the increase in self-selection produced by RJPs – it could be the *best* people who drop out);
(3) people are impressed by the honesty of the organization and want to become and remain a member of it.

Wanous (1989) has referred to 'ten tough choices' in implementing an RJP. The choices include:

(1) Descriptive or judgemental content? Wanous argues that inclusion of the latter (e.g. people's feelings about working weekends) does not exclude the former, and therefore recommends its use.
(2) High or medium negativity? Wanous says that he has never seen a high negativity RJP. Use of one could increase self-selection too much, and/or make coping seem impossible.
(3) Written or audio-visual? According to Wanous this is the only choice for which there is clear research evidence. Audio-visual is easier to comprehend and may improve work performance.
(4) Late or early in the selection process? Using an RJP late in the process costs less and reveals negative information about the organization to fewer people. On the other hand it also means applicants will have invested more of their time and commitment into trying to get the job, and be less inclined to self-select. For this reason, early is better.

Like everything else, RJPs are not without problems. The issue of high vs. medium negativity hints at one of them – whose reality is reflected in an RJP? Not everyone who does or has done the job has the same view of it, so there are choices about what to say in an RJP. One danger of course is that an RJP would end up very watered down. Another issue is more ethical in nature. Although an RJP might seem like an enlightened thing to do on the part of an organization, it is in fact putting the entire burden of adjustment on to the individual. The organization is effectively saying this is how we are; take us or leave us. An alternative would be to change the things which appeared to be causing discontent and disillusion.

Research on RJPs has gone rather quiet at the time of writing this. But there is likely to be continuing and perhaps increasing use of them as concern about fulfilling the psychological contract (see Chapter 3) becomes more widespread. On the other hand, like many interventions RJPs are based on the notion of the job as a relatively fixed set of activities and role requirements. As the 21st century beckons, RJPs may have to be used rather more flexibly to demonstrate what an organization is like as a whole, and the activities members might be asked to perform.

ENCOUNTER

Plenty of anecdote and also research (e.g. Nicholson and West, 1988) supports the notion that informal social interactions help a newcomer learn much more than formal induction programmes and written information.

Several more recent research studies have focused on the content and strategies of information-seeking used by newcomers. Some of these are exhaustive in their classification of different sources and types of information (and quite exhausting to read at times!). Ostroff and Kozlowski (1992) found that newcomers tend to focus their efforts primarily upon acquiring information about their own task and role as opposed to group and wider organization. To illustrate the importance of information-seeking, they also found that acquisition of knowledge from superiors and knowledge about the task was associated with newcomers' satisfaction and commitment. Morrison (1993a) used a slightly different classification of types and sources of information. She distinguished five types of information a newcomer may seek:

(1) technical information – how to perform the required work tasks;
(2) referent information – the expectations and demands of others in the organization specifically concerning the newcomer's role;
(3) normative information – the expected behaviours and attitudes in general in the organization: the norms and values;
(4) performance feedback – evaluations of the newcomer's work performance;
(5) social feedback – evaluations of the newcomer's general behaviour, such as how well he or she is fitting in.

Morrison also distinguished between three ways of getting information:

(1) monitoring – observing and/or listening;
(2) enquiry – asking questions;
(3) consulting written documents.

In a sample of 205 accountants 1, 3 and 6 months into their jobs, Morrison (1993a) found that the amount of information respondents reported they had obtained in the first three months predicted their satisfaction, performance and intention to stay after six months. This was especially true of referent, normative and social information (i.e. information to do with norms and acceptable social behaviours), and especially that obtained through monitoring.

One frequently discussed feature of the encounter stage is surprise (Louis, 1980). As we have already seen, effective use of RJPs can reduce the surprises (especially nasty ones) experienced by newcomers. But not all surprises are nasty. Arnold (1985) found that graduates entering their first full-time employment were often pleasantly surprised by the informality of their work-place and the friendliness of co-workers. The nature of the work and their own reactions and feelings were relatively rarely surprising, though when they were surprising they tended to be unpleasant and big surprises. The graduates' own work performance was also comparatively rarely a surprise to them, and when it was, it tended to be because they were doing better than they expected. The least pleasant surprise overall was the way communications and decisions seemed to be handled in the organization: not rationally but politically and/or chaotically. Schein (1964, 1978) long ago identified coming to terms with the less than rational elements of work organizations as a key task for newcomers. Nicholson and West (1988) found that communications and decisions remained a frequent and very negative source of surprise for managers changing jobs, which suggests that it doesn't get any easier with experience.

ADJUSTMENT AND STABILIZATION

The term adjustment is often used to denote emotional well-being, but in the context of work-role transitions it more commonly refers to the approach a person takes to doing his or her job. Edgar Schein again supplies the origins of some of this. Schein (1971) distinguished between three orientations a person may adopt:

(1) *Custodian* The person does the job strictly in conformity with how it has been done before, and/or how the job description states that it should be done.
(2) *Content innovator* The person accepts as given the purpose of the job and how it fits into wider organizational functioning, but changes the way in which it is done.
(3) *Role innovator* Here the person seeks to change the whole purpose of the job – what it aims to do. An example might be a human resources manager who wants to change his or her role from personnel administrator to strategic manager of the flow of human resources through the organization.

Many organizations claim to want people who are innovative, but there must be doubts about whether they are serious. As Schein (1971) pointed out, role innovators are often unpopular people because they threaten quite far-reaching and big changes. Custodianship is only really a viable strategy when there is a reasonable amount of information available about how the job has been or should be done. The frequency of organizational changes noted by Nicholson and West (1988) and Inkson (1995), plus the fact that Nicholson and West found that a third of job changes were into newly created jobs, casts doubts upon the scope for being a custodian. In fact it casts doubts on all of Schein's categories, since his definitions of innovation concern reacting against some predefined way of doing things. This all highlights the need these days for newcomers to find their own ways of doing things, and for organizations to facilitate that. The adjustment stage of the transition cycle is a real task, not just a theoretical notion, and it is probably becoming increasingly significant.

But of course Schein's (1971) three-way classification remains relevant to many, perhaps most, work-places. In practice, the two types of innovation are often put together into one category. Many have argued that innovation is increasingly necessary in many work organizations, particularly in the Western world, which cannot on the whole compete on cost and therefore must do so on ideas (e.g. Herriot, 1992). How can work-role transitions be

| | | Role change | |
		Low	High
Personal change	Low	Replication	Determination
	High	Absorption	Exploration

Figure 8.3   Four modes of adjustment
Source: Adapted from Nicholson (1984)

handled in ways which foster an innovative orientation in newcomers? Nicholson (1984) suggested it was helpful to identify four personal outcomes of work-role transitions. These are shown in Figure 8.3. People can be changed by transitions (personal change) and/or they can seek to change the nature of their work role (role change, or role innovation). Incidentally, we should note that role innovation is a narrower notion than the usual definition of innovation, which normally refers to 'a tangible product, process or procedure within an organization' (King and Anderson, 1995, p. 3), though clearly related to it.

Nicholson (1984) made some predictions which seemed to suggest that outcomes of work-role transitions were largely a product of pre-existing factors and therefore not very open to being managed. Having high discretion in how to carry out the new role predisposes toward role change (particularly if the person is accustomed to high discretion in earlier roles), whilst high novelty of new role to the person makes personal change more likely. A person who has a high level of desire for control would tend to change the role, whilst high desire for feedback would predispose toward personal change. Nicholson's theory has often been cited but less often tested. The tests that have been reported suggest only limited support. Munton and West (1995) found only a small tendency for novelty to be associated with personal change and discretion with innovation in a longitudinal study of relocators. Ashforth and Saks (1995) found that graduates who reported that they had high discretion did indeed also report that they had changed the role, as Nicholson predicted. But other than that there was little support for the theory. The authors suggested that it would be better to see factors such as desire for control as elicited by circumstances rather than being fixed characteristics of the person. They also noted that Nicholson's theory is quite asocial – it de-emphasizes social processes. It also refers to the *amount* of personal and role change. Presumably those involved in managing work-role transitions will be interested in *how* things change as well as *how much* they change.

Another approach to explaining why people adopt more or less innovative approaches to a new job is derived from what was once termed the 'people processing' or socialization strategies of organizations. In broad terms, newcomers can be socialized in either an 'institutionalized' fashion or an 'individualized' one. The former refers to where a newcomer is treated in quite a formal way, subjected to carefully planned experiences along with other newcomers with events occurring to a timetable known in advance. The latter refers to a less formal (and perhaps less organized) strategy,

Table 8.1 Socialization tactics in organizations

Dimensions of 'institutionalized' socialization	vs. Dimensions of 'individualized' socialization
Collective All newcomers have common learning experiences	*Individual* Each newcomer has a unique set of learning experiences
Formal Newcomers are segregated from other members of the organization during the learning stage	*Informal* Newcomers become part of workgroups very early on and learn on the job
Sequential Newcomers get explicit information about the sequence of future activities	*Random* The sequence of stages is unknown to newcomers
Fixed Newcomers get precise information about future timetable	*Variable* Newcomers have no knowledge of future timetable
Serial Experienced members of the organization act as role models	*Disjunctive* No role models are available to newcomers
Investiture Members of the organization support newcomers and affirm their identity	*Divestiture* Newcomer identity is redefined by negative social experiences

Source: Adapted from Van Maanen and Schein (1979)

where a newcomer is treated more like an ordinary member of the organization, learning more on the job and in relative isolation from any other newcomers there may be, with the timing of events uncertain (Van Maanen and Schein, 1979; Jones, 1986). There is not quite complete agreement about exactly how specific socialization strategies fit together, but Table 8.1 shows the general flavour.

Research (e.g. Jones, 1986; Ashforth and Saks, 1996) shows that institutionalized socialization tactics tend to produce a custodial orientation in newcomers, whilst individualized tactics predispose towards an innovative orientation. However, it should be noted that this research, like much in organizational behaviour, is based upon people's self-reports of the nature of their socialization and of their orientation to their work role, not on direct observation of those things. Institutionalized tactics are thought to produce a custodial response because they ensure that newcomers are exposed mostly to the 'official' views of the organization, and because their experiences reflect on orderly sequence of learning about the organization. The problem is that the use of institutionalized tactics also seems to help newcomers to feel committed to the organization (see the next section for a discussion of commitment). This may be partly because institutionalized tactics bring less stress for newcomers than individualized ones (Ashforth and Saks, 1996). So the conundrum becomes how to socialize newcomers so that they are both committed and innovative. Allen and Meyer (1990) suggested on the basis of their findings that the best way might be to provide investiture but avoid the other institutionalized tactics.

This is all very well, but it reflects the way in which socialization is carried out rather than its content. Chao *et al.* (1994) have reported a large study of the content. They identified six topic areas in which newcomers can be socialized:

(1) performance proficiency: learning and performance of the tasks required in the job;
(2) people: establishment of successful and satisfying work relationships with organizational members;
(3) politics: understanding of formal and informal work relationships and power structures within the organization;
(4) language: understanding of the necessary technical language and organization-specific acronyms, slang and jargon;
(5) organizational goals and values: learning what the organization is trying to achieve and what its members value;
(6) history: knowledge of the past of the organization and of particular organization members.

Chao *et al.*'s longitudinal data showed that the extent to which newcomers reported being socialized in most of these areas had a positive impact on their involvement in their career and the clarity of their self-concept. However, the amount of history socialization experienced by newcomers seemed if anything to be a handicap, perhaps because it reflected a tendency of unhealthy organizations (or alienated people within them) to focus upon the past to the exclusion of the present.

One problem with socialization is the ambiguity surrounding exactly what it is. There is general agreement that it concerns learning by newcomers about the organization and how to perform their role within it. But does this mean learning *what* to do, learning *how* to do it, learning to *want* to do it, believing it is the right thing to do, or viewing oneself as the kind of person who does it? These could be seen as increasingly 'deep' levels of socialization, travelling from cognitive learning through performing certain behaviours to internalizing values and a changing sense of self. Writers in this field seem rather careless in that they refer to newcomers' learning without being specific (and sometimes being contradictory) about which level or levels they mean.

There are some interesting issues about what socialization will become as we enter the 21st century. Much literature and practice of socialization has assumed that there is a relatively fixed role and organization for newcomers to be socialized into, and that those concerned with socialization are physically present in the place or places where the organization operates. This does not reflect well the trends toward 'virtual' organizations, teleworking and flexible work roles. Nor does the fact that much socialization is, or has been, delivered through processes of social interaction. On the good side, the changing nature of organizations may mean that people are less likely to have their innovativeness drummed out of them. The other side of the coin is that the traditional strategies and content of socialization may not be well suited to so-called postmodern organizations. The problem is at two levels: (1) whether traditional socialization methods are sufficient, and (2) whether they are even appropriate to organizations of the 21st century. Most of the strategies described in Table 8.1 would be hard to apply to a person joining, for example, a loosely organized consultancy firm and working principally from home.

Finally, for this section, Dawis and Lofquist (1984) have proposed the Theory of Work Adjustment (TWA), which has its enthusiasts, not least because the authors have carefully developed questionnaires to measure the key concepts. TWA takes a person–job fit approach to adjustment. The person and the job are described principally in terms of the needs and abilities they require and offer. Both person and job are assumed to be relatively static. The key notions of TWA are:

(1) satisfaction of the person with his or her environment, based principally on the extent to which the environment satisfies his or her needs;
(2) satisfactoriness of the person in his or her environment, based principally on his or her work performance, as assessed by the person's superiors.

If both these are present, there is said to be a state of correspondence. The process by which the person seeks to attain and maintain correspondence is called adjustment. Variables located in both the person and the environment can affect the adjustment process – the so-called 'adjustment style dimensions'. These include:

(1) flexibility: willingness to tolerate discorrespondence without doing something about it;
(2) activeness: in acting to increase correspondence;
(3) perseverance: willingness to tolerate discorrespondence without parting company.

TWA states that a person's tenure in a job and/or organization is a joint function of satisfaction and satisfactoriness, and of the perseverance of person and environment. Also, as tenure increases, correspondence tends to as well. In other words, people mould their jobs to fit them better and conversely environments mould people so that they fit better. This adjustment process is of course exactly the focus of much of the material covered in this chapter, but the process itself is not central to TWA.

The theory appears to be moderately good at predicting a person's satisfactoriness, and slightly better at predicting his or her satisfaction. On the other hand it has a slightly old-fashioned mid-twentieth-century feel, particularly in the apparent assumptions that people and jobs are relatively unchanging, and that a person's 'default option' is to stay in the job as long as he or she experiences correspondence.

ORGANIZATIONAL COMMITMENT

As briefly noted above, as well as innovation, commitment to the organization on the part of the newcomer is a potential outcome of the adjustment stage of the transition cycle. Indeed, it is an outcome that many organizations seek, though the wisdom of doing so is sometimes questioned (see, for example, Coopey and Hartley, 1991). Organizational commitment has been defined by Mowday, Porter and Steers (1982) as the relative strength of an individual's identification with, and involvement in, a particular organization. Over the years a variety of theoretical perspectives have been brought to bear on organizational commitment, and this has led to recognition that it is a multifaceted concept. Probably the most widely accepted breakdown is that of Meyer and Allen (1991), who have distinguished between:

(1) affective commitment – a person's emotional attachment to his or her organization;
(2) normative commitment – a person's felt obligation and responsibility to the organization;
(3) continuance commitment – a person's perceptions of the risks and costs associated with leaving his or her current organization.

The first two are more positive than the last, in the sense that they imply the person *wants* to be part of the organization whereas continuance commitment has connotations of feeling that one has no choice. Many HR managers seem inclined to assume that high commitment produces high work performance, and there is a little evidence for that (Ostroff, 1992; Leong, Randall and Cote, 1994), particularly where performance includes elements of being a good organizational citizen such as helping others and working extra hours in a crisis. The connection between commitment and performance is stronger for affective and, to a lesser extent, normative commitment than for continuance commitment. Perhaps the most obvious feature of committed people is that they are more likely to stay in the organization than less committed people. The evidence for that is very strong and consistent (see, for example, Mathieu and Zajac, 1990). Again, it is particularly the case for affective commitment rather than continuance commitment.

The definitions of commitment given above may suggest either that socialization can operate at quite deep levels or that people arrive in an organization with a propensity to be committed. But over and above that, commitment is partly a response to whether membership of the organization provides the individual with outcomes he or she values. The question then arises, what experiences in an organization are most likely to enhance commitment, and can these be managed? Research suggests that many experiences in the work-place have some measurable impact upon commitment (Mathieu and Zajac, 1990). But which things matter most of all? Naturally this will vary somewhat between individuals, but on the whole it seems to be factors concerned with the intrinsic nature of the job (for example, skill development and challenge) and with the clarity and attractiveness of career prospects within the organization, especially in relatively highly educated samples (Arnold and Mackenzie Davey, 1996). Other experiences at work such as pay, role clarity and perceptions of the wider organization seem on the whole less important. The only form of commitment that can be bought with money is perhaps continuance commitment – highly paid people are more likely to perceive high financial costs of leaving.

As we enter the 21st century, it becomes ever more difficult for organizations to think in terms of long-term career prospects for employees. But this reality does not yet seem to have reduced the value placed on this factor by employees. Perhaps the comparative rarity of long-term career paths will perversely further increase the importance of career factors – organizations that can offer them may have a real competitive advantage in generating and sustaining employee commitment.

ENTERING EMPLOYMENT

Over the years a lot of attention has been paid to the transition from education to employment (see Arnold, 1990, for a review). Even more than most transitions, this has been seen as fraught with difficulty. Due partly to the historic separation of education from employment in order to eradicate the use of child labour, young people leaving education are said to be quite naive about the world of employment. They might also be regarded as relatively inexperienced in coping with life events. Yet if we revisit the characteristics of transitions described earlier in this chapter, we can see that the transition from education to employment is often anticipatable in terms of timing (if not always its exact form). It is often viewed as a 'good' step associated with growing up. There are plenty of people around who have already made the transition to act as role models or advice givers. The transition is not a taboo subject. Perhaps then it is not surprising that long ago Ashton and Field (1976, p. 15) stated that the issues faced in this transition 'do not differ significantly from problems of adjustment young people have already faced and will continue to face in both work and non-work situations'.

Historically, there has been a tendency to view the transition for school-leavers as being all about how they get to grips with working life and come to terms with boring, routine jobs. Frequent job-changing was seen as dysfunctional behaviour on their part. For university graduates, however, research focused much more on how employers could attract and retain these valuable people. Job-changing was viewed as a problem for employers. Things have moved on a bit now. Many of the routine jobs filled by school-leavers have disappeared. As education and employment become more interspersed, it is less realistic to refer to *the* transition from education to work. Transitions are made back and forth. In any case, much research on socialization and work adjustment is often carried out with recent graduates because they are relatively accessible to university researchers. So in that sense quite a high proportion of this chapter draws on people making transitions from education to work even though the research is not normally cast in those terms.

In spite of research showing that moving from education to employment is typically not traumatic, it is probably the case that, on average, young people making a first transition from (full-time) education to (full-time) employment will have more learning to do than more experienced job-changers. Some research has suggested that the first year or so of employment may be a critical period which greatly influences success much later (e.g. Berlew and Hall, 1966). On the other hand it is not clear whether this is because a successful transition boosts a person's self-confidence and motivation (Hall, 1971), or whether it gets him or her noticed and then favourably treated by organizational human resource systems (Rosenbaum, 1989). Schein (1978) has suggested that the following issues may be especially salient for newcomers to the work-place:

(1) accepting the reality of the human organization (e.g. politics, disorganization);
(2) dealing with resistance to change;
(3) learning how to work;
(4) dealing with the boss;
(5) deciphering the reward system;
(6) locating one's place in the organization, and developing an identity.

To the extent that a young person lacks knowledge, skill or experience regarding features that are common to all work-places, we would expect that more socialization and adjustment will be required for that person than for an older job-changer. But if, for example, the expected style of relationships with the boss varies significantly from setting to setting, we might expect no more difficulty for a person straight from education than for others. In fact there might be *less* difficulty, due to the absence of a requirement to unlearn earlier behaviours.

RETIREMENT

Retirement did not meaningfully exist until the very late 19th and 20th centuries. In 1889 Germany introduced the first old-age insurance legislation, and this included a standard retirement age of 70. Retirement has been defined in various ways, and not all the definitions adequately reflect the complexity of the transition these days. For a start it is possible to distinguish between retirement as a transition (becoming retired) and as a state (being retired). Also, relatively objective definitions such as Atchley (1982, p. 264) 'substantial reduction in employment accompanied by income from a retirement pension or personal savings', may not coincide with a person's subjective opinion of his or her employment status, or indeed with his or her financial position.

Retirement is another transition that social scientists tended to view as stressful, only to discover in their own research that for most people it isn't. Bosse *et al.* (1991) studied a sample of 1,516 men, 45% of whom were retired. Retirement as a transition was found to be the least stressful of 31 possible life events experienced by the respondents in the previous 12 months. Indeed, work seemed to present over twice as many problems as retirement.

Nevertheless, for some people the transition into retirement *is* a problem, and there is also some research that suggests satisfaction with retirement tends to dip after an initial 'honeymoon period' of six months or so (Bosse *et al.*, 1991).

It is not hard to see why retirement at least has the potential to be difficult. For people involved in their work to the exclusion of all else it may mean the withdrawal of a central aspect of their identity. But it is not just identity that matters – it is also activity. Satisfaction with retirement tends to be higher amongst people who engage in a number of activities and roles. Indeed, a person may already be fulfilling some of them before retirement and the continuity this provides itself contributes to adjustment after retirement (Atchley, 1989). So the loss of the work-role may not, in itself, be crucial (Taylor-Carter and Cook, 1995).

In fact, the best predictors of adjustment to and satisfaction with retirement appear to be good health and adequate finance, presumably because these enable a person to participate in a range of activities and roles during retirement, and perhaps because retirement without these factors would probably have been neither sought nor desired by the person (Talaga and Beehr, 1989). There is some research evidence suggesting that finance is the most commonly anticipated problem by people approaching retirement (Parker, 1983).

The importance of having positive reasons for retirement has been emphasized by Hanisch (1994). She found in a sample of 150 retirees that most of their stated reasons for retirement fell into three categories: (poor) health; personal reasons such as wanting to travel or spend more time with family; and work reasons such as job dissatisfaction or being tired of working. Not surprisingly, the second group reported having done more planning for retirement and engaging in more activities post-retirement than the other two groups.

The importance of planning for retirement is another consistent theme. It again illustrates how the preparation stage of the transition cycle can be used to good effect. Unfortunately, relatively few employing organizations offer assistance in planning for retirement (Parker, 1983) though the number may well have increased since 1983. Where planning is offered, it tends to focus on financial rather than psychosocial matters (Rowan and Wilks, 1987). It is difficult to evaluate the impact of pre-retirement programmes due to all the other things that happen in people's lives that might obscure that impact, and because of the rarity of opportunities to compare people who attend such programmes with similar people who do not. However, Kamouri and Cavanaugh (1986) did achieve such a comparison and found that people who attended a pre-retirement programme tended to remain satisfied with their retirement for longer than those who did not.

Retirement is an increasingly ambiguous transition, and this trend is likely to continue into the 21st century. Sometimes through choice and sometimes through necessity, many people disengage gradually from employment. This may present a very welcome opportunity to ease the transition, and perhaps a necessary one since some soothsayers predict that, at least for people with marketable skills, the era of early retirement is largely over. The changing demographic structure of populations in most Western countries and global competition may well mean that paid work continues well into people's 60s, though not necessarily on a full-time basis, in various forms of so-called bridge employment (Feldman, 1994). This requires, amongst other things, flexible pension provision. In particular, schemes which place heavy emphasis on final salary, and financial systems which prohibit pension payments whilst a person is still earning, substantially inhibit the flexibility that is required. Many countries have taken steps to facilitate gradual retirement (Reday-Mulvey and Taylor, 1996). For example, in France the government supplements salaries of older people who shift to part-time work with their employer, so long as the employer hires new people to work the time freed up. The insurance company AXA offers certain employees 65% of their salary to be 'semi-retired'. They can be called in at any time (for example to replace staff on leave), and they receive 100% of their salary for the time they are working. There may be great potential for such schemes to provide mutual benefits for employers and retirees.

RELOCATION

Relocation can be defined for our purposes as a geographical change of job location by one or more employees of an organization. The employees remain employed with the same organization. They may or may not perform the same job in their new location, and the move may or may not be at their own instigation. Munton *et al.* (1993) have concluded that, taking families into account, over one million people relocate each year in the UK, at a total annual cost to British industry of something like £7.5 billion. Brett, Stroh and Reilly (1992) reported that American companies relocate something like half a million employees per year. The number climbed during the 1980s and levelled off subsequently.

A considerable quantity of research has been devoted to identifying the factors affecting an employee's likely willingness to relocate. This is partly a response to perceptions that over recent years staff are becoming less willing to relocate just because their employer wants them to (Johnson, 1990). The research has produced somewhat variable findings, but overall the picture accords closely with what some might call common sense. Brett, Stroh and Reilly (1992) have concluded that those managers and professionals most willing to relocate are characterized by:

(1) high career ambition;
(2) a belief that their future with the organization is bright;
(3) a belief that moving is necessary to get ahead;
(4) partner support for moving, or no partner;
(5) no or few children;
(6) non-employed partner, or partner with low income;

(7) young age;
(8) being male;
(9) few community ties.

This is fair enough, but it is also important to remember that for some people willingness to relocate is much more simply explained. It may be a case of relocate or lose your job. In this case probably all that matters is how much the person relies on his or her work income to survive.

Regarding the experience (as opposed to anticipation) of relocation, Munton *et al.* (1993) reported that relocators' worries focused mostly on non-job factors such as property transactions and guilt about forcing children to move. Lawson and Angle (1994) also found that family and other non-job concerns were the best predictors of adjustment to relocation. Their research and that of Fisher and Shaw (1994) revealed that prior experience of relocation helped adjustment to the present one, probably because that prior experience both enabled relocators to appreciate the key tasks they faced and reinforced their confidence that they could tackle them. On the other hand R. Martin (1995) argued that it may be possible to have too much of a good thing. He found that adjustment to relocation was most difficult for those with the least *and* those with the most experience of it. In the former case, lack of know-how and disruption of community ties were probably to blame. For the latter group it may have been more of a case of being worn down by yet another round of tedious and taxing tasks. However, we must be cautious here because Martin's sample was small compared with most other research.

The management by organizations of mass relocation of staff needs to be handled carefully. Merrick (1995) reported how the Mobil Oil Company in the UK organized a move of over 200 employees from central London to Milton Keynes, about 80 kilometres north-west. An official announcement about the move was made (though the probability of the move was already well known) and, immediately after that, all staff were sent a video showing the new work location and town. Staff had previously been surveyed to find out their likely reactions and perceived difficulties if the move went ahead. Consultants were used to help with house buying and selling and with education for families with children. Staff who chose not to relocate (nearly half of the 400 employed in central London) were offered a full redundancy package with outplacement services. Whilst Merrick's article does not reveal the extent to which the move could be regarded as a success, it is clear that responding promptly and flexibly to staff anxieties in a well-funded manner was important. The experience of British Telecom also hints at the importance of sticking to commitments to employees. Like Mobil, BT planned to move out of central London in a project called Workstyle 2000, but there were some difficulties when some financial supports were less generous than staff had expected. Also, transport to one of the new sites posed some problems, which rather contradicted the aims of Workstyle. Research by Daly and Geyer (1994) has suggested that in large measure employee reactions to relocation are determined by the fairness with which they perceive the relocation to have been planned and implemented.

Of course, increasing numbers of relocations involve moves between countries. Brett and Stroh (1995) found that managers' willingness to relocate internationally was (not surprisingly) principally a product of their general attitude to moving and their spouse's willingness to relocate. Biographical variables such as age, education and number of children at home were less significant. For many reasons, including cultural and language differences, international relocation is likely to present more problems of management and adjustment than domestic relocation. In a wide-ranging review, Black, Mendenhall and Oddou (1991) estimated that somewhere between 16 and 40% of American employees sent overseas return early, and between 30 and 50% stay in their assignments but are considered ineffective or only marginally effective. There is no particular reason to think that the figures for expatriates from many other countries would be much different, so it looks as if international relocation almost qualifies as a disaster zone!

From the point of view of individuals, research has distinguished between relocators' feelings of psychological comfort (adjustment) and the extent to which relocators interact with the people and culture of their host country. Brewster (1994) has suggested that expatriates may adopt the behavioural styles of their host country much more quickly and completely than was previously thought. Janssens (1995) among others has pointed out that whilst company head offices might want relocators to feel well adjusted, there is also a concern that relocators may immerse themselves *too* thoroughly in the host culture, effectively 'going native' and losing the wider company perspective. Janssens found that the amount of interaction reported by relocators with members of the host country increased consistently as their time in the relocated position increased. This was true up to at least five years' tenure, which suggests that true integration with the host culture takes a long time, even if (as Brewster suggested) adoption of behavioural styles is much quicker.

Even more clearly than for domestic relocation, recent research has demonstrated the importance of non-work factors in adjustment to international relocation. In particular, the adjustment of family members seems crucial to the work and general adjustment of the relocatee. Nicholson and Imaizumi (1993, p. 130) have referred to this as 'a significant flow of adjustment from the domestic to the employment sphere' in their study of Japanese managers working in the United Kingdom. Consistent with this, Arthur and Bennett (1995) found that the family situation was perceived by a sample of 338 international relocators in 45 multinational companies as more important in determining the success of an international relocation than job knowledge and motivation, relational skills, flexibility/adaptability and even extra-cultural openness.

The concept of cultural distance is also relevant here, though its effect may not be straightforward. The influential work of Hofstede (1980) has led to a number of attempts to identify the key dimensions upon which (national) cultures may differ. Subsequent research (e.g. Trompenaars, 1993) has deviated somewhat, but not fundamentally, from Hofstede's dimensions, which are:

(1) power distance – the extent to which people of high status have more power than those with low status;
(2) uncertainty avoidance – the extent to which people feel threatened by unusual situations;
(3) individualism – the extent to which people are expected to 'do their own thing' irrespective of the expectations of others;
(4) masculinity – the extent to which people are expected to behave in assertive and competitive ways as opposed to caring and nurturing ones.

It is a reasonable bet that adjustment is more difficult the bigger the differences between the relocator's home and host culture. On the other hand Janssens (1995) found that immersion by European managers in the host country's culture (though not necessarily their sense of well-being) tended to be greater in Africa and Asia than it was in Europe, where because of less distance and better communications it was easier to maintain the social network in their home country.

Black, Mendenhall and Oddou (1991) presented a model of international adjustment which attempted to bring together relevant concepts from various fields. It is shown in Figure 8.4. Most of the concepts should be familiar by now.

In particular, the following are noteworthy:

(1) Three aspects of the individual are seen as important: sense of self-efficacy (perhaps derived from past relocations); skills in relating to other people; and skills in perceiving behaviours and values exhibited by other people. All too often it seems staff are selected for overseas assignments solely on the basis of their technical performance in the job tasks.
(2) The potential importance of culture, both general and organization-specific.
(3) The inclusion of socialization, and the use of the distinction made earlier between tactics and content.
(4) The inclusion of non-work factors.
(5) The distinction between the type of adjustment (e.g. innovator vs. custodian) and degree of adjustment (i.e. how well adjusted the person feels).

This model is of course speculative, and it may turn out that not all of it matters. Note also that, like much research on international relocation, it seeks to predict adjustment, not quality of work performance. The assumption seems to be that work performance is, at least partly, a product of adjustment.

The consultants Arthur Andersen have produced a helpful benchmarking study (Andersen, 1996) of the international assignment policy documents of

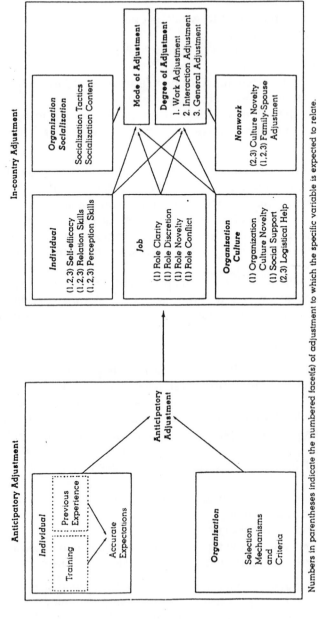

Numbers in parentheses indicate the numbered facet(s) of adjustment to which the specific variable is expected to relate.

Figure 8.4 Framework of international adjustment
Source: Black, Mendenhall and Oddou (1991)

Table 8.2 International assignment policy documents

(1) Policy areas typically scarcely addressed:
   Classification of different types of assignments
   Definition of terms used in the policy document
   The terms of the assignment contract
   Responsibilities for assisting the relocatee
   Medical cover
   Termination
   Others (e.g. spousal assistance)
(2) Policy areas typically covered, but often only sketchily:
   Introduction to the policy
   Remuneration
   Income tax
   Travel
   Car
   Education
   Repatriation
(3) Policy areas covered to a variable extent, sometimes moderately thoroughly:
   Pre-assignment preparation
   Freights, removals and storage
   Accommodation
   Leave

Source: Andersen (1996)

60 organizations based in various countries. A total of 194 policy elements, grouped in 19 policy areas, were identified. Like many such documents, it is partly a marketing exercise. It also suffers from the apparent assumptions that the more specific and detailed the policy document the better, sometimes irrespective of what the policy actually is, and that if something is not in the policy document it probably does not happen. Nevertheless, some useful observations emerged. The 19 policy areas were defined and rated as shown in Table 8.2. Notice that the policy areas themselves largely neglect the more behavioural and people-orientated dimensions of work-role transitions that have been the main focus of this chapter. It is noteworthy that only a quarter of the companies made policy statements about who might be eligible for assignments and how they would be selected. Policy documents were also short of information on:

(1) who was responsible for what during the assignment;
(2) whether cross-cultural training was provided;
(3) who was responsible for finding a role for the person when he or she returned;
(4) what assistance might be offered to a spouse or partner;
(5) whether any form of career guidance was available during the assignment.

If we accept the assumption that things not specified in policy documents are less likely to be delivered than those that are specified, it seems that there is plenty of scope for ambiguity and failure to meet some of the relocatees' main concerns.

SUMMARY

Job changes are happening with increasing frequency, and quite often involve big changes in location, role and work duties. It is tempting to see work-role transitions as potential crises for both individuals and organizations. But on the whole they seem to be experienced quite positively by individuals, with more feelings of growth than of threat. On the other hand organizations do not generally manage work-role transitions particularly well. The most important learning for newcomers occurs through daily social interactions and work experiences rather than organized training and induction, but that does not mean organizations are powerless to influence the process of adjustment. Careful choice of social context and work assignments of newcomers, coupled with realistic portrayal of the job and organization before their arrival, can substantially affect newcomers' attitudes to their work as well as their strategies for carrying it out. The early 21st century is likely to see modest further increases in the incidence of work-role transitions, and also greater frequency of 'partial' work-role transitions where a person completes one project that occupies part of his or her work time and moves to another whilst some other components of his or her work remain unchanged. Increasingly, globalization will probably mean more international job moves and greater attention from managers and academics to the role of national and organizational cultures in the transition process.

---------- 9 ----------

DIVERSE PEOPLE, DIVERSE CAREERS

Some of the material presented in earlier chapters has been based, explicitly or implicitly, on the assumption that people differ. So, for example, people may have different career decision-making styles. They may have different career management needs, and respond differently to any particular career management intervention. On the other hand, much theory and practice in career management also suggests that much is constant across different groups and individuals. So, for example, a development centre might be seen as something that 'works', so long as its technical design is up to scratch. Lifespan theories, although more flexible than they once were, have tended to view a person's life as passing through more or less inevitable phases.

Throughout this book I have tried to point out instances where the assumption that certain ideas apply to everyone is just a little too hard to swallow. For example, women's lives may not typically follow the same pattern as men's. The uses of a mentor for a member of an ethnic minority may be different from (and greater than) for a member of the ethnic majority. But many career management interventions and theories might nevertheless have general applicability if they can be framed in terms sufficiently broad to encompass quite different people. Also, career management interventions can help people to manage their own careers more flexibly if they reflect the real conditions and constraints of their lives.

In this chapter I analyse these issues in general terms. The fact that this chapter is near the end of the book should not be taken to mean the issues are somehow peripheral. They are central, and are best understood in the light of the previous chapters. I start with the concept and practice of managing diversity, and subsequently work towards the more specific concerns of dual-career couples and then women. More detailed analyses of issues concerning other specific constituencies can be found in, for example, Davidson and Burke (1994) for women, Iles and Auluck (1991) for ethnic minorities, and McHugh (1991) for people with a disability. I then change gear a little and examine the career dynamics of other 'special' groups, specifically entrepreneurs and self-employed people, and technical specialists. Finally I will also review the impact of unemployment, since this is a prominent feature of increasing diversity in careers. Quite simply, a greater proportion of the work-force experiences it than has been the case during most of the second half of the 20th century.

MANAGING DIVERSITY

Numerous labour market statistics (some of which are quoted in Chapters 2 and 3, and later in this one) show that work-forces in many countries are changing. They are becoming more equally balanced between genders, and more multicultural. The age profiles of work-forces are also changing, with an increase in the average age but also possibly a slight drop in the proportion over 55. Awareness of the special problems faced by, for example, people with a disability and gay and lesbian people is growing, albeit slowly. In short, there is growing awareness, at least in some quarters, that employees are very varied in terms of their needs, characteristics and potential. Furthermore, there is a growing belief that this diversity must be harnessed within organizations, not ignored or suppressed. The lines of reasoning here vary a bit between organizations, but include the following (Cox and Blake, 1991; Kandola, 1995):

(1) Recruitment of able staff. In a more diverse work-force, it would be counterproductive to exclude, or be unattractive to, significant parts of the population.
(2) Retention of able staff. Following on from point (1), it is costly and damaging to lose able employees because they feel unappreciated or oppressed.
(3) Ethics. The upholding of individual and group differences can be seen as a crucial ingredient of democratic societies.
(4) Marketing. Organizations with diverse staff will be better placed to communicate well with diverse markets.
(5) Innovation and problem-solving. Organizations with diverse staff will be able to capitalize upon a variety of thinking styles and perspectives.
(6) Flexibility. Organizations capable of accommodating the styles, needs and lifestyles of diverse staff will by definition be sufficiently flexible to respond to changing environmental conditions. (See Hall and Parker (1993) for a discussion of the connections between flexibility and diversity.)

By and large, then, managing diversity is justified in terms of the business case in its favour, rather than by conformity to statutory requirements which is perhaps more characteristic of equal opportunities (EO) and affirmative action (AA). But what exactly is managing diversity all about, and is it really so different from EO and AA? You may not be surprised to hear that definitions of diversity and its management differ to some extent. However, Greenslade (1991, p. 28) sums up the thrust of the argument: 'an environment in which individual differences are evident, different means to an end are respected, and the talents and attributes of people from different backgrounds and heritages are fully valued, utilized and developed'. So diversity is fundamentally about differences between individuals rather than subgroups. The personal styles of everyone, including white males, should be equally valued. In principle, the concept of diversity goes well beyond readily identifiable subgroup membership such as gender, ethnicity, religion, sexual orientation and disability. It can also include personality, lifestyle, and ways of working, thinking and communicating. Indeed, in some organizations it is taken that way (Dodds, 1995). In one sense then, managing diversity suggests that no *group* should be treated with special favour. This is of course different from affirmative action. On the other hand, it can be argued that the human resource systems in most organizations (or perhaps the people operating them) have historically operated in favour of white males, and that something more than an in-principle acceptance of individual differences is required to correct this. Ford (1996, p. 34) quoted a (presumably) fictional manager to make this point: 'I already do this. My team (of white men aged 35 to 45 who are just like me) are already treated with fairness and respect, and their individual differences are recognised – so there is nothing more for me to do.'

Diversity initiatives

In practice, then, diversity initiatives often include substantial attention to differences between specific groups, particularly based upon gender and/or ethnicity. Ellis and Sonnenfeld (1994) among others have described the interventions characteristic of diversity initiatives. They include:

(1) multicultural workshops designed to improve understanding and communication between cultural groups;
(2) multicultural 'core groups' which meet regularly to confront stereotypes and personal biases;
(3) support groups, mentoring and relationships and networks for women and cultural minorities;
(4) advisory councils reporting to top management;
(5) rewarding managers on the basis of their record on developing members of targeted groups (in the US, Tenneco and Prudential have both taken steps to assess and reward managers in this way);
(6) fast-track development programmes and special training opportunities for targeted groups.

There is a significant difference between learning to like diversity and learning to manage it. The former is difficult enough, and much social psychological research has shown how most of us tend to equate different from ourselves as being worse or wrong. But even if we learn to love people who differ from us in important ways, we do not necessarily know how to manage them. For example, a manager may appreciate the variety of perspectives of his or her diverse group of subordinates, but be unable to marshal these to produce agreed solutions at team meetings. Assessors at a development centre may struggle to appreciate that the same behaviour by two assessees may mean different things because they come from different backgrounds.

The jumps from awareness to appreciation to management of diversity are therefore considerable. At an interpersonal level, McEnrue (1993) has argued that key factors include acceptance of the relativity of one's own knowledge and perceptions, tolerance for ambiguity, ability to demonstrate empathy and respect, and willingness to change one's behaviour and beliefs. These characteristics are of course generally applicable to most interpersonal interactions. Possession of them should help staff to operate human resource systems fairly, but even so, characteristics of the organization and its people in general can be a help or a hindrance here (Kandola, 1995). A diversity-orientated organization is likely to include the following features:

(1) people who understand the importance of organizational culture and its impact upon individuals;
(2) devolved decision-making and power;
(3) consistent use of participation and consultation;
(4) tolerance of different values and cultures;
(5) flexibility with respect to working patterns;
(6) orientation towards the long term, including an acceptance of social responsibilities.

There is some ambiguity about whether such a description is *in itself* a diversity-orientated organization, or whether it specifies the characteristics required for an organization to operate in a diversity-friendly manner. The latter point of view might be more viable, since the characteristics listed above are likely to facilitate the achievement of the following (Thomas, 1990):

(1) Equal access opportunities for everyone to jobs in the organization.
(2) Equal treatment once in it.
(3) Structural integration, i.e. all groups represented in all parts of the organization. This is not yet the case on the whole. In the US, for example, 41% of all managers are women, but only 3% of top managers (Segal and Zellner, 1992). Figures for the UK are 20% of all managers and 4% of middle/senior ones. Similar patterns occur for ethnic minorities (Martin, 1991; Iles and Auluck, 1991).
(4) Adaptation of organizations to individuals as well as vice versa. Strong socialization and culture change programmes can put the onus of change well and truly upon the individual, and thus eliminate some of the diversity that is supposed to be valued.
(5) Human resource policies which are responsive to work–family issues (see also a later section of this chapter).
(6) Low levels of inter-group conflict, and where conflict does occur, it should be on the basis of ideas not power struggles or stereotypes.

In turn, these characteristics help to achieve the business-related benefits itemized near the start of this section on diversity. Or do they? Kandola (1995) has argued that some of those benefits are much more often asserted than demonstrated. Although claims of recruitment and retention benefits seem to have some weight behind them, the others do not. Kandola is particularly sceptical about claims concerning the superiority of diverse work teams over homogeneous ones, which are not consistently supported by research on decision-making groups. This is not to say that diverse groups are *incapable* of doing better – only that improvements in team performance do not follow automatically.

Some cautions and speculations

There seems to be an emerging consensus that although managing diversity indeed has a significantly different flavour from equal opportunities and affirmative action, it will usually include some focus on promoting the interests of specific groups of people in the organization. In turn, this carries some risks. One is of a white male backlash. It might be argued that feeling like a threatened group for once might do white men some good, but a more sympathetic response than that is probably advisable. Careful avoidance of any attack on the personal integrity and past conduct of individuals together with emphases on business benefits and the attempt to create a level playing field (as opposed to one sloping in the opposite direction) should help. So should the wholehearted support of top management, who are, after all, usually predominantly white and male. The notion of top management support is a bit of a cliché, but it has some validity since effective harnessing of diversity involves the culture and practices of the whole organization. A token gesture here and there will certainly not suffice.

Another tricky issue is that promoting the interests of subgroups of staff can perpetuate or even accentuate stereotypes that are a cause (or perhaps a symptom) of past problems. Workshops on cultural differences, for example, can serve the useful purpose of showing how groups may have different values and interpret their own and other people's behaviour in different ways. But they may also imply that everyone in a certain cultural group thinks or behaves that way. Moreover, significantly different cultural groups, e.g. 'Asians', may be lumped together inappropriately, resulting in rather grotesque generalizations. One way around these problems may be to define groups selected for special attention in terms of their positions in the organization. For example, a bank may target the customer service managers in branches as a previously neglected group. The chances are that these people are predominantly women, but the point is that any action aimed at promoting their interests is based on their organizational status, not their gender.

It is appropriate to assert that employees should be judged solely on their work performance rather than on irrelevant background and group membership criteria – appropriate, but a bit too easy. If judgements of work performance are based on narrow and fixed conceptions about how work should be done, the problem is hardly solved. Although biases in judgements appear not to be major in most cases, there is nevertheless a tendency to attribute the successes of women and cultural minorities to luck rather more than those of white men (e.g. Greenhaus and Parasuraman, 1993). It is therefore vital that work performance is assessed on what has been achieved rather than on how visible the person has been in the work-place, or the exact methods used to reach his or her goals.

Given current population trends and the need for skilled and innovative staff, there seems little doubt that concerted attempts by organizations to manage diversity will become increasingly common as the 21st century gets under way. But the prevailing use of the 'business case' for managing diversity could be twisted so that diversity is valued only at middle and higher organizational levels. At lower levels, particularly where there are casualized and low-skilled workers who have little or no contact with customers, it might be argued that diversity has no particular value since people are readily replaceable and as individuals can inflict little damage on the organization. Quite apart from its dubious ethical tone, use of this argument could undermine the whole of an organization's attempt to manage diversity. It is difficult to confine an organizational culture to certain levels only, and this rather cynical approach to staff management would probably spill over beyond its intended boundaries.

DUAL-CAREER COUPLES AND FAMILIES

Greenhaus and Callanan (1994, p. 252) have defined a dual-career couple as two people who share a lifestyle that includes an ongoing love relationship, cohabitation, and a work role for each partner. As they point out, this definition can include couples of the same sex as well as unmarried couples of opposite sexes. Nevertheless, much of the research and management practice concerning dual-career couples focuses on married people, usually with children. Much of it also concentrates on such couples who have managerial or professional jobs as opposed to less exalted ones. In many ways the tone was set long ago by Rapoport and Rapoport (1971), who, in their analysis of dual-career families, defined careers as occupations with a developmental sequence requiring a high level of commitment and having high personal salience. As we saw in Chapter 2, this is an overly restrictive concept of career, which is one reason why Greenhaus and Callanan's approach is superior. Dual-career couples constitute about 60% of the total number of UK households with couples, up from about 40% in the early 1970s.

Life in a dual-career household can have many rewarding aspects. Both partners may derive a sense of autonomy and fulfilment from their work, such that neither feels unduly reliant upon, or outstripped by, the other. Household income is of course usually considerably greater than it would be if only one partner was working. This may bring welcome 'extras' to the partners' lives. Or it may simply (but importantly) allow them to keep their heads above water in financial terms. If there are children, the parents may have more equal relationships with them than if one was out and the other at home all day.

On the other hand, most members of dual-career couples can quickly point to a number of not-so-good features of this way of living. The extent to which problems exist and to which supports are available is not solely due to the characteristics of the people involved. As Lewis (1992) has pointed out, there are cultural and national differences concerning:

(1) the extent to which gender divisions are reflected in social institutions including, for example, welfare systems;
(2) the value placed on work and family life;
(3) the value placed on women's participation in the work-force;
(4) receptivity to change.

In Sweden, for example, income differentials between men and women are comparatively low, and men are taking a greater role in child-care. Social and employment policies tend to support this via, for example, paternity leave. The UK government has tended to be non-interventionist, which in practice means that male-orientated employment practices and expectations prevail.

But Lewis (1992) also concluded that a common theme across countries is continuing gender inequality. To a greater or lesser extent, women retain the major responsibilities for child-care and domestic duties. Research suggests that men enjoy more leisure time than women, and that mothers in dual-career couples spend over 50% more time per week than fathers on home and child-care (Burden and Googins, 1987; Swiss and Squires, 1993). To the extent that men are involved in household chores, it tends to be the traditionally male domain of repairs and improvements. Women's income tends to be lower than men's, and even where a women earns a relatively high proportion of household income this does not necessarily increase her authority. Many couples, and certainly their employers and their children's schools, seem to assume that it is the woman who will down tools if a child is sick or some other crisis occurs (Cooper and Lewis, 1993). Benign employers and line managers might be sympathetic to women's requests for flexibility in order to accommodate these eventualities, but this simply reinforces the expectation that it is the woman's responsibility to deal with them. In the long run, of course, this might be seen as a reason not to employ mothers of young children. Izraeli (1992), for example, has shown how this phenomenon occurs in Israel. Similarly, employment of low-paid and low-status nannies by dual-career couples may help to liberate both partners (particularly the woman) but paradoxically it does absolutely nothing for the more general status and role of women in society (Hertz, 1986).

Tricky issues can arise concerning job moves and job seeking by one or both members of dual-career couples. As we have already implied, the man's career often takes precedence, but not always. A few dual-career couples take turns to have their way in such dilemmas. Others have a more general agreement that over time both partners will have a fair crack of the whip. The availability of suitable work for one partner but not the other at a given location sometimes results in weekly commuting, which in some circumstances can put considerable strain on the couple and their relationship (Gerstel and Gross, 1984). A practice seen as enlightened in some quarters is for organizations to offer employment to both members of a couple

(Sekaran, 1986). In a sense this is family-friendly since it reduces the risk of working away from home. But it could drive a coach and horses through an organization's equal opportunities policies. This is particularly the case if it badly wants one member of the couple, and is prepared to take the other as part of the price of getting the favoured one. Other perhaps better candidates do not get a look in.

We have seen that significant conflicts can all too easily arise for dual-career couples. These conflicts can be of an interpersonal nature if the partners have not agreed in general terms how they will handle routine and non-routine situations. Hall and Hall (1979) long ago suggested that the key factor was for members of dual-career couples to shift their thinking from 'I' to 'we' in making decisions and establishing priorities. This is an elegant expression of the problem rather than a solution to it, but it does suggest some useful tips. High and approximately equal levels of practical and emotional support should be offered by each partner. Full feedback and openness without undue offence being taken are also needed. Yet these are difficult to achieve, particularly since there are always practical tasks that need doing. The temptation is to leave relationship issues to a tomorrow which never comes. This is particularly the case when the partners are experiencing considerable pressure, including competing demands on their time. Fatigue and stress from one domain of life can easily spill over into another. So can patterns of behaviour, which can mean that a partner behaves at home in the same way that he or she is expected to at work. This may be deemed neither appropriate nor welcome by the other partner.

Other conflicts can arise from expectations of others. Many members of dual-career couples, particularly women, experience a sense of guilt that they are neglecting the traditional roles they feel they should be fulfilling. This is often derived from the values and role modelling of their own parents – factors which are at work principally during childhood but often into adulthood as well. More diffuse but nevertheless influential are societal norms, which may themselves conflict. A professional woman may feel she ought to be a full-time homemaker and carer, but also that she shouldn't waste her education and training. A woman accustomed to low-paid work on, for example, a factory floor may experience a conflict between staying at home with her children and a societal expectation that people should earn their living rather than rely on welfare benefits. Research evidence has clearly shown that children's development and well-being are not impaired by the absence of parents for a number of hours during the day (Rutter, 1981). This conclusion rests on the assumption that a child's care-givers do a decent job, but many parents can attest to its truth despite initial anxieties when the child is 'handed over' on the first day.

Many employers have little provision to help dual-career couples and others with family responsibilities (which can include care of elderly relatives, not just children). Nevertheless, increasing numbers of employers take the view that supporting family need is a duty and/or serves their interests in attracting and retaining effective performers. Policies supporting family responsibilities and some of the issues surrounding them will now be examined a little more closely.

Leave entitlements

Some organizations offer maternity and paternity leave over and above any statutory requirements. If such statutory requirements exist, the leave permitted (particularly maternity leave) may be quite limited in terms of duration, the number of employees covered by the requirement and employees' qualifying conditions including tenure and/or working hours. F. Schwartz (1989) observed that only 36% of the US full-time work-force was covered by a maternity leave policy, and 17% by a paternity leave policy. In the UK, up to 18 weeks of statutory maternity pay is available, though two years' full-time service is required for the right of reinstatement, which applies up to 29 weeks after the birth. Cooper and Lewis (1993) found that some women returning from maternity leave were shunted around less desirable and more disjointed assignments than those they experienced before taking leave. There were some other instances where work was simply allowed to pile up while the woman was away, giving her a very nasty surprise when she returned. Of course, it does not *have* to be the woman who stops work to care for a baby. Sweden has seen the concept of parental leave, where the father and/or the mother have a leave entitlement which they can split between them or not as they choose. Most countries are less flexible, but some employers have parental leave schemes.

Child-care facilities

Friedman (1990) noted a ninefold increase in the number of US employers supporting child-care activities between 1982 and 1990, though this still represented only about 12% of organizations with 100 or more employees. Many employers are justifiably proud of their provision of child-care facilities at or near their premises, but as Cooper and Lewis (1993) have observed, a work-place crèche alone can be a token gesture – albeit a fairly expensive one. In the UK only one child in 250 has access to an employer-sponsored nursery, and state and local authority child-care is not particularly plentiful relative to some other European countries. The number of places with day nurseries and registered childminders doubled between 1985 and 1992, but even so less than half of children aged 3 to 5 have access to day care (Davidson, 1996). Some parents are able to make satisfactory child-care arrangements elsewhere, often enlisting relatives through choice or economic necessity. Child-care at the work-place has obvious convenience, but can again reinforce the role of the woman as an on-call care-giver if something goes wrong – after all, if the child-care is at her work-place, she is easily summoned. And, as has already been noted, family problems and crises are the eventualities which stretch parents most. Some employers (for example, in the US, Du Pont) therefore include a 'hospital wing' for sick children in their child-care facilities.

Career breaks

Only a small population of women return to work immediately after the statutory period of maternity leave. Most others return later, or would do so if they had the chance. Some organizations, most notably in the financial services sector, facilitate this by organizing career breaks of up to several years. This is almost invariably taken up by women – when men start doing it, the world really will be changing! Some organizations offer a choice between one long career break (e.g. for five years) and two shorter ones. People taking career breaks are expected to stay in touch with the organization, to do at least a couple of weeks per year of paid relief work, and perhaps to attend a limited number of training and updating sessions. From the organization's point of view, career breaks are thought to enhance the payoff of prior training investment, and to help in the recruitment of ambitious young people, particularly women. On the other hand, some confidence is required that suitable positions can be found for returning career-breakers. Also, although F. Schwartz (1989) rightly pointed out that five years is only a small proportion of a total career that may span more than 40 years, five years is a big gap if there is an expectation of relatively short tenure in the organization, which of course is increasingly the case.

Training

Quite often training is best directed at managers in order to increase awareness of the difficulties faced by dual-career couples (Cooper and Lewis, 1993). For members of dual-career couples themselves, training often focuses on how to deal with the potential conflicts described earlier. This can include stress management techniques such as prioritizing, time management and adjusting one's expectations (for example reducing the standard of housekeeping one sees as appropriate). It can also involve assertiveness training as a means of politely but firmly warding off too numerous and/or incompatible demands on the person's already taxed time and energy.

Flexible working patterns

One potential measure here is flexitime, which is relatively common. The amount of flexibility varies quite a lot according to the specific scheme in operation. The general idea is that a person has some discretion over the timing and/or duration of his or her working day. Often this is within quite tight limits such as core times when everyone must be present and latest and earliest starting and finishing times. However, in principle it can be much broader, even extending to a prescribed total annual hours with wide discretion about how it is distributed. The amount and type of flexibility offered depend partly upon organizational cultures and managers' assumptions about human nature, and also of course on the labour needs of the organization. This latter factor seems rather neglected in some discussions of work and family issues. After all, in an increasingly competitive and customer-responsive business environment, the first requirement is to meet customer demands. These may not be compatible with highly flexible work patterns. That said, some employers are no doubt inclined to overestimate the constraints and thus fail to introduce flexibility that could be appropriate.

Various forms of part-time working are also a possible solution. One example is term-time contracts. A person (yet again, usually a woman) is employed during school terms only. This on its own does not recognize the important truth that school hours and 'normal' working hours do not match. Indeed, in some ways child-care becomes more difficult once the child is at school. So along with term-time working, work hours are often geared to the school day, with the person working, for example, from 9 to 3. More generally, as we saw in Chapter 2, part-time work is on the increase, but much of it is mundane and low-paid. Such work is no kind of solution for people accustomed to work requiring high skill and responsibility. Some employers, though not many, therefore offer carefully constructed opportunities for part-time workers. The UK's National Health Service, for example, has provided a part-time route for some medics.

Another form of part-time work is job sharing. Some job advertisements specifically state that a job-share will be considered, though in practice recruiters take some convincing that the job-sharers will be able and willing to ensure that their efforts complement one another. A further form of flexible working is teleworking. There are over twice as many women teleworkers in the UK than men (Labour Force Survey, 1994), and most teleworkers are in professional and managerial levels of work, not manual. Working at or from home is becoming more common (see Chapter 2) and after some initial start-up costs can be quite a cheap option for employers. In itself it does not eliminate a need for child-care, since one key factor in the success of teleworking is the worker's willingness to shut him- or herself off from interruptions. Nevertheless, particularly if children are at school, it may enable a parent to fit work and home duties more easily than if he or she were based at the employer's premises. Again, the nature of many people's work does not easily allow teleworking, so this solution may be strictly limited. But working at home on days when a child is sick (to the extent that working is possible) should probably be permitted more often than it is.

Fostering a family-friendly culture

Widespread use of the provisions described above probably both reflects and encourages organizational and national cultures supportive of compatibility between work and home lives. Some of the provisions such as teleworking and also special leave (see below) may also require an atmosphere of trust where line managers are confident that the opportunities will not be abused. In the US, Johnson and Johnson are well known for facilitating flexible working, and evaluative work by the Families and Work Institute (1993) showed that between 1990, when the initiatives were introduced, and

1992 supervisors became more supportive. The proportion of employees saying they paid a price for using the initiatives decreased from 44% to 32%.

Some concerted initiatives have been launched in the UK to try to get things going. Opportunity 2000 is a campaign organized by Business in the Community which aims to promote the successful implementation of equal opportunities policies in organizations. It is difficult to disentangle cause and effect, but organizations participating in Opportunity 2000 (they cover about a quarter of the UK work-force) have much better representation of women at senior levels than other organizations (Opportunity 2000, 1994).

Another initiative is called Parents at Work, which has more than 300 corporate members, and membership is growing. Through the 1990s Parents at Work has made annual awards to organizations which do most to reconcile work and family life. A 1995 winner was the North British Housing Association, which has offered enhanced maternity benefits for 11 years, and paternity leave and other family leave arrangements for six (Crabb, 1995). Maternity leave is available for 44 weeks, 11 weeks before the birth and 33 after. Full salary is paid for the first 12 weeks, and then half pay plus statutory maternity pay for another 6. Five days' paternity leave is available, and so is unpaid special family leave for the care of dependent relatives. Child-care vouchers are available to both men and women employees, up to a total of about £90 a month – more if late working is required. There are about 50 job-sharers, including five men.

Wakefield Council is another UK organization in the vanguard of family-friendly policies (Bigwood, 1996). The council surveyed its employees' needs in 1992 and found that they most valued flexibility to cope when regular arrangements fell through. Flexitime, job sharing, maternity and paternity leave, career breaks and time off for religious festivals had been available since the late 1980s. In response to the survey, up to 15 days per year paid short-term leave was introduced. A maximum of five days at a time are allowed. The leave is in addition to holiday entitlement, but managers may take uncommitted holiday entitlement into account when considering a request for paid short-term leave. Also available are unpaid longer-term leave, term-time working and temporary negotiated hours (for up to 12 months, without any change to the employee's contract). A total of 112 employees made use of these options during their first year of operation, and most of these took paid short-term leave. The total cost was just £18,000, or £1.20 per employee, and that did not take into account savings from reduced salary payments. On the same theme, Hammond and Holton (1991) have reported that a major UK bank's costs of providing child-care were exceeded by the savings on recruitment and training of new staff.

Evaluation work in the US has also shown that the benefits of family-friendly policies probably exceed the costs. For example, Bond (1987) found that women working in the most family-friendly companies reported higher job satisfaction, less sick leave and greater likelihood of returning to work after childbirth. Galinsky and Stein (1990) concluded that the most consistent benefit of family-friendly policies is enhanced employee retention. On the other hand, D. Schwartz (1996) has pointed out that the impact upon longer-term career prospects of using family-friendly initiatives is unknown at present. Certainly there is some anecdotal evidence that users are viewed as not serious about their career, though Schwartz also noted that people who had used the initiatives were less fearful on this score than those who had not.

The future

As is the case with several other career management interventions (see Chapters 4 and 5), some current trends in careers encourage the use of family-friendly interventions whilst others might do the opposite. There is no doubt that the increasing participation of women in the work-force, together with the need to utilize available talent, will serve to increase the pressure on organizations to facilitate compatibility between work and family. If staff really are seen as the organization's competitive edge, then well-chosen family-friendly policies are an essential part of HR strategy to recruit and retain good performers. The increasing availability and sophistication of communications technology and the growing incidence of project work and portfolio careers tend to increase opportunities for flexible work patterns.

On the other hand, some provisions in this area such as career breaks and job sharing may pay off for an organization only if the people concerned remain members for a reasonably long time. Even though Wakefield Council found that the costs of family-friendly policies were low, this might not always be the case. If cost-cutting remains a high priority in many organizations, it must be tempting to discourage employees from demanding childcare and other provision, and to avoid hiring people who are likely to do so.

On balance, though, a steady extension and expansion of flexible forms of working can be expected. The demand from potential employees is increasingly evident, and so is public recognition for employers who make better than average provision. But future government policies on matters such as parental leave will also be significant. They *may* herald further blurring of the boundaries between gender roles. Progress will be fastest if and when men take up the issues in earnest.

WOMEN'S CAREER SUCCESS

We have already noted that women's participation in the work-force is increasing (see Chapter 2). For example, in the UK, women's employment rose 16% between 1984 and 1993 whilst men's employment remained static. Over approximately the same period, the proportion of UK mothers with children over 16 who were economically active increased from 55% to 64% (Davidson, 1996). Yet, as noted in an earlier section of this chapter, women's representation at higher levels of organizational and occupational hierarchies is much smaller than that at lower levels. Some of the ways in which the odds are stacked against women have already been described in this chapter and in earlier ones. To recap briefly:

(1) Because women tend to have greater involvement in, and responsibility for,

child-care, they tend to be seen by men as less committed to their careers.

(2) On average, women tend to have less self-belief than men, particularly about their ability to perform in occupations dominated by the opposite sex.

(3) Women are more likely than men to interrupt their careers, and this reduces the amount of relevant work experience they can offer. It may also increase the risk of their skills being out of date.

(4) It is well documented that women are paid less on average than men (Rubery, Fagan and Grimshaw, 1994). On the face of it this might make them more attractive to employers, but within dual-career couples their earnings are lower than the man's, whose career therefore takes priority.

(5) Women may have different definitions of success and different life concerns from men (see Chapters 6 and 7). Particularly in early adulthood, women may be concerned with connectedness and interdependence with other people, whilst men focus on achievement and independence – concepts which more closely reflect the usual definitions of career success (Powell and Mainiero, 1992). On a similar theme, women's interpersonal styles may on average be more co-operative and less assertive than men's – again men's style is seen as more appropriate for career success.

(6) Women tend to have less access to influential informal networks than men (see also Chapter 5).

(7) Women's achievements may be rated less positively than men's, and their successes seen as less to do with their ability.

Some research suggests that even after all legitimate or potentially legitimate reasons for men's success being greater than women's are taken into account, there is still some residual difference that can only be attributed to straightforward discrimination. An example is Stroh, Brett and Reilly (1992). They studied over a thousand male and female managers in leading US companies. They were chosen for participation in the research if they had relocated in 1987/8, so it cannot be said that the women were not prepared to move with their company for success. The researchers found that the women's salary increases between 1984 and 1989 (though not their rate of promotion) lagged behind the men's, even after the following trends within the sample were taken into account:

(1) women's lower education and training;

(2) women's longer spells out of employment;

(3) women's income being lower than their partners';

(4) women's tendency to work in lower paid industries than men.

Research along similar lines by Schneer and Reitman (1995) tells a similar story. They studied a sample of nearly 700 MBA graduates up to 18 years post-MBA. The women earned on average 19% less than men, and only a small part of this could be explained by possibly legitimate factors such as years of post-MBA work experience and number of hours worked per week. But as the authors noted, even these factors might be considered a product of gender stereotypes and discrimination. For example, women might have worked less hours per week because of their disproportionate share of household work.

Earlier research with another sample of MBA graduates by the same authors (Schneer and Reitman, 1993) bore out the well-established findings that men's career progression is enhanced by having a non-employed partner. But to their surprise, single women earned less than women with partners but no children. Less surprising, the earnings of women with partners and children were lower on average than of those with partners but no children. Other research has also shown that, whereas for men having a partner and family is broadly supportive of their careers, the reverse tends to be the case for women. Successful women are much less likely to be married and/or have children than are successful men (Nicholson and West, 1988).

Overall it seems that our understanding of the determinants of women's career success is much more limited than of those of men's success. For example, in a study of 513 women and 501 men managers in Australian organizations, Tharenou, Latimer and Conroy (1994) found that the amount of training and development experienced influenced the men's career advancement (in terms of level in the organizational hierarchy) much more than the women's. The same was true for work experience and level of education. Also, level of education influenced how much training and development men received, but not how much women received. Duties in the home had a significant but small negative impact on women's advancement, though the authors pointed out that this sample of women was highly self-selected, and in the population as a whole the impact would probably be bigger. The women also seemed to be more reliant upon career encouragement than the men. Overall, these findings and others suggest that most occupational environments are more conducive to men's success than women's. Within such environments, men's success has a lot to do with their individual characteristics. But women are more reliant upon situational factors such as someone to encourage them or their home circumstances. This is not an inherent characteristic of women, but a consequence of the way the world currently works.

In the present and future things may even out a bit. Factors like promotions, organizational levels attained and salary are becoming less viable as criteria of career success as delayered structures, project teams and short-term contracts become more common. More personal criteria such as employability and career satisfaction may be becoming more useful, and men's career patterns are shifting more towards the rather fragmented patterns more commonly experienced by women. The labour market in the early part of the 21st century may well be a much more level playing field in this respect than ever before.

UNEMPLOYMENT

In many countries one prominent consequence of global competition has been an increase in the number of people who experience one or more spells of involuntary unemployment. Although unemployment rates vary with the economic cycle, underlying trends have been upward in the last twenty years of the 20th century. In OECD countries the mean unemployment rate rose from under 6% in 1980 to over 8% three years later, back down to just over 6% in 1990 and then up again to nearly 10% in 1993 (Winefield, 1995). Of course, even a rate of 6% represents a relatively common experience, especially if movement into and out of employment is fluid, which would mean that the 6% of the labour force who are unemployed tend to be different people month by month. Even during a period of relatively rapid economic growth, 4.3 million people in the United States lost their jobs between 1985 and 1989 (Herz, 1991, cited in Latack, Kinicki and Prussia, 1995).

An enormous volume of research has shown that unemployment is normally associated with relatively poor mental and physical health, life satisfaction, self-esteem and many other variables (for reviews, see Feather, 1990; Winefield, 1995). As Latack, Kinicki and Prussia (1995, p. 312) have put it: 'Despite moderating factors, the impact of job loss is generally detrimental to individuals by virtually any criteria a researcher chooses to examine.' Having said that, it probably isn't all one-way traffic. There is also some evidence that people who experience unemployment tend to have poorer mental health even before unemployment occurs (Dooley, Catalano and Hough, 1992; Arnold, 1994). This might be for a variety of reasons. A relatively low sense of well-being may sometimes manifest itself in a rather distracted approach to work (making being chosen for redundancy more likely) and perhaps sub-optimal job-search strategies (thus prolonging duration of unemployment).

Although it is helpful to remind certain politicians and others that unemployment is not a joy-ride, the available evidence does not conclusively show *why* it is typically an unpleasant experience. Following on from pioneering work in the 1930s, Jahoda (1982) has suggested that employment has certain 'latent' functions as well as the 'manifest' one of providing an income. These latent functions include the imposition of activity, time structure, goals and purposes on the day and the opportunity for regular social contact and social status outside the family. This analysis implies that any job is better than no job, but there is mounting research evidence that this is not the case – some jobs are no more pleasant than being unemployed (e.g. Schaufeli and Van Yperen, 1992). Also, many of the latent functions of employment may actually be damaging at high levels. For example, the level of social contact may be so great that it makes a person irritated, disorientated, overloaded or distracted (Warr, 1987).

Fryer (1986) has forcefully argued that the latent functions of employment do not necessarily assist people to achieve goals that matter to them. That is why some jobs do not seem to foster well-being even though they provide some time structure, social contact and the other latent functions of employment. Fryer's approach may help to explain why some researchers have found it difficult to identify any specific factor other than reduced income which makes unemployment an unpleasant experience (Kessler, Turner and House, 1987). In most societies a low income not only reduces the comfort in which people live, it also makes it more difficult to resource the achievement of personal goals in any realm of life. This is most obviously so if one's personal goals involve the accumulation of substantial wealth, possessions and status, but equally true for more modest materialistic goals, and also those concerning other pursuits such as leisure or service.

The lack of psychological and material resources of many unemployed people clearly threatens their careers in significant ways. It is therefore not surprising that few people make a transition from unemployment to self-employment, and a disproportionate number of those who do so then experience business failure (C. Gray, 1989; see also next section of this chapter). Nevertheless, it can be done. Imaginative financial supports and the availability of entrepreneurial advice can play a key role in helping people from unemployment. For example, an outfit operating in north-east England called Initiative Management (IM) selects long-term unemployed people who seem suitably motivated for self-employment (*Sunday Times*, 3 November 1996). By arrangement with the Department of Social Security, the newly self-employed keep their entitlement to benefits while the business starts up. They can call upon modest financial resources and advice on how to run their business from IM staff.

There is some evidence that mental health and well-being during unemployment can be improved by certain psychological techniques which focus on changing a person's beliefs about the likely causes and consequences of unemployment. For example, Saam, Wodtke and Hains (1995) examined the impact of what they referred to as a cognitive stress reduction programme, and found that this reduced unemployed managers' anxiety and anger more than the receipt of less structured counselling. It was also associated with quicker re-employment. This suggests that outplacement programmes at least have the potential to have a positive impact on redundant people (see Chapter 4 for further discussion of outplacement).

Bennett *et al.* (1995) followed earlier writers in distinguishing between problem-focused coping and symptom-focused coping. The former involves attempts to eliminate the cause of stress, and the latter concerns attempts to decrease the amount of stress experienced. The distinction seems clear conceptually, but becomes cloudy when applied to unemployment. Bennett *et al.* classified job-search activity and considering relocation as problem-focused strategies, whilst seeking financial assistance and engaging in community activism were regarded as symptom-based. In a sense, community activism might be seen as problem-focused, since at least some forms of such activism are directed at changing public and/or corporate policies on employment. Job-search activity might be seen as problem-focused for the individual but not for society more generally. Bennett *et al.* found that, contrary to their prediction, unemployed people who perceived that the procedures adopted by their ex-employer were fair and that (US) government assistance programmes were adequate, were *less* likely than others to use problem-focused strategies. People who blamed themselves for being made redundant were more likely than others to engage in community activism. The authors noted that their findings contradicted much of the literature on stress and coping, and also suggested that the content of government and corporate programmes for un-employed and about-to-be unemployed people should be reviewed since they seemed not to encourage job-seeking.

Eby and Buch (1995) studied 456 men and 59 women in the United States who were asked to look back on a period of unemployment after they had been re-employed, and evaluate the extent to which, with hindsight, the gains of having been unemployed outweighed the losses. On the whole they did, and most of the sample reported that family and friends had been supportive. For the women, having a family whose members were suffi-ciently flexible to change roles and behaviours to cope with their unemploy-ment and an (eventual) positive financial impact of being forced to find a new job were the most powerful helps, whilst for men the key factors were financial impact, being able to accept the job loss emotionally and remaining active after it happened. These findings neatly show how money, self and family all contribute to the career impact of unemployment.

But of course there is a dilemma here. Enabling people to cope better at a personal level with unemployment may also tend to reduce the probability that they will challenge the policies and conditions that led to their unem-ployment. Helping individuals to deal with unpleasant situations does not usually reduce the probability of those situations recurring – rather the opposite in fact. Also, training of unemployed people in job-related skills assumes that the labour market has the capacity to absorb at least some of them. This assumption has been challenged (Dooley and Catalano, 1988).

The increasing prevalence of unemployment is one reason for ceasing to treat it as an abnormal event, as it has been in the past. It is important that, whilst unemployed, people have the resources necessary to maintain or enhance their employability if that is a realistic strategy. Whether or not it is realistic depends on their attributes, the state of the labour market and government policies (if any) for creating employment. There are big choices to be made at societal levels about whether or not employment (sporadic or continuous) for all is to be a goal (Watts, 1987). This issue goes beyond the scope of this book, but obviously has high relevance to what careers people experience. If employment is not to be for everyone, alternative lifestyles need to be identified and resourced. If it *is* to be for everyone, unemploy-ment in the 21st century must be a potential source of career growth, not just a downward spiral into poverty and low self-confidence. Development of job-search skills, job-search facilities, support for community and occupa-tional networking, opportunities for training and retraining, psychological assistance to retain self-belief and an income which permits all this and an adequate (if modest) lifestyle are required here.

ENTREPRENEURSHIP AND SELF-EMPLOYMENT

Many people are entrepreneurs at some point in their working lives, though fewer sustain that role for long periods. However, there isn't complete con-sensus about what entrepreneurship is (Churchill and Lewis, 1986). For some it is characterized by risk-taking. Others think of it as concerning innovation of a new product or service. Others again view ownership of the enterprise as the defining feature.

Self-employment is clearly one element of entrepreneurship, and is often equated with it for practical purposes. As we saw in Chapter 2, self-employment has been on the increase. But it does not necessarily involve the innovation or perhaps even the risk-taking inherent in some definitions of entrepreneurship. As C. Gray (1989, p. 6) put it: 'very few self-employed or small business managers are truly entrepreneurial. An entrepreneur is always an innovator – whether of product, process, organization or marketing – but few small businesses and even fewer self-employed can claim to be genuinely innovative.' Further, a person can be self-employed or an entrepreneur in one job, and simultaneously an employee in another. Indeed, in the USA about 20% of self-employed people also have a waged or salaried job. Given the short life of many small businesses (see Chapter 2) this is probably a wise strategy.

Whatever the exact definition of entrepreneurship, considerable efforts have been made to identify the personal characteristics and backgrounds of entrepreneurs and whether these differ from those of non-entrepreneurial workers. In many cases the evidence is rather mixed and inconclusive (Cromie, 1987). As has been pointed out, almost by definition, entrepreneurs are an idiosyncratic bunch about whom it is difficult to generalize. For example, it is sometimes hypothesized that entrepreneurs will have a greater risk-taking propensity than other people. In a sense this is the case, but there is also some indication that entrepreneurs have sufficient belief in themselves to perceive that they are not really taking risks. Entrepreneurs are significantly more likely than other people to be first-born children in business-owning families. Some entrepreneurs turn their hobby into their work when they start their own enterprise, and some are motivated by dissatisfaction with their earlier work, but in both cases it is very important that the potential entrepreneur assesses whether there really will be a market for his or her product or service. On its own, a desire to escape from something else is a dangerous reason for moving to self-employment.

Hyatt (1992) has spelt out the questions a potential entrepreneur should ask. These include:

(1) Do I have the required management skills?
(2) How will my family react?
(3) How much money do I need?
(4) Are my business ideas viable?

Like anyone, entrepreneurs need to establish career goals and make clear decisions. The processes are no different from those for other people. Some psychometric tests and interest inventories (see Chapter 6) provide a measure of a person's suitability for entrepreneurial work, so some guidance is available.

Tolerance for ambiguity is one aspect of personality that does distinguish between entrepreneurs and others, with entrepreneurs having higher tolerance on average. They also score higher on desires for autonomy and independence. However, as implied earlier, this is not the only element of entrepreneurship. Katz (1994) has pointed out that there may be at least two 'breeds' of entrepreneur: those who want to be autonomous, and those who want to be creative. Schein (1985a) reported that, in terms of his career anchors (see Chapter 7), 8% of his sample of Massachusetts Institute of Technology business graduates had an entrepreneurial anchor (i.e. creative) whilst 11% had an autonomy anchor, which suggests that both are relatively rare and approximately equally so. Katz suggested that the work histories of these two groups might look quite different. The 'true' entrepreneurs are more likely than the autonomy-seekers to enjoy increases in status, to head up firms which grow substantially in terms of turnover and employees, and to own multiple firms simultaneously. Certain entrepreneurs of this kind are quite unusual people, suggesting that at least some entrepreneurs are distinctive in important ways from an early age. Consider the following from the *Sunday Times* of 7 January 1996:

> With his 19th birthday barely behind him, Lars Windhorst now runs a business empire with a turnover of more than £80m a year. . . . Aged eight he was trying to market a liquid toothpaste he had invented. In his early teens he was spending pocket money on shares rather than sweets. . . . 'I consider myself quite normal' he said. 'Some people my age have a fantastic feel for the tennis ball. I just have a particularly good instinct for business.'

Whether or not Herr Windhorst continues to be successful is more or less beside the point. He has made it in a big way and at a very early age through a whole series of business successes, not just one lucky break.

There is some evidence that women and men entrepreneurs are pretty similar in terms of psychological characteristics. However, women seem more likely than men to be driven to entrepreneurship by dissatisfaction with some features of corporate life, and more likely to use entrepreneurship as a part-time and/or family-friendly way of earning a living (Kaplan, 1988). But again it is hard to generalize. A sample of sixty Australian women entrepreneurs investigated by Langan-Fox and Roth (1995) fell into three distinct groups:

(1) Managerial entrepreneurs. These women exhibited moderate levels of need for achievement, but were high on needs for influence and power, and in resistance to subordination. As an aside, Furnham (1992) among others has argued that influencing skills are essential to continued success as an entrepreneur.
(2) Pragmatists. This group consisted of women who were entrepreneurs for practical reasons such as the work fitting family demands.
(3) Need for achievers. These women wanted to achieve results they could measure by taking on personal challenges that were difficult but not impossible.

Not all entrepreneurs and self-employed people are in that position by choice. Some are 'refugees' who are trying to make a living after redundancy, and would take a waged or salaried position if one was available (Hakim, 1988). For example, Granger, Stanworth and Stanworth (1995) studied 371 freelance home-based teleworkers in the UK book publishing industry, nearly all of whom had previously been in conventional employment. They found that close to half their respondents were 'refugees'. Less than 20% had chosen to quit an employed position in favour of their self-employed one. But just over a quarter were converts who had not entered self-employment willingly, but who were now convinced of its merits, because of the independence and control it offered. Even though none of these people were in businesses involving anyone else, some had, as Granger, Stanworth and Stanworth put it, learned to talk the language of enterprise. They referred to the excitement of managing their own business and taking on new projects.

The proportion of people who are self-employed or entrepreneurs is likely to increase as the 21st century unfolds, partly through choice and partly because of the opportunities presented by the labour market. There are clear needs for education and training in forming and managing small businesses, and to a large extent the education systems of Western countries have responded to this need in recent years. Formal and informal support networks are needed because self-employed and entrepreneurial people are often relatively isolated. Some such networks already exist. But, perhaps most of all, it should be realized that many self-employed and entrepreneurial people are only in those roles for quite a short time. They are not on the whole a breed apart from other people, though as noted earlier, some are clearly different from most of their peers from quite an early age.

CAREERS OF TECHNICAL SPECIALISTS

People who have training in specific areas of expertise often experience careers where the expectations, demands and opportunities presented by employing organizations on the one hand and professional bodies on the other are quite different from each other. A common argument is that there is a conflict between professional and organizational demands which makes it difficult or impossible to honour both in one's career. This general idea was expressed long ago by Gouldner (1957) in his distinction between locals (those who identify with the employing organization) and cosmopolitans, whose primary allegiance is to some body or cause outside the organization. More recent research suggests that conflicts of loyalty may be the exception rather than the rule. For example, Wallace (1993) found that commitment (see Chapter 8 for more on commitment) to profession and to organization tended to go together. That is, specialists who reported a sense of commitment to one tended also to be committed to the other. Nevertheless, managing the careers of specialists such as scientists, engineers, medics and allied professionals does have its own special complications, both for those people themselves and for others attempting to manage them.

In Chapter 7 we looked in some depth at developmental approaches to careers. Dalton, Thompson and Price's (1977) model of careers of professionals in organizations could be considered one such, but is placed here because of its specific relevance to the concerns of this chapter. Dalton, Thompson and Price conducted a detailed study of 550 professionals working in organizations in the USA. They identified four distinct career stages of specialist careers:

(1) *Apprenticeship.* At this stage the person works under the supervision of a more senior professional on part of a project. He or she is not responsible for the project as a whole. Instead, he or she carries out the detailed and routine work.
(2) *Independence.* People at this stage are considered expert in one or more areas of work. They are responsible for projects or significant parts of them, and work independently of a supervisor. They gain a reputation amongst other professionals for their work.
(3) *Mentoring.* Specialists at this stage work in more than one area of expertise, and/or on more than one project. They develop a breadth of skills and also knowledge of how to apply them. They deal with other organizations on colleagues' behalf and they help other more junior specialists to develop.
(4) *Strategic.* Specialists at this stage influence organizational decisions and directions, and provide strategic insights. They have considerable power and may also be involved in sponsoring promising individuals.

It might seem reasonable to expect a strong tendency for specialists at the later stages to be considerably older than those at the earlier stages. In fact this was not the case – average ages did increase with stages but only from about 39 to 42. What was more, a specialist's job title in the organization did not necessarily faithfully reflect his or her stage. Noting that there is a breakpoint from a specialist into a more general managerial role between stages 2 and 3, Dalton (1989, p. 98) observed that:

> in several of the organizations studied, more than half of those described as being in Stage III held no formal supervisory or management positions. In a number of high-technology organizations, the investigators even found a number of individuals who were described as being in Stage IV who had no management or supervisory positions.

Nevertheless, there was a tendency for the work of specialists at the later stages to be more highly valued than that of those at the earlier stages. In effect by the time they reach stage 4 (and to a lesser extent stage 3) they are more like general managers than specialists. Many professionals never progress beyond stage 2. Indeed, many do not wish to, particularly if they have in Schein's terms a technical–functional career anchor (see Chapter 7) in which professional reputation and development of specialist skills are valued above all else. Whilst there may be a distinction to be made between those who choose to remain a specialist and those who remain so because they are not considered suitable for anything else (Mainiero, 1986), the major dichotomy is normally thought of as being between those who remain technical specialists and those who become managerial generalists. Some organizations have dealt with this by offering a separate career ladder for specialists, so that those who wish to remain specialists can do so without sacrificing promotion opportunities. There are, however, some problems with this. As already noted, the contribution to the organization of specialists operating at the later stages of Dalton, Thompson and Price's (1977) model is generally seen as being greater than that of those at earlier stages. This creates difficulties if a specialist career ladder is to go as high as a general managerial one. Yet if it does not go that high, it may not be attractive to the specialists. Also, it is not clear whether it is even possible let alone desirable to keep specialist work sufficiently distinct from managerial work to justify a separate career ladder.

On the other hand it could be argued that having a specialist career ladder helps to avoid the unpleasant situation for individuals of having to drop their specialism in favour of general managerial work. Badawy (1988) has asserted that many specialists exhibit poor interpersonal skills and have difficulty delegating and making decisions in the absence of complete information, so perhaps the consequence of such individuals being promoted to managerial roles will be unpleasant for the employing organization too! Whilst Badawy's view might be seen as encouraging stereotypes of specialists, concern about the transferable personal skills of, for example, engineers is quite widespread, and various attempts have been made to deal with this, including via education (Keenan, 1994). A longitudinal study of one organization by Roberts and Biddle (1994) has, however, suggested that technical and managerial aptitudes are more similar than often thought. They found that the better technical performers were at least as good at managerial jobs as the less good technical performers. Also, partly because of good training opportunities, the most able technical workers did not on the whole leave the organization when they reached the top of the technical career track.

All this prompts some wider questions. Should a specialist who is really so bad at managerial skills be allowed to remain so? Surely, it might be argued, there is no room for out-and-out boffins in these days of projects and teamwork. Even if there is, specialists might feel almost as alienated if they remain specialists in a managerially orientated organization as they would if they played the management game. In any case, there is considerable evidence from research on scientists (Pelz, 1988) that their best performance does not occur when they are able freely to do their own thing in a cocooned environment. Instead, their best work seems to be done when they are challenged by tensions such as balancing the demands of the real world and pure science, and maintaining their independence whilst also being influenced by others' opinions.

Roberts and Fusfeld (1988) have tried to go beyond the management vs. specialist dichotomy. They identified five crucial activities which must occur if an organization is to be innovative: (1) generating ideas; (2) championing an idea within the organization; (2) project leading; (4) collecting information from the environment; (5) sponsoring or coaching others. The roles do not fit precisely into either specialist or managerial job descriptions. (3) and (5) are characteristics of Dalton, Thompson and Price's (1977) later stages, but are not logically confined to them, even if that occurred in practice at the work-sites investigated by Dalton, Thompson and Price. So, people can develop their skills within either specialist or general managerial work by broadening and deepening their contribution to the five activities. Perhaps this a much more rounded way of viewing specialist careers than a simple specialist vs. manager distinction.

SUMMARY

Work-forces in most Western countries are becoming more diverse in terms of ethnicity, gender, family circumstances and lifestyle. There is a move afoot to embrace diversity in these and other respects such as age and disability. The case for this is typically made in terms of business benefits as well as fairness. Managing diversity means recognizing, valuing and utilizing individual differences of all kinds. It needs awareness of what these differences are and skill in managing them, since most of us are inclined to think that different from ourselves is also less good than ourselves. At their best, diversity initiatives maximize the chances of all employees to fulfil their potential and develop through their work. One aspect of diversity is a more equal numerical balance between the sexes in the work-place, and in turn this means increasing prevalence of dual-career couples. In most couples the man's career tends to take priority and the woman performs the bulk of the housework and child-care. Demands upon and difficulties for members of dual-career couples are often quite intense (particularly if they have children), but can be eased by a variety of flexible working arrangements. It is also arguable that these arrangements lead to better work performance, and that their benefits to the employer exceed their costs. The literature on career success does suggest that women are still at a disadvantage compared with men. However, the increasingly fragmented nature of careers may be evening things out, not least because women are more accustomed to such careers than men are. Other aspects of diversity in careers include more common experience of self-employment, entrepreneurship and spells of unemployment. Skills and resources for coping with all three of these seem to be underdeveloped in many countries, and they need to be seen as more normal events. Even so, the number of people in Western countries with an entrepreneurial career orientation may be quite small, and some self-employed people are not that way by choice. Technical specialists also face career transitions that may cause them difficulty, particularly the one from predominantly specialist to predominantly managerial work.

POSTSCRIPT

The words of Hall and Mirvis (1995b) sum up the position taken in this book: Careers are dead; long live careers! In other words, orderly, predictable upwardly mobile careers are dead, but careers in a wider sense are alive and kicking. In fact they are kicking hard, prompting employing and other organizations, individuals and governments to think afresh about exactly what to do with them.

At the widest level there are important choices to be made about how to maintain social cohesion. Work is becoming harder to find and increasingly dominated by those who have marketable skills. Education and training provision in many countries needs to expand and improve in order to meet the changing skill requirements of work. But that provision can pay off only if there is a pervasive culture supporting lifelong learning. In the absence of such a culture, and in the absence of a willingness to share work around, and perhaps to pay for previously unpaid work such as child-rearing, any society is likely to develop a deprived underclass, with serious implications for social justice and public order.

EDUCATION AND CAREER GUIDANCE

Education, whether compulsory or post-compulsory, should incorporate two particularly career-relevant features. These are already often evident, though some (e.g. Confederation of British Industry, 1989) would argue not evident enough due partly to the historical role of education as a brake on child labour and therefore separate from employment. The first feature is the application of what is being learned to the world of work. Young people, and indeed older ones, can benefit from being shown how classroom learning can be utilized at work. The most obvious ways of doing this are through examples and exercises based on work-place issues, and work experience built into education (though in the latter case it is often the experience of working *per se* that is most valued by students: the links between work and education are sometimes difficult for them to discern). Employers have an obvious role to play here if they want to do more than lament the sorry state of education, and many have engaged wholeheartedly in partnerships with education. The second feature of career-relevant education is a combination of learning how to learn and valuing learning for its own sake. Insights into one's preferred styles of learning, reflection on the learning process, and training in how to go about learning are all involved here. In one sense these activities represent a respite from the relentless vocationalism implied earlier in this paragraph. But in another sense they are the most vocational of all in rapidly changing work environments. Taken as a whole, career-friendly education means the integration of careers education into the curriculum as a whole, and may also mean some changes in teacher-training, particularly towards familiarity with a wider range of occupations.

The provision of affordable careers guidance services for people of all ages, either directly by public services or indirectly through private providers, is another way in which governments may choose to contribute to an appropriate infrastructure for managing careers. This would recognize the reality that significant decisions and changes are required right through adulthood, and that many people simply do not currently have the skills or other personal resources to handle this. It can be argued that careers guidance providers need to be impartial in the sense that they do not have a vested interest in the decisions and subsequent actions taken by individual clients (Watts, 1996). Governments may have well-founded aims, for example, to improve citizens' familiarity with information technology or to improve skills of entrepreneurship and small business management. It would be appropriate for careers guidance providers to point this out to clients. However, decisions and action plans about careers should be owned by individuals. This suggests that careers guidance providers should not be funded on the basis of, for example, the proportion of clients who embark upon a particular kind of training. This would encourage the providers to steer clients toward certain conclusions thus jeopardizing their sense of independence and ownership: 'They sent me on a training course because everyone has to do it' is not the kind of perception needed for career management in the 21st century.

INFORMATION TECHNOLOGY

Continuing technological change is likely to play a pervasive part in 21st-century career management. Although some have argued that the major technological changes wrought by the microchip have already happened, others take a different view. Van der Spiegel (1995) has stated that the information revolution is still in its infancy. The capacity and sophistication of integrated circuits continue to increase. The differences in computing power between PCs and mainframes are dwindling. In the future computers are likely to become ever more portable and with wider bandwidth, so that multiple functions such as phone, fax, computer, video-conference and email are all available on one machine. Some tasks such as vision, speech and natural language processing currently remain very difficult for computers, and although the neurons in human brains operate slowly compared with microchips, future computers are likely to mimic biological structures in important ways. In particular, the brain processes information from a variety of sources (the senses) and stores it in highly distributed fashion using the multiplicity of connections between neurons. Eventually we can expect computers which can process speech, learn, adapt, guess, and deal with ill-defined problems.

It is vital that people are able to afford and use technology. This does *not* mean that each of us must be well versed in the most up-to-date hardware and software. That is too much to ask. Instead, we need to be familiar with the potential and general principles of operation of the latest generation of technology. We need to be able to use the parts most relevant to us and, most important, be able and unafraid to learn new applications when required. The declining cost of information technology and some of the trends described in the previous paragraph may help to make it more accessible to more people. But this must not be assumed. Opportunities to become familiar with technology at low cost must always be available.

Information technology is highly relevant to career management as well as the narrower range of skills required to do a particular job. The opportunities for self-presentation via electronic media are becoming ever wider, and it is becoming ever more necessary to use them if one wants to be taken seriously by potential employers and other contacts. Career management by individuals can therefore include activities such as setting up one's own worldwide web page, searching the internet for information and contacts, and participating in electronic mailing and discussion groups relevant to one's career. Another activity is the preparation and revision of a curriculum vitae (CV; also known as a résumé) to meet specifications set by, for example, employers who use scanning packages which require certain information to appear in certain positions on the CV. Computer packages for aiding career exploration and decision-making are of course already available (see Chapter 6). There is much scope for them to become more sophisticated. Multimedia packages can offer individuals considerable insight into what various occupations are like. In the future virtual reality technology may take that process a stage further – though whether it will be economic to create virtual reality simulations of occupations is not at all clear.

But it is unlikely that information technology will fully take over from more traditional methods of networking, job search and career exploration. Predictions about the impact of new technology often turn out to be exaggerated at both societal or organizational levels of analysis. I could look pretty stupid in twenty years' time, but I suspect that many employment opportunities in the 21st century will still be publicized by traditional methods of newspaper advertising, notices in windows and word of mouth. This will particularly but not solely be the case for work requiring local labour and relatively limited skills. It will be a long time before electronic communication, even of a visual kind, is routinely considered to be a complete replacement for physical presence particularly in non-routine interactions such as negotiations or job interviews. Nevertheless, things are certainly moving in that direction.

INDIVIDUALS

The previous section makes it clear that, for individuals managing their own 21st-century careers, effective use of information technology is at the very least useful and in some fields essential. But there are other important lessons for individuals too. The changing role of employers in career management (see especially Chapter 3) means that each of us must truly take responsibility for and the initiative in looking after our own careers. To some extent it was always thus of course. 'Cradle to grave' employment was always something of a myth, and the smart employee never waited for organizational human resource systems to deliver what he or she wanted. But the game has changed significantly, and many people are more on their own than has been the case in the past.

Some of the implications for what you or I should actually do to manage our careers have been described in earlier chapters. If we have an employer, we should take advantage of whatever is offered in terms of career management and use it to our advantage. Career workshops, career action centres, personal development plans and mentoring are examples. For mentoring in particular, it may be possible to create opportunities for ourselves even if they are not formally organized. As we saw in Chapter 5, mentoring seems to work best as an informal relationship rather than as part of an organized scheme. Supports for career management may also come from elsewhere, such as professional associations, community groups, local careers services and libraries. It is important to be aware of what they can offer and take up Handy's (1994) advice, not to wait until we are reaching the point of dire need before we take advantage of them.

Decisions (if we have that luxury) about what work opportunities to take up should be made in strategic fashion. It is not only what we feel comfortable with right now that matters. It is also what skills and experiences we need in order to remain employable in fields that appeal to us, and what patterns of working best fit our chosen or enforced lifestyle. All this requires a perceptive appreciation of current and future labour market trends, and of our own characteristics including which we value most and which we can compromise on. External indicators of career success will be more elusive, so again we must know what matters to us and what we regard as constituting satisfactory achievement.

Work has of course always had implications for other arenas of a person's life – for example in terms of standard of living, the amount and distribution of leisure time available, and one's position in society. But now work and other roles are becoming more interpenetrated. For many people it is now difficult to earmark some blocks of time for work and other blocks for other activities. Technology has partly freed some work from restrictions of time and place. In turn this requires the skills and motivation for time management, and sensitive negotiation and agreement with significant others in our lives. Hage (1995) has pointed out that macroeconomic changes, shorter product cycles, changing work methods and enforced changes in the type of work a person does have all served to make life more complicated and relationships more superficial and short term, leading to more fragmented families. So for many of us, the day-to-day management of life and career involves more creative and co-operative problem-solving than in the past. It also requires us to understand and appreciate different possible ways of living because many examples are all around us. Increasingly, people seem to be feeling a need to establish or re-establish a personal morality now that the formerly small number of 'approved' lifestyles has grown. This is partly a recognition of the reality that children are profoundly affected by the nature and longevity of their relationships with adults.

Some of the skills required for effective management of one's career can be learned relatively easily, but many require a substantial shift in mindset. Telling a person that it would be a good idea to embrace the possibility of alternative lifestyles, or to be more flexible in terms of the types of work he or she can envisage doing, does not necessarily enable him or her to change, even if such a change is desired. This underscores the need for education to reflect the demands of 21st-century careers early in a child's life. As Hall and Mirvis (1995b) have put it, to earn a living a person must also learn a living. The increasing pace of change should also increase both the requirement and the reward for learning among older workers. The requirement reflects the need to stay employable. The potential reward derives from the likelihood that the best employers can hope for from skill development is relatively short-term advantage, so if other things are equal there is no added benefit in investing in a young person rather than an older one.

Other skills for individual career management concern the negotiation of mutual expectations with employers (see Chapter 3). Like some other career management skills, these are based on a good understanding of one's own compromisable and uncompromisable preferences as well as the strength or otherwise of one's labour market position.

One tension for many people is the need on the one hand to perform well in work right now, and on the other to seek ways in which to develop. Up to a point this can be resolved by taking on assignments that demand the development of new skills, thus killing two birds with one stone – so long as one's limitations in the early days and weeks in the job are not so great as to prevent satisfactory levels of performance. All in all though it is difficult to avoid the conclusion that career management and day-to-day work will tend to make greater demands on us in the 21st century than they did during most of the 20th. This is especially difficult for people to accept in societies which have enjoyed steadily increasing standards of living since the Second World War.

ORGANIZATIONS

We saw in Chapter 3 that employing organizations have tended to step back from managing the careers of employees, and that this could involve either an aggressive 'you're in it on your own' posture or a more supportive orientation with an emphasis on facilitating individuals' self-development efforts. It was also recognized that some employers are re-entering career management in recognition that an overly *laissez-faire* approach is unlikely to meet their human resource requirements. The career management interventions available to organizations are many and varied. They were analysed in several chapters, especially 4 and 5, so the details will not be repeated here.

Aside from the technical merits of the career management interventions they use in the 21st century, employing organizations can help to set a context which serves both their interests and those of their employees. It is easy to assume that this mutual benefit will automatically occur if intentions are good, but this is not the case. In particular, career management interventions must be designed to enhance people's long-term adaptability as well as short-term fit with their job. This includes the learning how to learn skills described earlier in this postscript, in the section on education. Perhaps the most sure-fire way to achieve this is to combine developmental work assignments with self-reflection aided perhaps by personal development planning, mentoring or career workshops. But this requires a strong organization-wide commitment to the value of learning. The commitment includes understanding that permissible costs of developmental assignments include some loss of performance (including perhaps the odd mistake), especially early in the assignment, and investment in support and perhaps training in key 'getting started' skills.

Another contextual issue concerns how much investment of identity employers demand of employees. Hage (1995) has noted that people tend these days to be conscious of the many aspects of their self-identity, and to carry this consciousness around with them rather than automatically suppressing some aspects when not in situations which immediately evoke them. This rather abstract point has practical consequences. It means that organizations are ill-advised to expect total commitment, as some do, or to establish cultures which are not only distinctive but which also intrude into employees' lives. Especially now most people realize that their employment is not necessarily secure, they will not in any case wish to invest their identity too exclusively in the realm of employment. For employers, the key is to manage employee behaviour more than attitudes and values. After all, ultimately employers want employees to *do* things, not simply believe them or feel positive about them. Further, analytical reflection rather than uncritical acceptance is a key contributor to employee flexibility as well as career management. Employers should therefore value a certain detachment, as opposed to alienation, from their staff.

We noted earlier that profound changes have been occurring in organizational structures (see especially Chapters 2 and 3). Delayering and downsizing have important implications for careers. More subtly, though, we also saw earlier that boundaries within and between organizations are breaking down. It is not always clear exactly who is a member of an organization. For example, how short term does a person's contract have to be for him or her to be merely a visitor rather than member? Is an individual on a two-year project-based contract a member of the organization? If you have regular work as a cleaner in a particular organization but are employed by another because cleaning has been outsourced, of which organization(s) are you a member? Joint ventures, mergers and more local events such as representatives of supplying companies working on projects within the companies they supply are other examples of the blurring of organizational boundaries.

Questions are therefore raised about exactly who is entitled to participate in an organization's career management interventions. In some cases the response is to treat everyone the same by opening up career management interventions (especially off-the-job ones) to all comers, and charging on a pay-as-you-use basis. Organizations may co-operate in the provision of some interventions such as career action centres. They may also open up career paths which cross the boundaries between them. This enhances opportunities for personal, and hence organizational, learning from new experiences. More employers are becoming sympathetic to the idea that staff may leave and later return – indeed some (e.g. Price Waterhouse) are said to treat departed staff as something akin to alumni. Organizations other than the employer may play a role in career management too. Some trade unions and professional associations provide career-related services to members, and this role may develop in certain cases into acting as an individual's agent in negotiations with a potential employer.

Some of the literature on career management seems more readily applicable to large organizations than to small ones. This is unfortunate in an era when small organizations are becoming more prevalent. References to career paths, career workshops, succession planning and development centres do tend to evoke images of large or at least medium-sized organizations. Other interventions, such as developmental assignments and mentoring, are perhaps more obviously applicable to small organizations, though even here opportunities to make them may be more haphazard and unpredictable than in large ones. Leaders of small organizations need to resist the temptation to shrug and conclude that career management is not for them. They can combine efforts and resources with other small organizations, and need to do so for the reasons described throughout this book.

The notion of organization as a loosely connected network of individuals is made more real by advances in communications technology which enable some people to work at home or in other places that are not the organization's premises. Career management interventions in such distributed organizations may serve even more diverse purposes than in other ones. They may bring people together for information and skills sharing that would not otherwise happen. They may cement working relationships that are normally conducted at a distance. They may help to acquaint individuals with career opportunities and the organization's present and future procedures and skill requirements. In short, the benefits of career management interventions for individual development and organizational competitiveness in 'distributed' organizations may be that much greater than in more situated outfits. This is the case even though interventions may seem a less natural activity, and require more arranging, in distributed organizations than situated ones.

Finally, there are some general rules of thumb for organizations in managing careers (Hirsh, Jackson and Jackson, 1995). These have been described in Chapters 3 and 9. It is better to have a few well-resourced interventions than many poorly resourced ones. The interventions must have clear aims – in particular whether they primarily concern vacancy filling or longer-term development needs. They must have payoffs for individuals as well as organizations. The interventions must have links with other human resource practices whilst preserving individual control and responsibility for outcomes wherever possible. They need to be evaluated in terms of their impact on individual behaviour and organizational performance, and over reasonably long time-frames. In short, as for individuals, career management by organizations requires substantial effort and an eye to the future as well as the present.

REFERENCES

Adams, J. D., Hayes, J. and Hopson, B. (1976) *Transition: Understanding and Managing Personal Change*, Martin Robertson, London.

Adler, P. S. (ed.) (1992) *Technology and the Future of Work*, Jossey-Bass, San Francisco.

Adler, S. (1994) The contingent worker. Keynote address at 23rd International Congress of Applied Psychology, Madrid.

Alexander, J. A. and Lee, S. D. (1996) The effects of CEO succession and tenure on failure of rural community hospitals, *Journal of Applied Behavioral Science*, Vol. 32, pp. 70–88.

Alleman, E. (1989) Two planned mentoring programs that worked, *Mentoring International*, Vol. 3, pp. 6–12.

Allen, N. J. and Meyer, J. P. (1990) Organizational socialization tactics: a longitudinal analysis of links to newcomers' commitment and role orientation, *Academy of Management Journal*, Vol. 33, pp. 847–58.

Alwin, D. F. (1994) Aging, personality and change: the stability of individual differences over the adult life span, in D. L Featherman, R. M. Learner and M. Perlmutter (eds.) *Life-Span Development and Behavior*, Vol. 12, Erlbaum, Hillsdale, N.J.

Andersen, A. (1996) *International Assignment Policies – A Benchmark Study*, Arthur Andersen, London.

Argyris, C. P. (1960) *Understanding Organizational Behavior*, Dorsey Press, Homewood, Ill.

Arnold, J. (1985) Tales of the unexpected: surprises experienced by graduates in the early months of employment, *British Journal of Guidance and Counselling*, Vol. 13, pp. 308–19.

Arnold, J. (1990) From education to job markets, in S. Fisher and C. L Cooper (eds.) *On the Move: The Psychology of Change and Transition*, Wiley, Chichester.

Arnold, J. (1994) Opportunity for skill use, job changing and unemployment as predictors of psychological well-being amongst graduates in early career, *Journal of Occupational and Organizational Psychology*, Vol. 67, pp. 355–70.

Arnold, J. and Bye, H. (1989) Sex and sex role self-concept as correlates of career decision-making self-efficacy, *British Journal of Guidance and Counselling*, Vol. 17, pp. 201–6.

Arnold, J. and Johnson, K. (1997) Factors affecting the benefits of mentoring reported by graduate protégés in early career, *Human Resource Management Journal*, in press.

Arnold, J. and Mackenzie Davey, K. (1992) Self-ratings and supervisor-ratings of graduate employees' competences during early career, *Journal of Occupational and Organizational Psychology*, Vol. 65, pp. 235–50.

Arnold, J. and Mackenzie Davey, K. (1994) Graduate experiences of organisational career management, *International Journal of Career Management*, Vol. 6, pp. 14–18.

Arnold, J. and Mackenzie Davey, K. (1996) Graduates' work experiences as predictors of organisational commitment and intention to leave: which experiences really matter? Unpublished manuscript.

Arthur, M. B. (1994) The boundaryless career: A new perspective for organizational enquiry, *Journal of Organizational Behavior*, Vol. 15, pp. 295–306.

Arthur, M. B., Hall, D. T. and Lawrence, B. S. (eds.) (1989) *Handbook of Career Theory*, Cambridge University Press.

Arthur, W. and Bennett, W. (1995) The international assignee: the relative importance of factors perceived to contribute to success, *Personnel Psychology*, Vol. 48, pp. 99–114.

Aryee, S. and Chay, Y. W. (1994) An examination of the impact of career-oriented mentoring on work commitment attitudes and career satisfaction among professional and managerial employees, *British Journal of Management*, Vol. 5, pp. 241–9.

Ashforth, B. E. and Saks, A. M. (1995) Work-role transitions: a longitudinal examination of the Nicholson model, *Journal of Occupational and Organizational Psychology*, Vol. 68, pp. 157–75.

Ashforth, B. E. and Saks, A. M. (1996) Socialization tactics: longitudinal effects on newcomer adjustment, *Academy of Management Journal*, Vol. 39, pp. 149–78.

Ashton, D. N. and Field, D. (1976) *Young Workers: From School to Work*, Hutchinson, London.

Atchley, R. C. (1982) Retirement as a social institution, *Annual Review of Sociology*, Vol. 8, pp. 263–87.

Atchley, R. C. (1989) A continuity theory of normal aging, *The Gerontologist*, Vol. 29, pp. 183–90.

Badaracco, J. L. (1988) Changing forms of the corporation, in J. R. Meyer and J. M. Gustafson (eds.) *The US Business Corporation: An Institution in Transition*, Ballinger, Cambridge, MA.

Badawy, M. K. (1988) Why managers fail, in Katz (1988) op. cit.

Ball, B. (1996) *Assessing Your Career: Time for a Change?*, British Psychological Society, Leicester.

Baltes, P. B. and Smith, J. (1990) Toward a psychological wisdom and its ontogenesis, in Sternberg (1990) op. cit.

Bandura, A. (1977) Self-efficacy: toward a unifying theory of behavioral change, *Psychological Bulletin*, Vol. 84, pp. 191–215.

Bartram, D. (1992) The personality of UK managers: 16PF norms for short-listed applicants, *Journal of Occupational and Organizational Psychology*, Vol. 65, pp. 159–72.

Bennett, N., Martin, C. L., Bies, R. J. and Brockner, J. (1995) Coping with a layoff: a longitudinal study of victims, *Journal of Management*, Vol. 21, pp. 1025–40.

Bennetts, C. (1995) The secrets of a good relationship, *People Management*, 29 June, pp. 38–9.

Berlew, D. E. and Hall, D. T. (1966) The socialization of managers: effects of expectations on performance, *Administrative Science Quarterly*, Vol. 11, pp. 207–23.

Bigwood, S. (1996) The advantages of a caring approach, *People Management*, 16 May, pp. 40–1.

Bird, A. (1994) Careers as repositories of knowledge: a new perspective on boundaryless careers, *Journal of Organizational Behavior*, Vol. 15, pp. 325–44.

Black, J. S., Mendenhall, M. and Oddou, G. (1991) Toward a comprehensive model of international adjustment: an integration of multiple theoretical perspectives,

Academy of Management Review, Vol. 16, pp. 291–317.

Blunt, N. (1995) Learning from the wisdom of others, *People Management*, 31 May, pp. 38–9.

Blustein, D. L., Pauling, M. L., DeMania, M. E. and Faye, M. (1994) Relation between exploratory and choice factors and decisional progress, *Journal of Vocational Behavior*, Vol. 44, pp. 75–90.

Bolles, R. N. (1993) *The 1993 What Color is your Parachute?*, Ten Speed Press, Berkeley, California.

Bond, J. T. (1987) *Accommodating Pregnancy in the Work-Place*, National Council of Jewish Women, New York.

Bosse, R., Aldwin, C., Levenson, M. and Workman-Daniels, K. (1991) How stressful is retirement? Findings from a normative aging study, *Journal of Gerontology*, Vol. 46, pp. 9–14.

Breaugh, J. A. (1983) Realistic job previews: a critical appraisal and future research directions, *Academy of Management Review*, Vol. 8, pp. 612–19.

Brett, J. M. and Stroh, L. K. (1995) Willingness to relocate internationally, *Human Resource Management*, Vol. 34, pp. 405–24.

Brett, J. M., Stroh, L. K. and Reilly, A. (1992) Job transfer, in C. L. Cooper and I. T. Robertson (eds.) *International Review of Industrial and Organizational Psychology*, Vol. 7, pp. 323–62, Wiley, Chichester.

Brewster, C. (1994) The paradox of adjustment: UK and Swedish expatriates in Sweden and the UK, *Human Resource Management Journal*, Vol. 4, pp. 49–62.

Bridges, W. (1995) *Jobshift: How to Prosper in a Workplace Without Jobs*, Nicholas Brealey, London.

Brim, O. G. and Ryff, C. D. (1980) On the properties of life events, in P. B. Baltes and O. G. Brim (eds.) *Life-Span Development and Behavior*, Vol. 3, Academic Press, New York.

Burden, D. S. and Googins, B. (1987) *Balancing Job and Homelife Study: Managing Work and Family Stress in Corporations*, Boston University Center on Work and Family, Boston, MA.

Cagnoni, S. (1988) Young persons required, *Labour Research*, July, pp. 9–10.

Callanan, G. A. and Greenhaus, J. H. (1992) The career indecision of managers and professionals: an examination of multiple subtypes, *Journal of Vocational Behavior*, Vol. 41, pp. 212–31.

Campion, M. A., Cheraskin, L. and Stevens, M. J. (1994) Career-related antecedents and outcomes of job rotation, *Academy of Management Journal*, Vol. 37, pp. 1518–42.

Cannella, A. A., Jr. and Lubatkin, M. (1993) Succession as a sociopolitical process: internal impediments to outsider selection, *Academy of Management Journal*, Vol. 36, pp. 763–93.

Carlton, I. and Sloman, M. (1992) Performance appraisal in practice, *Human Resource Management Journal*, Vol. 2, pp. 80–94.

Carnegie, D. (1936) *How to Win Friends and Influence People*, Simon & Schuster, New York.

Carnevale, A. P. (1995) Enhancing skills in the new economy, in Howard (1995b) op. cit.

Carroll, G. R. and Teo, A. C. (1996) On the social networks of managers, *Academy of Management Journal*, Vol. 39, pp. 421–40.

Cascio, W. (1994) Long-term impact of downsizing organisations on people and markets. Keynote address at 23rd International Congress of Applied Psychology, Madrid.

Caudron, S. (1992) Working at home pays off, *Personnel Journal*, November, pp. 40–9.

Cawsey, T. and Inkson, K. (1992) Patterns of managerial job change: a New Zealand study, *New Zealand Journal of Business*, Vol. 14, pp. 14–25.

Cerella, J. (1990) Aging and information-processing rate, in J. E. Birren and K. W. Schaie (eds.) *Handbook of the Psychology of Aging* (3rd edn), Academic Press, London.

Chao, G. T., Walz, P. M. and Gardner, P. D. (1992) Formal and informal mentorships: a comparison on mentoring functions and contrast with non-mentored counterparts, *Personnel Psychology*, Vol. 45, pp. 619–36.

Chao, G. T., O'Leary-Kelly, A. M., Wolf, S., Klein, H. J. and Gardner, P. D. (1994) Organizational socialization: its content and consequences, *Journal of Applied Psychology*, Vol. 79, pp. 730–43.

Chapman, A. J., Sheehy, N. P., Heywood, S., Dooley, B. and Collins, S. C. (1995) The organizational implications of teleworking, in C. L. Cooper and I. T. Robertson (eds.) *International Review of Industrial and Organizational Psychology*, Vol. 10, Wiley, Chichester.

Churchill, N. C. and Lewis, V. L. (1986) Entrepreneurship research: directions and methods, in D. L. Sexton and R. W. Smilor (eds.) *The Art and Science of Entrepreneurship*, Ballinger, Cambridge, MA.

Clark, A., Oswald, A. and Warr, P. (1996) Is job satisfaction U-shaped in age?, *Journal of Occupational and Organizational Psychology*, Vol. 69, pp. 57–82.

Clawson, J. G. (1980) Mentoring in managerial careers, in C. B. Derr (ed.) *Work, Family and the Career*, Praeger, New York.

Clement, S. (1987) The self-efficacy expectations and occupational preferences of females and males, *Journal of Occupational Psychology*, Vol. 60, pp. 257–65.

Clutterbuck, D. (1993) *Everyone Needs a Mentor: Fostering Talent at Work* (2nd edn), Institute of Personnel Management, London.

Coe, T. (1993) *Managers Under Stress*, Institute of Management, Corby.

Collin, A. and Watts, A. G. (1996) The death and transfiguration of career – and of career guidance? *British Journal of Guidance and Counselling*, in press.

Collins, E. and Scott, P. (1978) Everyone who makes it has a mentor, *Harvard Business Review*, Vol. 54, pp. 89–101.

Colvin, C. R. and Block, J. (1994) Do positive illusions foster mental health? An examination of the Taylor and Brown formulation, *Psychological Bulletin*, Vol. 116, pp. 3–20.

Cooper, C. L. and Lewis, S. (1993) *The Workplace Revolution: Managing Today's Dual-Career Families*, Kogan Page, London.

Coopey, J. and Hartley, J. (1991) Reconsidering the case for organizational commitment, *Human Resource Management Journal*, Vol. 1, pp. 18–32.

Cordery, J. L. and Wall, T. D. (1985) Work design and supervisory practice: a model, *Human Relations*, Vol. 38, pp. 425–41.

Costa, P. T., Jr. and McCrae, R. R. (1980) Still stable after all these years: personality as a key to some issues in adulthood and old age, in P. B. Baltes and O. G. Brim (eds.) *Life-Span Development and Behavior*, Vol. 3, Academic Press, New York.

Costa, P. T., Jr. and McCrae, R. R. (1992) *NEO-PI-R Professional Manual*, Psychological Assessment Resources, Odessa, FL.

Court, G. (1995) *Women and the Labour Market: Two decades of change and continuity.* IES Report 294, Institute for Employment Studies, Brighton.

Cowden, P. (1992) Outplacement services assessment, *HRMagazine*, Vol. 37, no. 9, pp. 69–70.

Cox, T. H. and Blake, S. (1991) Managing cultural diversity: implications for organizational competitiveness, *Academy of Management Executive*, Vol. 5, no. 3, pp. 45–56.

Crabb, S. (1995) Four reasons to be family friendly, *People Management*, 6 April, pp. 40–3.

Cressey, R. and Storey, D. (1995) *New Firms and their Bank*, Centre for Small and Medium-Sized Enterprises, Warwick University Business School.

Crites, J. O. (1978) *Administration and Use Manual for the Career Maturity Inventory*, CTB/McGraw-Hill, Monterey.

Cromie, S. (1987) Motivations of aspiring male and female entrepreneurs, *Journal of Occupational Behaviour*, Vol. 8, pp. 251–61.

Dalton, G. W. (1989) Developmental views of careers in organizations, in Arthur, Hall and Lawrence (1989) op. cit.

Dalton, G. W., Thompson, P. H. and Price, R. (1977) The four stages of professional careers, *Organisational Dynamics*, Summer, pp. 19–42.

Daly, J. P. and Geyer, P. D. (1994) The role of fairness in implementing large-scale change: employee evaluations of process and outcome in seven facility relocations, *Journal of Organizational Behavior*, Vol. 15, pp. 623–38.

Davidson, M. J. (1996) Women and employment, in P. Warr (ed.) *Psychology at Work* (4th edn), Penguin, London.

Davidson, M. J. and Burke, R. J. (eds.) (1994) *Women in Management – Current Research Issues*, Paul Chapman, London.

Davies, D. R., Matthews, G. and Wong, C. S. K. (1991) Ageing and Work, in C. L. Cooper and I. T. Robertson (eds.) *International Review of Industrial and Organizational Psychology*, Vol. 6, Wiley, Chichester.

Davy, J. A., Anderson, J. S. and DiMarco, N. (1995) Outcome comparisons of formal outplacement services and informal support, *Human Resource Development Quarterly*, Vol. 6, pp. 275–88.

Dawis, R. V. (1992) The structure(s) of occupations: beyond RIASEC, *Journal of Vocational Behavior*, Vol. 40, pp. 171–8.

Dawis, R. V. and Lofquist, L. H. (1984) *A Psychological Theory of Work Adjustment*, University of Minnesota Press, Minneapolis.

Dawson, K. M. and Dawson, S. N. (1996) Maximising your outplacement ROI: how to select the best service, *HRMagazine*, January, Vol. 41, part 1, pp. 75–83.

Dinklage, L. B. (1968) Decision strategies of adolescents. Unpublished doctoral dissertation, Harvard University.

Dix, J. E. and Savickas, M. L. (1995) Establishing a career: developmental tasks and coping responses, *Journal of Vocational Behavior*, Vol. 46, pp. 93–107.

Dodds, I. (1995) Differences can also be strengths, *People Management*, 20 April, pp. 40–3.

Dooley, D. and Catalano, R. (1988) Recent research on the psychological effect of unemployment, *Journal of Social Issues*, Vol. 44, pp. 1–12.

Dooley, D., Catalano, R. and Hough, R. (1992) Unemployment and alcohol disorder in 1910 and 1990: drift versus social causation, *Journal of Occupational and Organizational Psychology*, Vol. 65, pp. 277–90.

Dreher, G. F. and Ash, R. A. (1990) A comparative study of mentoring among men and women in managerial and professional and technical positions, *Journal of Applied Psychology*, Vol. 75, pp. 539–46.

Dreher, G. F. and Bretz, R. D. (1991) Cognitive ability and career attainment: moderating effects of early career success, *Journal of Applied Psychology*, Vol. 76, pp. 392–7.

Eby, L. T. and Buch, K. (1995) Job loss as career growth: responses to involuntary career transitions, *The Career Development Quarterly*, Vol. 44, September, pp. 26–42.

Eden, D. (1991) Applying impression management to create productive self-fulfilling prophecy at work, in R. A. Giacalone and P. Rosenfeld (eds.) *Applied Impression Management: How Image-Making Affects Managerial Decisions*, Sage, California.

Egan, G. (1990) *The Skilled Helper*, Brooks/Cole, California.

Ellis, C. and Sonnenfeld, J. A. (1994) Diverse approaches to managing diversity, *Human Resource Management*, Vol. 33, pp. 79–109.

Ellison, R., Butcher, S. and Melville, D. (1995) British labour force projections: 1995–2006, *Employment Gazette*, August, pp. 153–67.

Employment Department (1995) *Labour Market and Skill Trends 1995–96*, Employment Department, London.

Engelbrecht, A. S. and Fischer, A. H. (1995) The managerial performance implications of a developmental assessment center process, *Human Relations*, Vol. 48, pp. 387–404.

Ericsson, K. A. and Smith, J. (1991) *Toward a General Theory of Expertise*, Cambridge University Press.

Erikson, E. H. (1959) Identity and the lifecycle, *Psychological Issues*, Vol. 1, pp. 1–171.

Erikson, E. H. (1980) *Identity and the Life Cycle: A Reissue*, W. W. Norton, New York.

Evans, M. (1995) Mentoring: unlocking organizational learning. Workshop presented at Achieving Business Growth Conference, London, June.

Families and Work Institute (1993) *An Evaluation of Johnson & Johnson's Work-Family Initiative*, Families and Work Institute, New York.

Farh, J. L., Dobbins, G. H. and Cheng, B. S. (1991) Cultural relativity in action: a comparison of self-ratings made by Chinese and US workers, *Personnel Psychology*, Vol. 44, pp. 129–47.

Feather, N. T. (1990) *The Psychological Impact of Unemployment*, Springer, New York.

Feldman, D. C. (1994) The decision to retire early: A review and reconceptualization, *Academy of Management Review*, Vol. 19, pp. 285–311.

Feldman, D. C. and Klich, N. (1991) Impression management and career strategies, in R. A. Giacalone and P. Rosenfeld (eds.) *How Image-Making Affects Managerial Decisions*, Sage, California.

Feldman, D. C. and Weitz, B. A. (1988) Career plateaus reconsidered, *Journal of Management*, Vol. 14, pp. 69–80.

Ference, T. P., Stoner, J. A. F. and Warren, E. K. (1977) Managing the career plateau, *Academy of Management Review*, Vol. 2, pp. 602–12.

Fine, S. A. and Wiley, W. W. (1971) *An Introduction to Functional Job Analysis*, W. E. Upjohn Institute, Kalamazoo.

Fisher, C. D. and Shaw, J. B. (1994) Relocation attitudes and adjustment: a longitudinal study, *Journal of Organizational Behavior*, Vol. 15, pp. 209–24.

Fletcher, C. and Williams, R. (1985) *Performance Appraisal and Career Development*, Hutchinson, London.

Floodgate, J. F. and Nixon, A. E. (1994) Personal development plans: the challenge of implementation – a case study, *Journal of European Industrial Training*, Vol. 18, no. 11, pp. 43–7.

Ford, V. (1996) Partnership is the secret of progress, *People Management*, 8 February, pp. 34–6.

Fosler, R. S., Alonso, W., Meyer, J. A. and Kern, R. (1990) *Demographic Change and the American Future*, University of Pittsburgh Press.

Fox, S. and Dinur, Y. (1988) Validity of self-assessment: a field evaluation, *Personnel*

Psychology, Vol. 41, pp. 581–92.

Franz, E. D. and White, K. M. (1985) Individuation and attachment in personality development: extending Erikson's theory, *Journal of Personality*, Vol. 53, pp. 224–56.

Friedman, D. E. (1990) Work and family: the new strategic plan, *Human Resource Planning*, Vol. 13, no. 2, pp. 79–89.

Fryer, D. M. (1986) Employment deprivation and personal agency during unemployment: a critical discussion of Jahoda's explanation of the psychological effects of unemployment, *Social Behaviour*, Vol. 1, pp. 3–23.

Furnham, A. (1992) *Personality at Work*, Routledge, London.

Galinsky, E. and Stein, P. J. (1990) The impact of human resource policies on employees, *The Journal of Family Issues*, Vol. 11, December, pp. 368–83.

Gallos, J. V. (1989) Exploring women's development: implications for career theory, practice and research, in Arthur, Hall and Lawrence (1989) op. cit.

Gati, I. (1986) Making career decisions – a sequential elimination approach, *Journal of Counseling Psychology*, Vol. 33, pp. 408–17.

Gerstel, N. and Gross, H. (1984) *Computer Marriage: A Study of Work and Family*, Guildford Press, New York.

Gibb, S. and Megginson, D. (1989) Inside corporate mentoring schemes: a new agenda of concerns, *Personnel Review*, Vol. 22, no. 1, pp. 40–54.

Gilligan, C. (1982) *In a Different Voice: Psychological Theory and Women's Development*, Harvard University Press, Cambridge, MA.

Goffee, R. and Scase, R. (1992) Organizational change and the corporate career: the restructuring of managers' job aspirations, *Human Relations*, Vol. 45, pp. 363–85.

Goldberg, L. R. (1990) An alternative 'description of personality': the Big-Five factor structure, *Journal of Personality and Social Psychology*, Vol. 59, pp. 1216–29.

Gouldner, A. W. (1957) Cosmopolitans and locals: towards an analysis of latent social roles, *Administrative Science Quarterly*, Vol. 2, pp. 282–92.

Gouldner, A. W. (1960) The norm of reciprocity: a preliminary statement, *American Sociological Review*, Vol. 25, pp. 161–78.

Granger, B., Stanworth, J. and Stanworth, C. (1995) Self-employment career dynamics: the case of 'unemployment push' in UK book publishing, *Work, Employment & Society*, Vol. 9, pp. 499–516.

Granrose, C. S. and Portwood, J. D. (1987) Matching individual career plans and organizational career management, *Academy of Management Journal*, Vol. 30, pp. 699–720.

Gray, C. (1989) From unemployment to self employment: a manageable change? Paper given at 4th West European Congress, Robinson College, Cambridge, 10–12 April.

Gray, W. A. (1989) Situational mentoring: custom designing planned mentoring programs, *Mentoring International*, Vol. 3, pp. 19–28.

Greenhaus, J. H. and Callanan, G. A. (1994) *Career Management* (2nd edn), Dryden Press, London.

Greenhaus, J. H. and Parasuraman, S. (1993) Job performance attributions and career advancement prospects: an examination of gender and race effects, *Organizational Behaviour and Human Decision Processes*, Vol. 55, pp. 273–97.

Greenslade, M. (1991) Managing diversity: lessons from the United States, *Personnel Management*, December, pp. 28–32.

Gregg, P. and Wadsworth, J. (1995) A short history of labour turnover, job tenure, and job security, 1975–93, *Oxford Review of Economic Policy*, Vol. 11, pp. 73–90.

Guest, D. and Mackenzie Davey, K. (1996) Don't write off the traditional career,

People Management, 22 February, pp. 22–5.

Gunz, H. (1989) The dual meaning of managerial careers: organizational and individual levels of analysis, *Journal of Management Studies*, Vol. 26, pp. 225–50.

Gutteridge, T. G., Leibowitz, Z. B. and Shore, J. E. (1993) *Organizational Career Development*, Jossey Bass, San Francisco.

Hackett, G. and Betz, N. E. (1981) A self-efficacy approach to the career development of women, *Journal of Vocational Behavior*, Vol. 18, pp. 326–39.

Hage, J. (1995) Post-industrial lives: new demands, new prescriptions, in Howard (1995b) op. cit.

Hakim, C. (1988) Self-employment in Britain: recent trends and current issues, *Work, Employment and Society*, December, Vol. 2, pp. 421–50.

Hall, D. T. (1971) A theoretical model of career subidentity development in organizational settings, *Organizational Behavior and Human Performance*, Vol. 6, pp. 50–76.

Hall, D. T. and Mirvis, P. H. (1995a) The new career contract: developing the whole person at midlife and beyond, *Journal of Vocational Behavior*, Vol. 45, pp. 328–46.

Hall, D. T. and Mirvis, P. H. (1995b) Careers as lifelong learning, in Howard (1995b) op. cit.

Hall, D. T. and Parker, V. A. (1993) The role of workplace flexibility in managing diversity, *Organizational Dynamics*, Vol. 22, no. 1, pp. 4–18.

Hall, F. S. and Hall, D. T. (1979) *The Two-Career Couple*, Addison-Wesley, Reading, MA.

Hamburg, D., Coelho, G. and Adams, J. (1974) Coping and adaptation: steps toward a synthesis of biological and social perspectives, in G. Coelho, D. Hamburg and J. Adams (eds.) *Coping and Adaptation*, Basic Books, New York.

Hammond, V. and Holton, V. (1991) *A Balanced Workforce*, Management Research Group, Ashridge.

Handy, C. (1989) *The Age of Unreason*, Business Books, London.

Handy, C. (1994) *The Empty Raincoat*, Hutchinson, London.

Hanisch, K. A. (1994) Reasons people retire and their relations to attitudinal and behavioural correlates in retirement, *Journal of Vocational Behavior*, Vol. 45, pp. 1–16.

Hansen, J. C. and Campbell, D. P. (1985) *The Strong Manual*, Consulting Psychologists Press, Palo Alto, California.

Harren, V. A. (1979) A model of career decision making for college students, *Journal of Vocational Behavior*, Vol. 14, pp. 119–33.

Hedge, J. W. and Borman, W. C. (1995) Changing conceptions and practices in performance appraisal, in Howard (1995b) op. cit.

Heise, D. R. (1987) Sociocultural determination of mental aging, in C. Schooler and K. W. Schaie (eds.) *Cognitive Functioning and Social Structure over the Life Course*, Ablex, Norwood, N.J.

Hermansson, G. (1993) Counsellors and organisational change: Egan's systems model as a tool in organisational consulting, *British Journal of Guidance and Counselling*, Vol. 21, pp. 133–44.

Herriot, P. (1992) *The Career Management Challenge*, Sage, London.

Herriot, P. and Pemberton, C. (1995) *New Deals*, Wiley, Chichester.

Hertz, R. (1986) *More Equal than Others: Men and Women in Dual Career Marriages*, University of California Press, Berkeley.

Herz D. E. (1991) Worker displacement still common in the late 1980s, *Monthly Labor Review*, Vol. 114, no. 5, pp. 3–9.

Higson, M. and Wilson, J. P. (1995) Implementing personal development plans: a model for trainers, managers and supervisors, *Industrial and Commercial Training*,

Vol. 27, no. 6, pp. 25–9.

Hirsh, W. (1990) *Succession Planning: Current Practice and Future Issues*, Institute of Manpower Studies, Brighton.

Hirsh, W., Jackson, C. and Jackson, C. (1995) *Careers in Organisations: Issues for the Future*. IES Report 287, Institute for Employment Studies, Brighton.

Hirsh, W. and Jackson, C. (1996) *Strategies for Career Development: Promise, Practice and Pretence*, Institute for Employment Studies, Brighton.

Hofstede, G. (1980) *Culture's Consequences*, Sage, London.

Holland, J. L. (1973) *Making Vocational Choices*, Prentice-Hall, Englewood Cliffs, N.J.

Holland, J. L. (1985a) *Making Vocational Choices* (2nd edn), Prentice-Hall, Englewood Cliffs, N.J.

Holland, J. L. (1985b) *The Occupations Finder*, Psychological Assessment Resources, Odessa, FL.

Holland, J. L. (1987) *Supplement Manual for the Self-Directed Search*, Psychological Assessment Resources, Odessa, FL.

Hopson, B. (1984) Transition: understanding and managing personal change, in C. L. Cooper and P. Makin (eds.) *Psychology for Managers*, BPS, Leicester.

Howard, A. (1995a) A framework for work change, in Howard (1995b).

Howard, A. (ed.) (1995b) *The Changing Nature of Work*, Jossey-Bass, San Francisco.

Howard, A. and Bray, D. W. (1988) *Managerial Lives in Transition: Advancing Age and Changing Times*, Guilford Press, London.

Hutton, W. (1995) *The State We're In*, Cape, London.

Hyatt, J. (1992) Should you start a business, *INC.*, February, pp. 48–58.

Iles, P. and Auluck, R. (1991) The experience of black workers, in M. J. Davidson and J. Earnshaw (eds.) *Vulnerable Workers*, Wiley, Chichester.

Iles, P. and Forster, A. (1994) Developing organizations through collaborative development centres, *Organizational Development Journal*, Vol. 12, no. 2, Summer, pp. 45–51.

Iles, P. and Mabey, C. (1993) Managerial career development programmes: effectiveness, availability and acceptability, *British Journal of Management*, Vol. 4, pp. 103–18.

Iles, P., Robertson, I. T. and Rout, U. (1989) Assessment-based development centres, *Journal of Managerial Psychology*, Vol. 4, no. 3, pp. 11–16.

Inkson, K. (1995) Effects of changing economic conditions on managerial job changes and careers, *British Journal of Management*, Vol. 6, pp. 183–94.

Institute of Manpower Studies (1990) Employers and the older worker, in *IMS News*, July.

Investors in People UK (1991) *The National Standard*, Department of Employment, Sheffield.

Isabella, L. A. (1988) The effect of career stage on the meaning of key organizational events, *Journal of Organizational Behavior*, Vol. 9, pp. 345–58.

Izraeli, D. N. (1992) Culture, policy, and women in dual-earner families in Israel, in S. Lewis, D. N. Izraeli and H. Hootsmans (eds.) *Dual-Earner Families: International Perspectives*, Sage, London.

Jackson, C. (1993a) *Development Centres: Developing or Assessing People?* IMS Report 261, Institute of Manpower Studies, Brighton.

Jackson, C. (1993b) The case for diversity in computer-aided careers guidance systems: a response to Watts, *British Journal of Guidance and Counselling*, Vol. 21, no. 2, pp. 189–95.

Jackson, C. and Barltrop, J. (1994) Career Workshops. Presented at Improving Career Development in Organizations Conference, London, February.

Jackson, T. and Vitberg, A. (1987) Career development, Part 2: challenges for the organization, *Personnel*, Vol. 64, pp. 68–72.

Jackson, C., Arnold, J., Nicholson, N. and Watts, A. G. (1996) *Managing Careers in 2000 and Beyond.* IES Report 304, Institute for Employment Studies, Brighton.

Jacobs, R. (1989) Getting the measure of management competence, *Personnel Management*, June, pp. 32–7.

Jahoda, M. (1982) *Employment and Unemployment: A Social-Psychological Analysis*, Cambridge University Press, London.

Janis, I. L. (1982) Counteracting the adverse effects of concurrence-seeking in policy planning groups: theory and research perspectives, in H. Brandstatter, J. H. Davis and G. Stocker-Kreichgauer (eds.) *Group Decision Making*, Academic Press, London.

Janis, I. L. and Mann, L. (1977) *Decision-Making: A Psychological Analysis of Conflict, Choice and Commitment*, Free Press, New York.

Janssens, M. (1995) Intercultural interaction: a burden on international managers?, *Journal of Organizational Behavior*, Vol. 16, pp. 155–67.

Jessup, G. (1991) *Outcomes: NVQs and the Emerging Model of Educational Training*, Falmer, London.

Johnson, A. (1990) *Relocating Two-Earner Couples: What Companies are Doing*, The Conference Board, New York.

Jones, G. R. (1986) Socialization tactics, self-efficacy, and newcomers' adjustments to organizations, *Academy of Management Journal*, Vol. 29, pp. 262–79.

Jones, R. G. and Whitmore, M. D. (1995) Evaluating developmental assessment centres as interventions, *Personnel Psychology*, Vol. 48, pp. 377–88.

Kahneman, D. and Tversky, A. (1984) Choices, values and frames, *American Psychologist*, Vol. 39, pp. 341–50.

Kamouri, A. L. and Cavanaugh, J. C. (1986) The impact of pre-retirement education programmes on workers' retirement socialization, *Journal of Occupational Behaviour*, Vol. 7, pp. 245–56.

Kandola, R. (1995) Managing diversity: new broom or old hat?, in C. L. Cooper and I. T. Robertson (eds.) *International Review of Industrial and Organizational Psychology*, Vol. 10, pp. 131–67, Wiley, Chichester.

Kanter, R. M. (1989) *When Giants Learn to Dance*, Simon & Schuster, New York.

Kaplan, R. (1988) Entrepreneurship reconsidered: the antimanagement bias, *Harvard Business Review*, May–June, pp. 84–9.

Katz, J. A. (1994) Modelling entrepreneurial career progressions: concepts and considerations, *Entrepreneurship Theory and Practice*, Vol. 19, part 2, pp. 23–39.

Katz, R. (ed.) (1988) *Managing Professionals in Innovative Organizations*, Ballinger, Cambridge, MA.

Keenan, A. (1994) Undergraduate education and the career orientation of professional engineers. Comparison between individuals from enhanced engineering courses and those from conventional engineering courses, *Journal of Occupational and Organizational Psychology*, Vol. 67, pp. 153–72.

Kesner, I. F. and Dalton, D. R. (1994) Top management turnover and CEO succession: an investigation of the effects of turnover on performance, *Journal of Management Studies*, Vol. 31, pp. 701–13.

Kesner, I. F. and Sebora, T. C. (1994) Executive succession: past, present and future, *Journal of Management*, Vol. 20, no. 2, pp. 327–72.

Kessler, R. C., Turner, J. B. and House, J. S. (1987) Intervening processes in the relationship between unemployment and health, *Psychological Medicine*, Vol. 17, pp. 959–61.

Kidd, J. M., Killeen, J., Jarvis, J. and Offer, M. (1994) Is guidance an applied science?:

the role of theory in the careers guidance interview, *British Journal of Guidance and Counselling*, Vol. 22, pp. 385–403.

Killeen, J., White, M. and Watts, A. G. (1992) *The Economic Value of Careers Guidance*, Policy Studies Institute, London.

King, N. and Anderson, N. (1995) *Innovation and Change in Organizations*, Routledge, London.

Kirkpatrick, D. (1991) The new executive unemployed, *Fortune*, Vol. 123, 8 April, pp. 36–48.

Klemp, G. O. and McClelland, D. C. (1986) What characterizes intelligent functioning among senior managers?, in R. J. Sternberg and R. K. Wagner (eds.) *Practical Intelligence*, Cambridge University Press.

Knowdell, R. (1991) *Designing Career Development Programs for Organizations*. Video with transcript available from Career Research and Testing, Inc., San José, California.

Kozac, M. (1994) *Not Just Nine to Five: A Survey of Shift Workers, Childcare Needs*, Daycare Trust, London.

Kraiger, K. and Ford, J. K. (1985) A meta-analysis of ratee race effects in performance appraisal, *Journal of Applied Psychology*, Vol. 70, pp. 56–65.

Kram, K. E. (1985) *Mentoring at Work: Developmental Relationships in Organizational Life*, Scott, Foresman & Co., Glenview, Ill.

Labour Force Survey (1994), HMSO, London.

Landy, F. J. and Farr, J. L. (1983) *The Measurement of Work Performance*, Academic Press, London.

Langan-Fox, J. and Roth, S. (1995) Achievement motivation and female entrepreneurs, *Journal of Occupational and Organizational Psychology*, Vol. 68, pp. 209–18.

Latack, J. C. and Kaufman, H. G. (1988) Termination and outplacement strategies, in M. London and E. M. Mone (eds.) *Career Growth and Human Resource Strategies*, pp. 289–313, Quorum, New York.

Latack, J. C., Kinicki, A. J. and Prussia, G. E. (1995) An integrative process model of coping with job loss, *Academy of Management Review*, Vol. 20, pp. 311–42.

Lawler, E. E., III. (1992) *The Ultimate Advantage: Creating the High-Involvement Organization*, Jossey-Bass, San Francisco.

Lawler, E. E., III. (1994) From job-based to competency-based organizations, *Journal of Organizational Behavior*, Vol. 15, pp. 3–15.

Lawler, E. E., III., Mohrman, S. A. and Ledford, G. E., Jr. (1992) *Employee Involvement and Total Quality Management: Practices and Results in Fortune 1000 Companies*, Jossey-Bass, San Francisco.

Lawson, M. B. and Angle, H. (1994) When organizational relocation means family relocation: an emerging issue for strategic human resource management, *Human Resource Management*, Vol. 33, pp. 33–54.

Legge, K. (1995) Rhetoric, reality and hidden agendas, in Storey (1995) op. cit.

Leong, S. M., Randall, D. M. and Cote, J. A. (1994) Exploring the organizational commitment-performance linkage in marketing: a study of life insurance salespeople, *Journal of Business Research*, Vol. 25, pp. 57–63.

Levinson, D. J. (1986) A conception of adult development, *American Psychologist*, Vol. 41, pp. 3–13.

Levinson, D. J., Darrow, C. N., Klein, E. B., Levinson, M. H. and McKee, B. (1978) *The Seasons of a Man's Life*, Knopf, New York.

Lewis, S. (1992) Introduction: dual-earner families in context, in S. Lewis, D. N. Izraeli and H. Hootsmans (eds.) *Dual-Earner Families: International Perspectives*, Sage, London.

Loan-Clarke, J. (1996) The Management Charter Initiative – a critique of management standards/NVQs, *Journal of Management Development*, Vol. 15, no. 6. In press.

London, M. and Stumpf, S. (1982) *Managing Careers*, Addison-Wesley, Reading, MA.

Louis, M. R. (1980) Surprise and sense making: what newcomers experience in entering unfamiliar organizational settings, *Administrative Science Quarterly*, Vol. 25, pp. 226–51.

Louis, M. R. (1982) Career transitions: a missing link in career development, *Organizational Dynamics*, Vol. 10, pp. 68–77.

Lowman, R. L. and Williams, R. E. (1987) Validity of self-ratings of abilities and competencies, *Journal of Vocational Behavior*, Vol. 30, pp. 1–13.

Mabe, P. A. and West, S. G. (1982) Validity of self-evaluation of ability: a review and meta-analysis, *Journal of Applied Psychology*, Vol. 67, pp. 280–96.

Mabey, C. and Iles, P. (1993) The strategic integration of assessment and development practices: succession planning and new manager development, *Human Resource Management Journal*, Vol. 3, no. 4, pp. 16–34.

Macaulay, S. and Harding, N. (1996) Drawing up a new careers contract, *People Management*, 4 April, pp. 34–5.

Mackenzie Davey, K. (1993) Women's accounts of personal change since starting work. Unpublished doctoral dissertation, UMIST.

Mackenzie Davey, K. and Guest, D. (1994) Self development and the career: a review of some issues. Paper prepared for the Careers Research Forum, available from the authors at Birkbeck College, University of London.

Mackenzie Davey, K. and Guest, D. (1995) Silicon Valley and the future of careers. Paper presented to Careers Research Forum, London.

Mainiero, L. A. (1986) Early career factors that differentiate technical management careers from technical professional careers, *Journal of Management*, Vol. 12, pp. 561–75.

Marrick, N. (1995) Making the best of the daily grind, *People Management*, 31 May, pp. 36–7.

Marshall, J. (1984) *Women Managers: Travellers in a Male World*, Wiley, Chichester.

Martin, L. (1991) *A Report on the Glass Ceiling*, US Department of Labor, Washington, DC.

Martin, R. (1995) The effects of prior moves on job relocation stress, *Journal of Occupational and Organizational Psychology*, Vol. 68, pp. 49–56.

Martin, S. (1995) A futures market for competencies, *People Management*, 23 March, pp. 20–4.

Martinez, F. (1994) New forms of employment in Spain. Paper presented at the 23rd International Congress of Applied Psychology, Madrid.

Mathieu, J. E. and Zajac, D. M. (1990) A review and meta-analysis of the antecedents, correlates, and consequences of organizational commitment, *Psychological Bulletin*, Vol. 108, pp. 171–94.

Mayo, A. (1991) *Managing Careers in Organizations*, IPM, London.

McCauley, C. D., Eastman, L. J. and Ohlott, P. J. (1995) Linking management selection and development through stretch assignments, *Human Resource Management*, Vol. 34, pp. 93–115.

McCauley, C. D., Ruderman, M. N., Ohlott, P. J. and Morrow, J. E. (1994) Assessing the developmental components of managerial jobs, *Journal of Applied Psychology*, Vol. 79, pp. 544–60.

McEnrue, M. P. (1993) Managing diversity: Los Angeles before and after the riots, *Organizational Dynamics*, Vol. 21, no. 3, pp. 18–29.

McEvoy, G. M. and Cascio, W. F. (1989) Cumulative evidence of the relationship between employee age and job performance, *Journal of Applied Psychology*, Vol. 74, pp. 11–17.

McHugh, M. F. (1991) Disabled workers: psychosocial issues, in M. J. Davidson and J. Earnshaw (eds.) *Vulnerable Workers*, Wiley, Chichester.

Merrick, N. (1995) The Mobil way to achieve mobility, *People Management*, 16 November, pp. 37–8.

Meyer, J. P. and Allen, N. J. (1991) A three-component conceptualization of organizational commitment, *Human Resource Management Review*, Vol. 1, pp. 61–89.

Miller, D. (1991) Stale in the saddle: CEO tenure and the match between organization and environment, *Management Science*, Vol. 37, pp. 34–52.

Miller, M. V. and Robinson, C. (1994) Managing the disappointment of job termination: outplacement as a cooling-out device, *Journal of Applied Behavioral Science*, Vol. 30, pp. 5–21.

Mintzberg, H. (1973) *The Nature of Managerial Work*, Harper & Row, New York.

Mischel, W. (1984) Convergences and challenges in the search for consistency, *American Psychologist*, Vol. 39, pp. 351–64.

Mitchell, L. K. and Krumboltz, J. D. (1990) Social learning approach to career decision making: Krumboltz's theory, in D. Brown and L. Brooks (eds.) *Career Choice and Development* (2nd edn), Jossey-Bass, San Francisco.

Morrison, E. W. (1993a) Newcomer information-seeking: exploring types, modes, sources and outcomes, *Academy of Management Journal*, Vol. 36, pp. 557–89.

Morrison, E. W. (1993b) Longitudinal study of the effects of information seeking on newcomer socialization, *Journal of Applied Psychology*, Vol. 78, pp. 173–83.

Mowday, R. T., Porter, L. W. and Steers, R. M. (1982) *Employee-Organization Linkages: The Psychology of Commitment, Absenteeism, and Turnover*, Academic Press, New York.

Munton A. G. and West, M. A. (1995) Innovations and personal change: patterns of adjustment to relocation, *Journal of Organizational Behavior*, Vol. 16, pp. 363–75.

Munton, A. G., Forster, N., Altman, Y. and Greenbury, L. (1993) *Job Relocation: Managing People on the Move*, Wiley, Chichester.

Murphy, K. R. and Cleveland, J. (1991) *Performance Appraisal: An Organizational Perspective*, Allyn & Bacon, Boston.

NACETT (1995) *Report on Progress towards the National Target*, National Advisory Council for Education and Training Targets, London.

Nathan, R. and Hill, L. (1992) *Career Counselling*, Sage, London.

National Council for Vocational Qualifications (1992) *National Vocational Qualifications at Level 5*, NCVQ, London.

Naylor, K. (1994) Part-time working in Great Britain – an historical analysis, *Employment Gazette*, Vol. 102, pp. 473–84.

Neugarten, B. L. and Neugarten, D. A. (1987) The changing meanings of age, *Psychology Today*, May, pp. 29–33.

Nicholson, N. (1984) A theory of work-role transitions, *Administrative Science Quarterly*, Vol. 29, pp. 172–91.

Nicholson, N. (1990) The transition cycle: causes, outcomes, processes and forms, in S. Fisher and C. L. Cooper (eds.) *On the Move: The Psychology of Change and Transition*, Wiley, Chichester.

Nicholson, N. (1993) Purgatory or place of safety? The managerial plateau and organizational agegrading, *Human Relations*, Vol. 46, pp. 1369–89.

Nicholson, N. and Imaizumi, A. (1993) The adjustment of Japanese expatriates to living and working in Britain, *British Journal of Management*, Vol. 4, pp. 119–34.

Nicholson, N. and West, M. A. (1988) *Managerial Job Change: Men and Women in Transition*, Cambridge University Press.

Nicholson, N., West, M. A. and Cawsey, T. (1985) Future uncertain: expected vs. attained job mobility among managers, *Journal of Occupational Psychology*, Vol. 58, pp. 313–20.

Noe, R. (1988a) An investigation of the determinants of successful assigned mentoring relationships, *Personnel Psychology*, 41, pp. 457–79.

Noe, R. (1988b) Women and mentoring: a review and research agenda, *Academy of Management Review*, Vol. 13, pp. 65–78.

Nordvik, H. (1991) Work activity and career goals in Holland's and Schein's theories of vocational personalities and career anchors, *Journal of Vocational Behavior*, Vol. 38, pp. 165–78.

Ohlott, P. J., Ruderman, M. N. and McCauley, C. D. (1994) Gender differences in managers' developmental job experiences, *Academy of Management Journal*, Vol. 37, pp. 46–67.

Opportunity 2000 (1994) *Opportunity 2000 – Third Year Report*, Opportunity 2000, London.

O'Reilly, B. (1994) The new deal: what companies and employees owe one another, *Fortune*, 13 June, pp. 44–52.

Ornstein, S., Cron, W. L. and Slocum, J. W. (1989) Life stage versus career stage: a comparative test of the theories of Levinson and Super, *Journal of Organizational Behavior*, Vol. 10, pp. 117–33.

Ostroff, C. (1992) The relationship between satisfaction, attitudes, and performance: an organizational level analysis, *Journal of Applied Psychology*, Vol. 77, pp. 963–74.

Ostroff, C. and Kozlowski, S. W. J. (1992) Organizational socialization as a learning process: the role of information acquisition, *Personnel Psychology*, Vol. 45, pp. 849–74.

Ostroff, C. and Kozlowski, S. W. J. (1993) The role in the information gathering processes of newcomers during early organizational socialization, *Journal of Vocational Behavior*, Vol. 42, pp. 170–83.

Parker, S. (1983) Retirement in Britain, in K. Markides and C. Cooper (eds.) *Retirement in Industrialised Societies*, Wiley, Chichester.

Parks, J. M. and Kidder, D. L. (1994) 'Till death do us part . . . ' changing work relationships in the 1990s, in C. L. Cooper and D. M. Rousseau (eds.) *Trends in Organizational Behavior*, Vol. 1, Wiley, Chichester.

Parsons, F. (1909) *Choosing a Vocation*, Houghton Mifflin, Boston, MA.

Pearce, J. L. (1993) Toward an organizational behavior of contract laborers, *Academy of Management Journal*, Vol. 36, pp. 1082–96.

Pelz, D. Z. (1988) Critical tensions in the research and development climate, in Katz (1988) op. cit.

Phillips, S. D., Friedlander, M. L., Pazienza, N. J. and Kost, P. P. (1985) A factor analytic investigation of career decision-making styles, *Journal of Vocational Behavior*, Vol. 26, pp. 106–15.

Phillips-Jones, L. (1989) Common problems in planned mentoring programs, *Mentoring International*, Vol. 3, pp. 36–40.

Piore, M. J. and Sabel, C. F. (1984) *The Second Industrial Divide: Possibilities for Prosperity*, Basic Books, New York.

Pollock, R. (1995) A test of conceptual models depicting the developmental course of informal mentor-protégé relationships in the work place, *Journal of Vocational Behavior*, Vol. 46, pp. 144–62.

Powell, G. N. and Mainiero, L. A. (1992) Cross currents in the river of time: conceptualizing the complexities of women's careers, *Journal of Management*, Vol. 18, pp. 215–37.

Prahalad, C. K. and Hamel, G. (1990) The core competence of the corporation, *Harvard Business Review*, Vol. 68, no. 3, pp. 79–93.

Prediger, D. J. and Vansickle, T. R. (1992) Locating occupations on Holland's hexagon: beyond RIASEC, *Journal of Vocational Behavior*, Vol. 40, pp. 111–28.

Premack, S. L. and Wanous, J. P. (1985) A meta-analysis of realistic job preview experiments, *Journal of Applied Psychology*, Vol. 70, pp. 706–19.

Ragins, B. R. and Cotton, J. L. (1991) Easier said than done: gender differences in perceived barriers to gaining a mentor, *Academy of Management Journal*, Vol. 34, pp. 939–51.

Rapoport, R. and Rapoport, R. N. (1971) *Dual Career Families*, Penguin, London.

Reday-Mulvey, G. and Taylor, P. (1996) Why working lives must be extended, *People Management*, 16 May, pp. 24–9.

Reddy, M. (1987) *The Manager's Guide to Counselling at Work*, BPS Books, Leicester.

Reinke, B. J., Holmes, D. S. and Harris, R. L. (1985) The timing of psychosocial changes in women's lives: the years 25–45, *Journal of Personality and Social Psychology*, Vol. 48, no. 5, pp. 1353–64.

Rice, B. (1985) Performance review: the job nobody likes, *Psychology Today*, September, pp. 30–5.

Roberts, E. B. and Fusfeld, A. R. (1988) Critical functions: needed roles in the innovation process, in Katz (1988) op. cit.

Roberts, K. and Biddle, J. (1994) The transition into management by scientists and engineers: a misallocation or efficient use of human resources?, *Human Resource Management*, Vol. 33, pp. 561–79.

Roberts, P. and Newton, P. (1987) Levinsonian studies of women's adult development, *Psychology and Aging*, Vol. 2, no. 2, pp. 154–63.

Robertson, I. T. and Iles, P. A. (1988) Approaches to managerial selection, in C. L. Cooper and I. T. Robertson (eds.) *International Review of Industrial/Organizational Psychology*, Vol. 3, pp. 159–211, Wiley, Chichester.

Robertson, I. T., Iles, P. A., Gratton, L. and Sharpley, D. (1992) The impact of personnel selection and assessment methods on candidates, *Human Relations*, Vol. 45, no. 9, pp. 963–81.

Robinson, S. L. and Rousseau, D. M. (1994) Violating the psychological contract: not the exception but the norm, *Journal of Organizational Behavior*, Vol. 15, pp. 245–59.

Robinson, S. L., Kraatz, M. S. and Rousseau, D. M. (1994) Changing obligations and the psychological contract: a longitudinal study, *Academy of Management Journal*, Vol. 37, pp. 137–52.

Roe, A. (1956) *Psychology of Occupations*, Wiley, New York.

Rogers, C. (1965) *Client-Centered Therapy*, Houghton Mifflin, Boston, MA.

Rosenbaum, J. E. (1989) Organization career systems and employee misperceptions, in Arthur, Hall and Lawrence (1989) op. cit.

Rosenfeld, P., Giacalone, R. A. and Riordan, C. A. (1995) *Impression Management in Organizations*, Routledge, London.

Rothwell, S. (1995) Human resource planning, in Storey (1995) op. cit.

Rounds, J. and Tracey, T. J. (1993) Prediger's dimensional representation of Holland's RIASEC circumplex, *Journal of Applied Psychology*, Vol. 78, pp. 875–90.

Rousseau, D. M. (1990) New hire perceptions of their own and their employer's obligations: a study of psychological contracts, *Journal of Organizational Behavior*, Vol. 11, pp. 389–400.

Rousseau, D. M. (1995) *Psychological Contracts in Organizations*, Sage, London.

Rousseau, D. M. and Wade-Benzoni, K. A. (1995) Changing individual-organization attachments: a two-way street, in Howard (1995b) op. cit.

Rowan, R. B. and Wilks, C. S. (1987) Pre-retirement planning: a quality of life issue for retirement, *Employee Assistance Quarterly*, Vol. 2, no. 4.

Rubery, J., Fagan, C. and Grimshaw, D. (1994) *Bulletin on Women and Employment in the E.U., No. 5*, European Commission, Brussels.

Russell, J. E. A. (1991) Career development interventions in organizations, *Journal of Vocational Behavior*, Vol. 38, pp. 237–87.

Rutter, M. (1981) *Maternal Deprivation Reassessed*, Penguin, Harmondsworth.

Saam, R. H., Wodtke, K. H. and Hains, A. A. (1995) A cognitive stress reduction program for recently unemployed managers, *The Career Development Quarterly*, Vol. 44, September, pp. 43–51.

Salthouse, T. A. (1987) Age, experience and compensation, in C. Schooler and K. W. Schaie (eds.) *Cognitive Functioning and Social Structure over the Life Course*, Ablex, Norwood, N.J.

Schaie, K. W. (1983) What can we learn from the longitudinal study of adult psychological development?, in K. W. Schaie (ed.) *Longitudinal Studies of Adult Psychological Development*, Guildford Press, New York.

Schaufeli, W. B. and Van Yperen, N. W. (1992) Unemployment and psychological distress among graduates: a longitudinal study, *Journal of Occupational and Organizational Psychology*, Vol. 65, pp. 291–305.

Schein, E. H. (1964) How to break in the college graduate, *Harvard Business Review*, Vol. 42, pp. 68–76.

Schein, E. H. (1971) The individual, the organization, and the career: a conceptual scheme, *Journal of Applied Behavioral Science*, Vol. 7, pp. 401–26.

Schein, E. H. (1978) *Career Dynamics*, Addison-Wesley, Reading, MA.

Schein, E. H. (1985a) *Career Anchors: Discovering your Real Values* (1st edn), Pfeiffer and Co., London.

Schein, E. H. (1985b) *Career Anchors: Trainer's Manual*, University Associates, San Diego, CA.

Schein, E. H. (1993) *Career Anchors: Discovering your Real Values* (revised edn), Pfeiffer and Co., London.

Schein, V. E., Mueller, R. and Jacobson, C. (1989) The relationship between sex role stereotypes and requisite managerial characteristics among college students, *Sex Roles*, Vol. 20, pp. 103–10.

Schlossberg, N. K. (1981) A model for analyzing human adaptation to transition, *The Counseling Psychologist*, Vol. 9, no. 2, pp. 2–18.

Schneer, J. A. and Reitman, F. (1993) Effects of alternate family structures on managerial career paths, *Academy of Management Journal*, Vol. 36, pp. 830–43.

Schneer, J. A. and Reitman, F. (1995) The impact of gender as managerial careers unfold, *Journal of Vocational Behavior*, Vol. 47, pp. 290–315.

Schor, J. B. (1991) *The Overworked American*, Basic Books, New York.

Schwartz, D. (1996) The impact of work-family policies on women's career development: boon or bust?, *Women in Management Review*, Vol. 11, no. 1, pp. 5–19.

Schwartz, F. N. (1989) Management women and the facts of life, *Harvard Business Review*, January–February, pp. 65–76.

Segal, A. T. and Zellner, W. (1992) Corporate women, *Business Week*, 8 June, pp. 74–8.

Segall, A. (1995) Career development interventions, cited in Jackson *et al.* (1995) op. cit.

Sekaran, U. (1986) *Dual Career Families: Contemporary Organizational and Counseling Issues*, Jossey-Bass, San Francisco.

Sharf, R. F. (1992) *Applying Career Development Theory to Counseling*, Brooks/Cole, California.

Sheehy, G. (1974) *Passages: Predictable Crises of the Adult Life*, Dutton, New York.

SHL (1982) *Occupational Interest Inventories: Manual and User's Guide*, Saville and Holdsworth Ltd., Esher.

Smart, R. and Peterson, C. (1994) Stability versus transition in women's career development: a test of Levinson's theory, *Journal of Vocational Behavior*, Vol. 45, pp. 241–60.

Smithers, A. and Robinson, P. (1991) *Beyond Compulsory Schooling: A Numerical Picture*, Council for Industry and Higher Education, London.

Somers, M. J. and Birnbaum, D. (1991) Assessing self-appraisal of job performance as an evaluation device: are the poor results a function of method or methodology? *Human Relations*, Vol. 44, pp. 1081–91.

Sonnenfeld, J. A. and Peiperl, M. A. (1988) Staffing policy as a strategic response: a typology of career systems, *Academy of Management Review*, Vol. 13, pp. 588–600.

Sonnenfeld, J. A. and Ward, A. (1995) Being successful at succession, *Directors and Boards*, Vol. 19, no. 4, pp. 17–21.

Spokane, A. R. (1985) A review of research on personality congruence in Holland's theory of careers, *Journal of Vocational Behavior*, Vol. 26, pp. 305–43.

Stern, R. (1995) On the swap floor, *Health Service Journal*, 10 August, pp. 20–1.

Sternberg, R. J. (ed.) (1990) *Wisdom: Its Nature, Origins, and Development*, Cambridge University Press.

Stewart, J. and Hamlin, B. (1992) Competence based qualifications: the case for established methodologies, *Journal of European Industrial Training*, Vol. 16, no. 10, pp. 9–16.

Storey, J. (ed.) (1995) *Human Resource Management: A Critical Text*, Routledge, London.

Stroh, L. K., Brett, J. M. and Reilly, A. H. (1992) All the right stuff: a comparison of male and female managers' career progression, *Journal of Applied Psychology*, Vol. 77, pp. 251–60.

Strong, E. K. (1943) *Vocational Interests of Men and Women*, Stanford University Press, California.

Stumpf, S. A., Colarelli, S. M. and Hartman, K. (1983) Career Exploration Survey, *Journal of Vocational Behavior*, Vol. 22, pp. 191–226.

Sugarman, L. (1986) *Life-Span Development: Concepts, Theories and Interventions*, Methuen, London and New York.

Summerfield, J. (1996) Lean firms cannot afford to be mean, *People Management*, 25 January, pp. 30–2.

Super, D. E. (1953) A theory of vocational development, *American Psychologist*, Vol. 8, pp. 185–90.

Super, D. E. (1957) *The Psychology of Careers*, Harper & Row, New York.

Super, D. E. (1973) The work values inventory, in D. G. Zytowski (ed.) *Contemporary Approaches to Interest Measurement*, University of Minnesota Press, Minneapolis.

Super, D. E. (1990) Career and life development, in D. Brown and L. Brooks (eds.) *Career Choice and Development* (2nd edn), Jossey-Bass, San Francisco.

Super, D. E., Thompson, A. S. and Lindeman, R. H. (1985) *The Adult Career Concerns*

Inventory, Consulting Psychologists Press, Palo Alto, California.

Super, D. E., Thompson, A. S., Lindeman, R. H., Jordaan, J. P. and Myers, R. A. (1979) *Career Development Inventory*, Consulting Psychologists Press, Palo Alto, California.

Swiss, D. and Squires, J. (1993) *Women and the Work/Family Dilemma*, Wiley, Chichester.

Talaga, J. and Beehr, T. A. (1989) Retirement: a psychological perspective, in C. L. Cooper and I. T. Robertson (eds.) *International Review of Industrial and Organizational Psychology*, Vol. 4, pp. 186–211, Wiley, Chichester.

Tamkin, P., Barber, L. and Hirsh, W. (1994) *Personal Development Plans: Case Studies of Practice*, Institute for Employment Studies, Brighton.

Taylor, K. M. and Betz, N. E. (1983) Applications of self-efficacy theory to the understanding and treatment of career indecision, *Journal of Vocational Behavior*, Vol. 22, pp. 63–81.

Taylor, S. E. and Brown, J. D. (1988) Illusion and well-being: a social psychological perspective on mental health, *Psychological Bulletin*, Vol. 103, pp. 193–210.

Taylor-Carter, M. A. and Cook. K. (1995) Adaptation to retirement: role changes and psychological resources, *The Career Development Quarterly*, Vol. 44, pp. 67–82.

Tharenou, P., Latimer, S. and Conroy, D. (1994) How do you make it to the top? An examination of influences on women's and men's managerial advancement, *Academy of Management Journal*, Vol. 37, pp. 899–931.

Thomas, D. A. and Kram, K, E. (1988) Promoting career-enhancing relationships in organizations: the role of the human resource professional, in M. London and E. M. Mone (eds.) *Career Growth and Human Resource Strategies*, Quorum Books, New York.

Thomas, R. R. (1990) From affirmative action to affirming diversity, *Harvard Business Review*, March–April, pp. 107–17.

Tokar, D. M. and Swanson, J. L. (1995) Evaluation of the correspondence between Holland's vocational personality typology and the five-factor model of personality, *Journal of Vocational Behavior*, Vol. 46, pp. 89–108.

Tomlinson, S. (1996) *Career Action Centres*. Workshop presented at conference entitled Innovative Approaches to Managing Careers, London, June.

Tranberg, M., Slane, S. and Ekeberg, S. E. (1993) The relation between interest congruence and satisfaction: a metaanalysis, *Journal of Vocational Behavior*, Vol. 42, no. 3, pp. 253–64.

Trompenaars, F. (1993) *Riding the Waves of Culture*, Nicholas Brealey, London.

Turner, J. C. (1991) *Social Influences*, Open University Press, Buckingham.

Vaillant, G. E. (1977) *Adaptation to Life: How the Best and Brightest Come of Age*, Little, Brown, Boston.

Van der Spiegel, J. (1995) New information technologies and changes in work, in Howard (1995b) op. cit.

Van Maanen, J. and Schein, E. (1979) Toward a theory of organizational socialization, *Research in Organizational Behavior*, Vol. 1, pp. 209–64.

Vancil, R. (1987) *Passing the Baton*, Harvard University Press, Boston, MA.

Vaughn, R. H. (1988) Linking employees and jobs: the career tree strategy, *Trainer's Workshop* (American Management Association), January–February, pp. 3–7.

Vaughn, R. H. and Wilson, M. C. (1994) Career management using job trees: charting a path through the changing organization, *Human Resource Planning*, Vol. 17, no. 4, pp. 43–55.

Veiga, J. F. (1981) Plateaued versus non-plateaued managerial career patterns, attitudes and path potential, *Academy of Management Journal*, Vol. 24, pp. 566–78.

Vondracek, F. W. and Schulenberg, J. (1992) Counseling for normative and non-normative influences on career development, *Career Development Quarterly*, Vol. 40, pp. 291–301.

Vondracek, F. W., Hostetler, M., Schulenberg, J. E. and Shimizu, K. (1990) Dimensions of career indecision, *Journal of Counseling Psychology*, Vol. 37, pp. 98–106.

Walker, L. (1996) Instant staff for a temporary future, *People Management*, 25 January, pp. 34–5.

Wallace, J. E. (1993) Professional and organizational commitment: compatible or incompatible?, *Journal of Vocational Behavior*, Vol. 42, pp. 333–49.

Wanous, J. P. (1980) *Organizational Entry*, Addison-Wesley, Reading, MA.

Wanous, J. P. (1989) Installing a realistic job preview: ten tough choices, *Personnel Psychology*, Vol. 42, pp. 117–33.

Ward, J. L. (1995/6) If the family falters, the business will falter: the succession dilemmas for the Masters family, *Small Business Forum*, Winter 1995/6, pp. 32–44.

Warr, P. B. (1987) *Work, Unemployment, and Mental Health*, Clarendon Press, Oxford.

Warr, P. B. (1993) Age and cognition, in M. Dunnette, L. Hough and H. Triandis (eds.) *Handbook of Industrial and Organizational Psychology*, Vol. 4, Consulting Psychologists Press, Palo Alto, California.

Warr, P. B. and Pennington, J. (1994) Occupational age-grading: jobs for older and younger non-managerial employees, *Journal of Vocational Behavior*, Vol. 45, pp. 328–46.

Waterman, R. H., Waterman, J. A. and Collard, B. A. (1994) Toward a career resilient workforce, *Harvard Business Review*, Vol. 72, no. 4, pp. 87–95.

Watts, A. G. (1987) Beyond unemployment? Schools and the future of work, *British Journal of Educational Studies*, Vol. 35, pp. 3–17.

Watts, A. G. (1993) The politics and economics of computer-aided careers guidance systems, *British Journal of Guidance and Counselling*, Vol. 21, pp. 175–88.

Watts, A. G. (1996) *Careerquake*, Demos, London.

Watts, A. G., Kidd, J. M. and Knasel, E. (1991) PROSPECT (HE): an evaluation of user responses, *British Journal of Guidance and Counselling*, Vol. 19, pp. 66–80.

Weatherly, K. and Beach, L. R. (1994) Making the right impression, *Contemporary Psychology*, Vol. 39, pp. 416–17.

Westbrook, B. W. (1985) What research says about career maturity: a response to Crites, Wallbrown and Blaha (1985), *Journal of Vocational Behavior*, Vol. 26, pp. 239–50.

Wheatley, M. (1992) *The Future of Middle Management*, Institute of Management, Corby.

Whitely, W., Dougherty, T. W. and Dreher, G. F. (1991) Relationship of career mentoring and socioeconomic origin to managers' and professionals' early career progress, *Academy of Management Journal*, Vol. 34, pp. 331–51.

Wick, C. W. (1989) How people develop: an in-depth look, *HR Report*, Vol. 6, no. 7, pp. 1–3.

Winefield, A. H. (1995) Unemployment: its psychological costs, in C. L. Cooper and I. T. Robertson (eds.) *International Review of Industrial and Organizational Psychology*, Vol. 10, Wiley, Chichester.

Wooler, S. (1985) Let the decision maker decide!: a case against assuming common occupational value structures, *Journal of Occupational Psychology*, Vol. 58, pp. 217–27.

Worsley, R. (1996) Only prejudices are old and tired, *People Management*, 11 January, pp. 18–23.

Yu, J. and Murphy, K. R. (1993) Modesty bias in self-ratings of performance: a test of the cultural relativity hypothesis, *Personnel Psychology*, Vol. 46, pp. 357–63.

Zajac, E. and Westphal, J. D. (1996) Who shall succeed? How CEO/board preferences and power affect the choice of new CEOs, *Academy of Management Journal*, Vol. 39, pp. 64–90.

INDEX

Authors' names are included where their work is discussed in some detail.

Abbey National, 37
adjustment, 161–5 (*see also* transition cycle)
Adult Career Concerns Inventory, 129, 130, 139, 142
Advanced Occupational Interest Inventory, 101
ageing, 9, 25–6, 143–6
Arnold, J., 35, 46, 88 ,106, 160, 166, 167, 192
Arthur Andersen, 173–5
Arthur, M., 29, 83
assessment centres (*see* development centres)
AT&T, 120, 142
attitudes, 123, 138
AXA, 170

BBC, 65, 80–1
Bray, D., 92, 142
British Telecom, 171

Cable & Wireless, 34, 81–2
career
  context, 1, 13, 15–18
  defined, 1
  structures, 23–4
career action centres, 5–6, 46, 47, 80–2
career anchors, 99, 112, 140–2
career breaks, 186
career concerns, 128–31
career decision-making, 95–122
  process, 114–19
  styles, 115–17
career decisions, 6–7, 62, 95–122
career development, 18–19

career exploration, 7, 96, 97–8, 114, 157
career guidance, 201–2
career management, 2–6, 13, 19–20, 44–54, 55–71, 72–94, 126–30, 135–6, 141–2, 146, 150, 155, 157, 169, 171, 175, 177, 184–9, 193–4, 195, 203–8
career maturity, 96–7
Career Orientations Inventory, 141
career paths, 23–4, 46, 167
career planning, 62, 96
career plateau, 91–4
career resilience, 82
career resource centres (*see* career action centres)
career stages, 128–9, 198 (*see also* life stages)
career workbooks, 46, 47, 62–4
career workshops, 4, 46, 47, 62–4
change
  in organizations, 21–2, 70
  in skill requirements, 24–5
  in working lives, 20–1
Chase Manhattan Bank, 37
chief executive officers, 56–8
child-care, 181, 183–5, 187
competencies, 24, 35–8, 61, 75, 79, 102, 110
computers in career management, 46, 63, 80–1, 120–1, 202–3
counselling, 4–5, 46, 47, 64, 67–70

decentralization, 32
delayering, 31–2
development centres, 4, 46, 59–62
development in adulthood, 123–47, 149–50, 157, 177
Developmental Challenge Profile, 73–5
developmental tasks, 124–5
developmental work assignments, 5, 46, 47, 72–6

diversity, 11–13, 25, 78, 89, 144, 177–82, 200
downsizing, 31–2
dual-career families, 25, 182–9
Du Pont, 185

education (*see* training and education)
empowerment, 22, 33
encounter, 159–61 (*see also* transition cycle)
entering employment, 167–8
entrepreneurs, 12, 26, 29, 194–7, 200
Erikson, E., 8, 96, 124–7, 131, 132, 136

fixed-term contracts (*see* short term contracts)
flexible work hours, 186–8

General Electric, 63
General Occupational Interest Inventory, 101
Greenhaus, J., 98, 102, 114, 181, 182
Guest, D., 23, 48
Gutteridge, T., 46–7, 63

Hall, D. T., 24, 126, 168, 184, 201, 205
Handy, C., 20, 28, 33, 204
Herriot, P., 20–1, 33, 39, 40, 43–5, 53, 161
Hirsh, W., 19, 24, 32, 38, 48, 50, 58, 78–80, 208
Holland, J., 7, 96, 101, 106–14, 119, 122
homeworking, 26–7
Howard, A., 24, 92, 142

identity, 124, 131, 157 (*see also* self-concept)
Iles, P., 45, 59, 60, 61
information technology (*see* computers in career management)
innovation, 33, 161–2, 199–200
insecurity, 27–8, 29
interests, 101–2, 110
internal vacancy notification, 46
Investors in People, 53

Jackson, Carole, 19, 24, 38, 48, 63, 208
Jackson, Charles, 19, 21, 24, 32, 38, 48, 50, 60, 70, 121, 208
job rotation, 46, 47, 73
Johnson and Johnson, 187–8

Kanter, R. M., 28, 29

Lawler, E., 36–7, 153
learning, 13, 74, 79, 152, 202, 205–6 (*see also* life-long learning)
leave, 185
Levinson, D., 8, 85, 86, 131–6, 138–9
life-long learning, 24, 26, 201 (*see also* learning)
life phases (*see* life stages)
life stages, 124–7, 128–40
life themes, 142–3
line managers, 51, 70, 73, 78

Mabey, C., 45, 61
Mackenzie Davey, K., 23, 46, 48, 82, 106
Mayo, A., 33–4, 43, 51, 52–4, 77, 86, 88
McCauley, C., 73–5
mentoring, 6, 46, 47, 85–91
mid-life crisis, 8, 133
Mirvis, P., 24, 126, 201, 205
Mobil, 171

National Health Service, 61, 187
networking, 6, 83–5
Nicholson, N., 91, 92, 149, 151, 152, 153, 155–7, 159, 161, 162, 191
North British Housing Association, 188

Opportunity 2000, 188
Organizational Analysis Survey, 75, 76
organizational commitment, 165–7, 197
outplacement, 4, 46, 64–7, 171, 193
outsourcing, 22–3, 34

Parents at work, 188
Pemberton, C., 39–40, 43–5
performance appraisal, 5, 76–8
personal development plans, 5, 46, 50, 78–80
personality, 99, 123, 195–6
preparation, 157–9 (*see also* transition cycle)
Price Waterhouse, 207
promotion, 32, 61, 73, 88, 91, 152
psychological contract, 2, 21, 39–44, 158, 159

realistic job previews, 10, 156, 158–9, 160
relocation, 162, 170–5
retirement, 26, 168–70
roles, 18, 128–31

Schein, E., 9, 53, 112, 131, 140–2, 158, 160, 161, 163, 168, 196, 198

SCO, 49–50
secondments, 72
self-assessment, 61, 64, 103–5, 110
self-concept, 130 (*see also* identity)
self-development, 3, 48–50, 58, 78
Self Directed Search, 104, 108–11,
    112
self-efficacy, 105–6
self-employment, 26, 193, 195, 196, 200
    (*see also* entrepreneurs)
short-term contracts, 23
small organizations, 26
socialization, 162–5, 173–4
Sonnenfeld, J., 51–2, 57–8
stabilization, 161–5 (*see also* transition
    cycle)
Strong–Campbell Interest Inventory,
    101, 108
succession planning, 3–4, 37, 46, 47, 56–9
Super, D., 8–9, 96, 99, 127–31, 136, 138,
    139, 142

talents, 102–3
technical careers, 12, 197–200
teleworking (*see* homeworking)

theory of work adjustment, 165
trade unions, 44, 207
training and education, 24, 29, 35–8, 46,
    81–2, 167, 186, 194, 197, 199, 201–2,
    205
transition cycle, 155–7
transitions (*see* work-role transitions)
TSB, 79–80

unemployment, 12, 29, 191–4

values, 99, 102
Vocational Preference Inventory, 108–9,
    112

Wakefield Council, 188
Watts, A. G., 70, 121, 194, 202
Wellcome, 63, 120
wisdom, 146–7
women's careers, 11, 25, 88–9, 105–6,
    111, 136–8, 189–91, 196
Woolwich Building Society, 79
workload, 21
work-role transitions, 9–11, 69, 74,
    148–76, 153–5, 148–53